CLASS, STATE, AND DEMOCRACY IN JAMAICA

POLITICS IN LATIN AMERICA
A HOOVER INSTITUTION SERIES

General Editor, **Robert Wesson**

Copublished with Hoover Institution Press,
Stanford University, Stanford, California

CLASS, STATE, AND DEMOCRACY IN JAMAICA

Carl Stone

PRAEGER SPECIAL STUDIES • PRAEGER SCIENTIFIC

New York • Westport, Connecticut • London

Library of Congress Cataloging-in-Publication Data

Stone, Carl.
  Class, state, and democracy in Jamaica.

  (Politics in Latin America)
  Includes index.
  1. Jamaica—Politics and government—1962-
2. Jamaica—Foreign relations—United States.
3. United States—Foreign relations—Jamaica.
4. Economic assistance, American—Jamaica.
5. Jamaica—Economic policy. 6. Caribbean Basin
Initiative, 1983-   . I. Title. II. Series.
JL639.A15S76 1986   972.92'06   85-19406
ISBN 0-275-92013-5 (alk. paper)

*The Hoover Institution on War, Revolution and Peace, founded
at Stanford University in 1919 by the late President Herbert
Hoover is an interdisciplinary research center for advanced study
on domestic and international affairs in twentieth century. The
views expressed in its publications are entirely those of the authors
and do not necessarily reflect the views of the staff, officers, or
Board of Overseers of the Hoover Institution.*

Library of Congress Catalog Card Number: 85-19406
ISBN: 0-275-92013-5

First published in 1986

Praeger Publishers, 521 Fifth Avenue, New York, NY 10175
A division of Greenwood Press, Inc.

Printed in the United States of America
∞

The paper used in this book complies with the Permanent
Paper Standard issued by the National Information Standards
Organization (Z39.48-1984).

10 9 8 7 6 5 4 3 2 1

FOREWORD

In a strict consideration of Latin America, English-speaking Jamaica would not enter. However, it has been included in the "Politics in Latin America" series because it geographically belongs to the region and has affinities with the Dominican Republic, Haiti, and Cuba; indeed, relations with the government of Fidel Castro have been a major source of controversy in Jamaican politics. Moreover, the problems of Jamaica closely parallel those of its Latin neighbors.

The political background of Jamaica differs from that of Latin America in the recency of its independence (1962), its British parliamentary tradition, and the absence of military interventionism. Yet Jamaican democratic practices are of great interest not only for students of Caribbean affairs but for Latin Americanists, as one observes how the party system has functioned in a society not only of great inequality but racial division as well. Jamaica is something of a political laboratory, an ongoing experiment that will show the prospects for democracy more and more clearly as time passes.

The present work, with its deep examination of Jamaican society and politics, is particularly relevant in view of the uncertainty surrounding Jamaica under the reformist leadership of Edward Seaga. No one is better qualified to penetrate Jamaican realities than Carl Stone, longtime political scientist at the University of the West Indies and the island's leading political commentator. He brings much new and valuable information to the growing body of knowledge in Jamaica studies.

Robert Wesson

PREFACE

The high-profile pro-Cuban foreign policy of the Manley government in the late 1970s and the even higher-profile pro-United States foreign policy of the Seaga administration in the 1980s have both guaranteed Jamaica extensive coverage in the North American media. The close relationship between U.S. President Ronald Reagan and Jamaica's Prime Minister Edward Seaga has been a key factor in the development of the Caribbean Basin Initiative and the U.S. effort to increase its influence in the Caribbean and to contain both Cuba and Marxist political tendencies.

Jamaica's receipt of aid from the United States has reflected this close political tie since 1980. In 1980 under Michael Manley's left-leaning government, Jamaica received a total of $U.S. 4.6 million in economic and military aid from the United States. In the first year of the Seaga administration this aid increased to $U.S. 75 million and doubled in 1982 to $U.S. 141 million. Paralleling this increase in U.S. aid, other loan assistance from U.S.-influenced international agencies also increased. World Bank loans grew from none in 1980 under Manley to $133 million in 1982 under Seaga. IDR loans increased from $7 million in 1980 to $87 million in 1982, again recording the increased level of international economic assistance Jamaica has attracted due to the close links with Washington.

Jamaica has been promoted by the Reagan administration as an example of democracy and free enterprise working for the benefit of the people and worthy of emulation by other Third World countries. After the defeat of the pro-Cuban Manley government in 1980, Reagan sought to cultivate the new Jamaican government to extend a flow of support that would help Jamaica to become an example of a country solving its problems by free enterprise economics and a continuing commitment to democracy.

In contrast to a glowing official image of Jamaica painted by the policy makers in Washington, there is a growing body of political analysis on Jamaica by foreign and local academics that projects an equally sharp but negative image of Jamaica as being an example of social exploitation, political manipulation by insincere leaders, and of a ravaged people suffering from an overdose of exploitative capitalism and imperialism.

Jamaica played a key role in the organizing of regional governmental support by the smaller Caribbean islands for the U.S. invasion of

Grenada in October 1983, which led to the removal of what remained of the leftist revolutionary regime after the surviving leaders had presided over the assassination of Prime Minister Maurice Bishop.

Jamaica's Third World standing has consequently declined because of the hostile reaction to her role as a strong ally of the conservative U.S. presidency, which is seen as being hostile to Third World interests by leaders in the developing countries. The U.N. Sea-Bed authority headquarters established in Jamaica largely because of the role of former Prime Minister Michael Manley (in the agitation for the New World Economic Order) is unlikely to be fully utilized for administrative purposes because of the hostility of Third World leaders towards the Seaga administration's close and collaborative ties with Reagan.

All this international focus on Jamaica and its leaders raises important questions about the character of the internal political life of the small island society with 2 million people which has managed to play a high profile role in the patterns of regional politics in the Caribbean area. This book attempts to provide some answers regarding the real character of Jamaican society and politics so as to remove the distortions projected by the exaggerated and misleading positive and negative profiles of Jamaica painted by the propaganda of Washington and propaganda of the Marxist left.

TABLE OF CONTENTS

INTRODUCTION

As a sparsely populated country of peaceful Arawak Indians, Jamaica was overrun by invading Spaniards in 1494 who later lost the island to Britain after the latter failed to take Hispaniola (the Dominican Republic) and easily took over the thinly populated and weakly defended Spanish colony in Jamaica. Established initially by the British as an outpost for buccaneers who concentrated on harassing Spanish territorial possessions in the region, the island became a sugar colony by the seventeenth century. By 1673 there were 57 sugar estates, and by 1740 some 430 sugar estates using African slave labor had been established.

Large fortunes were made from sugar in eighteenth century Jamaica but these surpluses were appropriated by mother Britain to help finance her Industrial Revolution and the local Jamaican economy remained starved for capital even in later periods despite this earlier era of high prosperity.

Internal pressures from constant slave revolts, and external pressures from declining profitability and markets, and a British abolition movement that eventually ended the African slave trade in 1807 all led to the abolition of slavery itself in 1838. The emancipation of the slaves and the decline of the plantation system that followed set the stage for the rapid growth of the peasantry, the diversification of local food production by the peasants, and a sharpening of political tensions between the privileged and powerful white planter class on the one hand, desperately seeking to preserve the status quo, and the brown or colored middle class and landowners who wished to see reforms. Increasingly, the blacks acquired both a stake in the system through a strong middle peasantry and leaders able to articulate their demands for change. A successful coalition was built around the brown middle class who wanted reforms and more power and the blacks who were largely left out of the old power structure controlled by the planters. It is this coalition between the middle and lower social classes in the society that has formed the social basis for the country's modern period of politics that emerged in the postwar period. The thrust of this push towards democracy was to transfer control over the governing institutions from the planter class to the middle class who gained political legitimacy by serving the needs of the majority classes.

In 1970 the Jamaican labor force consisted of the following main groupings broken down by percent as follows:

professionals and managerial	7
clerical and sales workers	15
service workers	16
nonfarm production workers	32
farmers and agricultural workers	30

The racial composition of the society consists of a majority 78 percent black or African, 15 percent brown or light-skinned colored, 3 percent Indian, 3 percent white, and 1 percent Chinese. Like the blacks, the majority of the Indians who were brought to Jamaica to replace blacks on the estates after emancipation remain poor. Although most of the blacks are poor, the blacks constitute the largest segment of the middle class. Most of the Chinese and the brown or colored people fall into the middle class of professionals, white collar workers, small business owners, and better-off middle level farmers. The whites tend to dominate ownership of land and bigger enterprises in industry, tourism, and services.

By Third World standards Jamaica is not a poor country. It is in fact a middle income Third World country. In a list of 213 countries worldwide Jamaica ranks number 107 in income per capita in 1979 with $1100; number 77 in kilowatt hours of electricity used with 2100 KWH's (MN); number 86 in length of roads in kilometers; number 97 in number of telephones, with 55 per 1000 persons; number 85 in number of television sets with 57 per 1000 persons; and number 81 in passenger cars with 49 per 1000 persons.

The postwar economic boom in Jamaica was built mainly around the expansion of bauxite and alumina production and the growth of tourism and traditional agricultural exports (sugar, bananas, and so on). Since then, all except tourism have fallen on hard times and lean inflows in hard currency earnings, thereby weakening the areas of production geared toward the domestic market because of the high level of import dependence for both production and consumption.

In 1958 Jamaica became a member of the now defunct West Indies Federation, but it was the first nation to pull out after a referendum vote in 1961 in which a majority of voters opposed continued membership. A separate independence from other Caribbean islands was only reluctantly claimed after the British made it clear that the country had an option. Some sense of the feelings of lack of preparation for independence is suggested by the JLP government's newspaper advertisements in 1962 advising the population regarding what independence meant. Independence came in August 1962 and since then there has been a pattern of continuous constitutional rule through parliamentary institutions.

Nationalism has always been lukewarm as neither Jamaica nor any of the English-speaking Caribbean countries managed to generate the intensity of national sentiment and anti-colonialism that developed in Africa or Asia. Lacking a strong traditional culture that preceded colonialism, and nurtured on strong feelings of loyalty to empire, the Jamaican political community has had neither a strong nationalist nor anti-imperialist political tendency. This partly accounts for the earlier preoccupation with race which began with the movement initiated by Marcus Garvey in the prewar years. But the seeming fixation with race was really a design to express demands for more equality of opportunity, to permit blacks to take their place among the elite in the society and to demand recognition and status for black cultural expression.

The Rastafarian black racial and religious movement has been in the forefront of this emphasis on racial consciousness; but in recent times, with the fulfillment of those two goals, defining black demands, this has reduced the militancy of the movement. The movement has focused more on cultural and religious self-expression rather than on political militancy. After being perceived in the period leading up to independence as a major threat to social and political stability, the Rastafarian movement is now widely accepted and tolerated as part of the fabric of the new Jamaican social structure with membership that cuts across the class barriers and increasingly attracts recruits from the middle class and from the nonblack ethnic minorities.

The mood of the country has fluctuated in cycles reflecting the trends in the economy. The years of the Great Depression and World War II were years of gloom, pessimism, anger, and protest about inequalities and social injustice. The postwar economic boom was followed by a mood of optimism and hopefulness as energies shifted from political agitation to efforts towards education and training, migration, self-improvement, and entrepreneurial activities. The slowdown of the economy in the late 1960s, which was followed by the oil price shocks and inflationary spiral of the 1970s, produced two divergent responses:

The first response was a return to political militancy and radicalism and a preoccupation with protest politics and the making of demands on the society for more justice and opportunity for the poor. After a period of high political mobilization and political agitation in the 1970s, the end of the decade saw a pattern of demobilization, political apathy, and withdrawal into cynicism and hopelessness as many lost faith in political causes, and lowered their expectations for benefits from the system, and expected less from political leaders. This scaling down of expectations and political demands stabilized the political mood and prepared the political community for a long uphill struggle to rebuild the Jamaican economy on a firmer footing with external assistance.

After the political turbulence of the 1970s the Seaga regime has been fortunate in having a climate of stability, passivity, and quiesence in which to attempt some structural adjustments to rebuild the economy along more export-directed emphases and with renewed efforts to revitalize the Jamaican private sector which had lost its self-confidence in the 1970s. This essentially stable political environment has adjusted to the harsh economic realities of the country's prolonged crisis, thereby permitting new policy measures to be tried in the desperate search for economic solutions.

The close interrelationship between economics and political trends provides the central theme around which I will attempt to examine the nature of the democratic political order developed in Jamaica in the post World War II period and how it has been influenced by, and has in turn affected, the efforts at building a capitalist economy in a small middle income Third World country.

The approach seeks to draw conclusions and inferences from personally researched facts about Jamaica's political and economic evolution. Most of these facts, which have been fruits of the author's 14 years of extensive empirical research in Jamaica, are being published for the first time.

It is therefore hoped that the information provided here and the conclusions drawn from it will clarify many areas of confusion about Jamaica generated by polemical leftist writings, the purpose of which has been self-serving, and by nicely packaged conservative propaganda on the virtues of Jamaican society and politics which better characterize aspirations than reality.

This work is dedicated to my wife Rosemarie whose support and encouragement have been important in the execution and completion of a manuscript that represents, thus far, my most ambitious academic undertaking.

Carl Stone
University of the West Indies, Mona Campus

DEMOCRACY AND CAPITALISM

DEMOCRACY AND CAPITALISM

Loss of faith in laissez-faire capitalist management caused by the traumatic experiences of the Great Depression in the 1930s, led to a great expansion of state interventionist welfare state policies throughout Western capitalism in the post-World War II period. This trend towards a more pronounced social democratic emphasis on capitalist economic management in core[1] capitalist countries was occurring at precisely the same period during which the independence movement was gathering strength and momentum in the Caribbean. These social democratic tendencies came to be srongly advocated by most of the emergent middle class intellegentsia[2] who led newly formed political parties in the region. Libertarian emphases in democracy took second place to such social democratic, political, and policy objectives in the building of democratic institutions in Jamaica and most of the Caribbean. As in Europe, the Caribbean bourgeoisie was more inclined to a libertarian view of democracy and this meant that conflicts would occur between these two tendencies as the newly emergent political leaders sought to fashion a tradition of public management that attempted to copy Western social democratic approaches to policy making. Big government, high taxes, high rates of public spending, high levels of public sector employment, and close government regulation and control of the private sector would inevitably become contentious issues once they became features of public management in circumstances in which private sector interests felt strong enough to challenge them.

The historical association of parliamentary democracy and Western capitalism raises important questions as to what factors contributed to this interrelated development in Western Europe and North America. To the extent that such factors can be isolated, this will clearly assist in establishing an understanding of the conditions under which parliamentary democracy and capitalism will co-exist and develop together in the Third World.

Various propositions have been put forward by theorists[3] of parliamentary democracy accounting for the historical link between Western capitalism and parliamentary rule. These include the following:

1. Economic wealth generated by industrial economies that permit class accommodation and negotiation of class conflicts by raising the living standards of the working class and reducing class inequalities in living standards.
2. Mass literacy which facilitates political communication and a shared political culture out of which political consensus can be established between divergent social interests.
3. An open class system permitting upward social mobility, thereby creating a social climate in which the poor identify with the rich by believing that the society gives everyone an opportunity to acquire wealth and power.
4. The creation of a large middle class that values political and social freedoms.
5. Rapid economic growth and full employment providing adequate opportunities for individual economic and social advancement, thereby reducing the propensity towards political alienation and radical class consciousness.
6. The high degree of support for democratic institutions among significantly large sections of the main classes who see such institutions as generating policies and political outcomes that favor their class interests. These main classes include the bourgeoisie, the petit bourgeoisie and the working class.

All of these factors acting together have reinforced the historical link between capitalism and parliamentary democracy in the core economies of world capitalism. The decline of parliamentary democracy in the aftermath of post-World War II transitions to independence in many African and Asian Third World states with capitalist economies has been interpreted also in terms of the above key factors. In the peripheral capitalist systems of the Third World most of these factors promoting democracy are either absent or undeveloped. Living standards remain low, illiteracy levels are very high, social mobility is minimal or negligible. Social systems are rigid, the middle class is small and neither rapid growth nor full employment have been achieved. Additionally, the privileged classes tend to support authoritarian rule to maximize the exploitation of labor and use their influence over the military to block democratic reforms usually supported by the working class and progressive sections of the middle class.

The link between capitalism and parliamentary democracy has therefore been reinterpreted as a link that is specific to core economies in the world capitalist system.[4] Implicit in the above, however, is the suggestion that the more modernized or semi-peripheral Third World capitalist societies should provide a social environment that is more hospitable to parliamentary democracy than the backward peripheral Third World societies. In the more modernized semi-peripheral societies[5] income levels will be higher, literacy will be more widespread, the class structures will be less rigid and more open to upward social mobility, the middle class will be larger and rates of economic growth and employment expansion should be more consistent with a social climate hospitable to democracy.

An alternative view[6] is that expectations for social change run ahead of available new social opportunities and widespread political mobilization sets the stage for instability, polarization between radical social movements and conservative property owning and middle class interests. Increasingly political turmoil is resolved by military rule backed by conservative capitalist interests. A third view[7] is that capitalist interests in these semi-peripheral states need authoritarian military rule to contain militant or radical peasant and workers movements that become highly organized under parliamentary democracy. They need militarism specifically to police the transition from import substitution policies to the structural adjustments associated with export-propelled industrialization which demands cheap labor. Strong initiatives towards export-led industrial policies[8] have tended in Latin America to follow the exhausting of growth prospects under import substitution industrialization in semi-peripheral economies. The dramatic successes of the newly industrialized countries of South Asia and the Far East have generated powerful international financial pressures (the World Bank, and IMF, and U.S. AID) supporting foreign and domestic capitalist interests bent on becoming more internationally competitive.

The Latin American experience with parliamentary democracy provides strong support for the first and the third of these propositions. These states have enjoyed independence since the nineteenth century. Up to the 1960s there was a high correlation between level of economic and social modernization and the degree of constitutional democratic rule in Latin America. The more advanced semi-peripheral states such as Costa Rica, Chile, and Uruguay have been shown in independent empirical studies[9] to have enjoyed high levels of democratic development in the postwar period between the 1940s and 1960s. Conversely, democratic advances were lowest in the most backward and peripheral states such as Guatemala, Haiti, Nicaragua, and Bolivia. These trends contradicted the second proposition which associated political instability with the highest levels of social modernization.

Since the 1960s a trend towards military rule in Latin America and the collapse of democratic rule in countries such as Chile and Uruguay with long traditions of constitutional government provided the basis for the third proposition which linked this accelerated pattern of militarism to the functional needs of dependent capitalism. In Chile, Uruguay, Argentina, and Brazil, conservative military regimes seized power from governments with leftist or strong social democratic tendencies against a background of class polarization between conservative pro-capitalist interests and radical worker or peasant-backed leaders and political parties. Unlike Western Europe, some structural factors appeared to be destroying the basis of the political consensus between labor and capital. This new pattern of modernizing authoritarian states in the more advanced semi-peripheral states gave rise to the persuasive thesis that its roots were to be found in political economy structures linked to dependent capitalism, increased investments by multinational corporations, and efforts by local and international capital to eliminate populist or social democratic tendencies in the management of these capitalist systems. In each case the emergence of such regimes led to structural adjustment policies that sought to dismantle import substitution and to reorient the economies towards export manufacturing strategies requiring cheap labor, reduced social expenditure, weak trade unions, and redistribution of income from labor to capital.

The Third World debt crisis has resulted in increasing financial dependence by these states on multilateral lending institutions such as the International Monetary Fund (IMF) and the World Bank. These latter institutions have attempted to use the leverage of control through debt capital to impose structural adjustment policies on financially debilitated Third World economies. The implication is a weakening or elimination of social democratic tendencies in economic management strongly supported by U.S. aid and the foreign policies of the Reagan administration in the United States. These structural adjustment policies prescribe tight monetary and fiscal policies, the removal of budget deficits, tight control over wages, reduced consumption levels among the working class, large cuts in public spending, social expenditure and public sector employment as well as reduced levels of social services and lower incidence of taxation on the rich to finance capital accumulation while increasing tax burdens on the poor. Their impact is to reverse policy trends developed in the management of capitalist economies to accommodate working class incorporation into the state and to achieve a minimal quality of life for the majority classes. The effect, therefore, is likely to be a weakening of support for democracy as efforts are made to impose the hegemony of capital over labor and capitalist interests seek ultraconservative economic policy options that are likely to be optimally achieved by authoritarian military regimes rather than by democratic governments accountable to working class and peasant voters.

Underlying this weakening of democracy in Latin America is the conflict between social democratic or populist prescriptions for capitalist economic management and laissez-faire free enterprise economic management strategies that are divorced from any commitment to political liberalism. The impulse to free capital from the burden of state populism, tax burdens, welfare expenditure, and income sharing with labor threatens to break and disentangle the historical association of capitalism with democracy and to support authoritarianism as a necessary condition for rapid capital accumulation in the peripheral and semi-peripheral states in the world system.

The early 1980s have witnessed a reversal away from militarism and towards the resumption of democratic rule in the Latin American region and notably in Uruguay, Argentina, Brazil, and Peru. Modernizing authoritarian regimes have proved no more capable of solving economic and political problems than the democratic regimes they replaced and these regimes collapsed in much the same way that democratic constitutional regimes collapsed under the weight of crisis pressures in the 1960s and early 1970s. This new trend, therefore, has temporarily reversed the disconnection between democracy and capitalism in the region's more socially modernized semi-peripheral states. Whether the new wave of democratic regimes survives remains to be seen. This is especially so as political instability has been endemic in Latin America where regime types tend to be dismantled and to disintegrate in periods of crisis. This is in contrast to the English-speaking Caribbean region where political regimes have shown greater resilience and survival capability under the stress of economic and political crisis.

THE CARIBBEAN STATES

As a region of small, mainly island states, black English-speaking populations and parliamentary democracies, the Caribbean represents an atypical Third World region. These small island states have had a close cultural, economic, and political link with Western European and North American capitalism and enjoy a middle income status within the Third World as semi-peripheral states that have been rapidly modernized and deeply incorporated into the world capitalist system as tourist resort areas, suppliers of agricultural exports, sources of mineral raw materials, suppliers of cheap labor and migrants and heavy consumers of Western culture and commodity exports.

Most developing countries that achieved independence in the post-

World War II period inherited Western European type constitutions with provision for elected governments, parliamentary representation, competitive political parties, and liberal-democratic political and juridical traditions. That inherited legacy was bequeathed by the association with Western European colonizers. The overwhelming majority of these states have since abandoned that inheritance in favor of military regimes, one-party rule and wide-ranging forms of authoritarian rule.

The English-speaking Caribbean remains the only area in the Third World where politics based on free elections, multiple parties, and liberal democratic freedoms are still predominant. What makes the region so interesting politically is that there exists as well a wide variety of other forms of political systems in non-English-speaking territories that provide sharp contrasts to the predominant pattern of liberal democratic regimes. The basis of this diversity of political regimes in the wider region is to be found in divergent history and political evolution of these states. Much of that historical influence that separates the experiences and character of government and politics of the individual Caribbean states is due to the impact of divergent British, French, Spanish, Dutch, and U.S. colonization in the Caribbean and the residual legacy it has left behind. In addition, some major differences in the nature of politics in these states is due to the character of the dominant political movements and their respective leadership and their ties with major world powers in the post-World War II period.

More importantly, the wider Caribbean[10] represents a zone of intense political rivalry between Western capitalist and Eastern communist influences in their efforts to establish client states and international allies or to weaken the network of international support for the respective rival power bloc. The emergence of Cuba in the region in the 1960s as a communist and radical Third World counterweight to the still-dominant North American and European Western influences has been a major factor here. Also important is the growing connection between Caribbean political leaders and the Third World nonaligned movement. Notions about Third World neutrality compete with traditional Caribbean pro-Western stances and the newer radical flirtation with the Eastern bloc via the Cuban connection. Understanding Caribbean politics, therefore, turns very much on having a grasp of these regional ideological currents and their contemporary impact.

The Caribbean region consists mainly of mini-states with small populations. The nature of their politics, therefore, reflects many of the features, problems, possibilities and potential of small states exercising authority and managing power with political communities that are considerably smaller than most cities and towns in industrial societies.

Caribbean societies have a long history of close contact with the North American mainland. The United States represents the most important current source of imports for the region as a whole and the largest export destination. As countries dependent on economic aid, foreign investment, and migration, the United States has been the major metropolitan center facilitating these economic linkages. The role played by the United States and U.S. interests in the region, and the perspective these interests bring to bear on Caribbean political issues are, therefore, an important feature of the Caribbean political environment.

More so than any other developing country area, the Caribbean has the largest concentration of territories that have voluntarily retained a colonial status by enjoying the benefits of colonial paternalism while postponing the burdens and responsibilities of independence. This compromise between the impulse for sovereignty and a pragmatic sense of economic realism has written an interesting chapter in the complex patterns of ambivalence that underlie the colonial connections in the Caribbean.

As a region deeply integrated into the world market economies the fortunes of Caribbean economies have fluctuated with the long-term and short-term cyclical trends in the world economy. The decades between the early 1950s and the late 1960s was a period of growth, diversification and expansion in trade, production, and real income for most territories in the region. The world price inflation of the 1970s and the world recession of the early 1980s have left a trail of declining incomes, reduced living standards, debt, balance of payments problems, and debilitated public sectors with substantially reduced capacities to finance public expenditure. This pattern of economic crisis has tested the capability of these states to govern and sustain political stability under the stress of economic hardships, increasing social problems (crime, unemployment, social alienation, drugs, violence, and so on) and severely limited resources for public management.

The decade of the 1970s was important as a period in which changes in the character of political regimes occurred across the region as governing coalitions and political leaders experienced increased difficulty in sustaining high levels of political support. The overall directions of these political changes express the dominant political and ideological impulses and trends that compete for ascendancy in the Caribbean. Competitive party systems dominated for years by a single party experienced electorial victories by opposition parties in some cases (St. Lucia, Antigua, Dominica). In others, liberal democratic rule collapsed and gave way to the installation of military rule and one-party states (Guyana, Suriname, Grenada). Hitherto stable political consensus in other states broke down under the pressure of ideological polarization to the accompaniment of increased levels of political violence (Jamaica, St. Lucia).

As a region where liberal democratic traditions are very well established in political life, the Caribbean provides an arena in which to assess how the institutional legacy of parliamentary government, free elections, and multiple parties actually works under Third World economic and social conditions. To be sure, these institutions have been adapted and modified by the social and cultural milieu of Caribbean societies and the contingent stresses and pressures of societies with limited social opportunities and surplus demand for jobs, social services, educational opportunities and the creature comforts of modernity. The end result of this process of institutional adaptation has been the creation of political traditions that bear some similarities with parliamentary government in Europe and North America but have distinctive features that are uniquely Caribbean.

Caribbean society has itself been undergoing some fundamental patterns of change. The traditional plantation society with its rigid social hierarchy dominated by a small handful of white landowners who preside over power structures with extreme social inequalities and entrenched privilege has been modified over the past five decades. It has given birth to more open societies with upward social mobility, significant middle class groupings, and a lower concentration of power in the hands of elites. These social changes have enhanced the prospects for strengthening democracy and deepening its social base of support. Most importantly, in many societies in the region, the wealthy have had to share power with the emergent middle class professional groups and to accept policy direction, control, and leadership from middle class politicians who control political movements representing broadly based working class and peasant interests. All of this has been facilitated by increasing urbanization, literacy levels, shifts in the concentration of power from plantations to urban based service and manufacturing activity, internal and external migration, and mass media exposure. All of these social trends have served to sharpen political awareness and increase pressures for democratic political expression and organization, especially among the lower socio-economic groupings. Out of this have come vibrant traditions of democratic party politics and highly politicized trade union movements. The long-term impact has been an enlargement of the rule of the state in economic and social management and a shift in power from property owners to the political directorate and technocrats who control the rapidly expanding domain of public power administered by state institutions.

As the largest of the English-speaking Caribbean democratic states, Jamaica represents an interesting case study in the development of democracy in a semi-peripheral Third World state where the transition from a backward peripheral slave economy to a more modern semi-peripheral capitalist economic structure was historically linked to the emergence of social forces supporting democracy. As one of the more indebted Third World economies, Jamaica has been passing through a severe economic crisis since the first major oil price increase in 1973. The first resonse to that crisis was an attempt to accelerate social democratic policies of economic management. The failure of that effort has been followed by attempts to install conservative structural adjustment policies backed by strong U.S. economic aid and IMF and World Bank support. The system of democratic government has survived both the economic crisis and the political crisis represented by sharply opposed ideological forces that have attempted to manage this economic crisis. What follows is an account of how this system of democratic political management emerged and how it has so far managed to cope with these internal crises. Unlike Latin America where there has been a visible de-linking of democracy from capitalist management in many states the strong democratic political traditions of Jamaica and the Caribbean has produced a continuing association betweeen democracy and capitalism. Whether this link will continue indefinitely in the future remains a difficult unanswered question. Clearly support for democracy may be threatened by the failure of social democratic policies in the 1970s and the conservative structural adjustment policies of the 1980s that have undermined the very foundations of the political consensus on which this democratic tradition was built in the postwar period. How and why Jamaica has not gone the way of Chile or Uruguay provides the main thrust of the analysis that follows.

Having elected a government in October 1980 which has shown a stubborn determination to implement far-reaching structural adjustment policies with the support of U.S. aid, the World Bank and the IMF, Jamaica will provide an interesting test case of what is the political impact of dismantling import-substitution industrial strategies for a more deregulated free market approach to economic management combined with a strong export reorientation of the economy. This case study will also provide an important commentary on the policy problems of making that adjustment as well as add an interesting chapter to the ongoing theoretical debate on the linkage of capitalism and democracy in semi-peripheral Third World states. The strength of the Jamaican democratic political tradition clearly offers a somewhat different environment in which to examine these relationships from that posed in the political environment of South America. The analysis therefore begins with an assessment of how that tradition evolved historically and its dominant features.

NOTES

1. The categories of core states, semiperipheral states, and peripheral states have been developed in the work of Immanuel Wallerstein in his effort to come to grips with the in-

ternational division of labor created by world capitalism. See Immanuel Wallerstein, *The Modern World System*, New York: Academic Press, 1974 and *The Capitalist World Economy*, Cambridge: Cambridge University Press, 1979. My use of the term *semiperipheral* differs from Wallerstein in that it groups together all relatively modernized Third World countries that are deeply incorporated into the world capitalist system and tries to distinguish them from the backward peripheral Third World economies with large traditional peasant communities and subsistence production.

2. See John Laguerre, *The Social and Political Thought of the Caribbean Intelligentsia*, Kingston, Jamaica: Institute of Social and Economic Research, 1975.

3. See Seymour Martin Lipset, *Political Man*, London: Heineman, 1959 for the classic statement of this thesis. Other contributors include Daniel Lerner, *The Passing of Traditional Society*, New York: Free Press, 1958, and D. Neubauer, "Some conditions for democracy," *American Political Science Review* 61 (1967): 1002–1009.

4. See James Malloy, ed., *Authoritarianism and Corporatism in Latin America*, Pittsburgh: University of Pittsburgh, 1977.

5. This follows, of course, from the definition of semiperipheral used in this analysis.

6. The best known exponent of this thesis is Samuel Huntington. See his *Political Order in Changing Societies*, New Haven: Yale University, 1968.

7. See Guillermo O'Donnell in James Malloy, ed., "Corporation and the Question of the State," in *Authoritarianism and Corporatism in Latin America*, op. cit. pp. 47–88.

8. For a comprehensive treatment of structural adjustment policies in Latin America, see Sidney Weintaub and William Cline, ed., *Economic Stabilization in Developing Countries*, Washington: Brookings Institution, 1981.

9. See Carl Stone, "Political determinants of social policy allocations in Latin America,"*Comparative Studies in Society and History* 17 (1975): 286–308.

10. By wider Caribbean I am referring to all the islands, including non-English-speaking territories and the mainland territories with close links with the region (Belize, Guyana, and others).

2

THE DEMOCRATIC ORDER

Jamaica is one of the nine independent, English-speaking island states in the Caribbean that at the end of 1983 had a constitutional parliamentary democracy with a relatively high level of political and civil rights. Emerging from three centuries of British Colonial rule (1655 to 1962), Jamaica is unique in the Caribbean in having a strong and stable two-party system that developed shortly before the end of World War II.

The independence constitution[1] of 1962 was the product of joint collaboration and design by the country's two dominant political parties, the Jamaica Labour Party (JLP) and the People's National Party (PNP). Under this constitution, the Queen of England is the titular head of state and her representative, a governor general, is appointed on the advice of the prime minister. Since independence in August 1962, the country has had two governor generals, both of whom have been retired politicians.

Administrative and executive power is vested in the hands of the prime minister and his cabinet of government ministers who are accountable to the lower house of the legislature, the House of Representatives. The members of parliament of MPs who occupy the lower house consist of 60 representatives elected in constituencies for five-year terms, on the basis of universal adult suffrage.

Prior to the achievement of independence in 1962, between 1958 and 1961, Jamaica was a member of the now defunct West Indian Federation. An elected majority in the lower house was introduced in 1944, ministerial government in 1953, and full internal self-government in 1959.

The upper house of the bicameral parliament consists of a Senate with 21 members appointed by the governor general. Thirteen of these appointees are selected on the advice of the prime minister and eight on the advice of the leader of the opposition. All money bills originate in the lower house and the Senate tends to operate as a mere political echo of the lower house because of the appointment of retired or active politicians with close ties of loyalty to the major political parties.

The two major political parties have alternated in power between 1944 and 1983, with each party winning two successive elections before losing power. In spite of recent trends towards partisan influence in the appointment and removal of civil servants, the public service is based on career appointments at all levels and public service personnel are expected to work with any political administration that is elected to office. Appointments are made by an independent Public Services Commission.

The island with its 2.2 million population and 4,232 square miles of territory is divided into 12 parishes and a Metropolitan municipal administration in the capital, Kingston. These parishes constitute the framework for local government administration. Election to these 13 local government bodies is monopolized by the two major political parties who treat local parish elections as an important test of political strength and an important source of leadership training and recruitment for party activists. The local government bodies have very little administrative or financial autonomy and are tightly regulated and controlled by central government.

The judicial system is relatively independent of party politics and the high court and appellate judiciary enjoy security of tenure from political interference. The system is headed by a Supreme Court with both primary and appellate jurisdiction and the members of both the Supreme Court and the Court of Appeals are appointed by the governor general on the advice of the prime minister. The legal system is based partly on English common law, an independent judiciary, and a written constitution that defines the authority of governmental bodies and makes provisions for political and civil rights of citizens. The constitution protects both property rights and personal freedoms, such as the right of free assembly, association, and expression of opinions.

The country's democratic traditions have preserved a respect for human rights. The 1982 Freedom House survey[2] of political rights and civil liberties ranked Jamaica as among the minority of free states in the Third World, with a rating 2 for political rights, and 3 for civil liberties on a scale of 1 to 7, ranging from high to low scores of political freedoms.

THE TRANSITION TO DEMOCRACY

The evolution of parliamentary democracy in Jamaica has a long history that parallels the transition from the feudal patrimonial state to liberal democracy in Western Europe. That history is tied up with the changing configuration of power between the classes and socioeconomic groupings within the society, influenced primarily by changes in the island's political economy.

Before examining the details of this process of political development, its essential character needs to be defined. The basic ingredient in this pattern of change between the late seventeenth century and the mid-twentieth century is the dismantling of a state apparatus geared to express the dominance or hegemony of a European plantocracy over a black slave society and its restructuring to accommodate and reflect the majority interests of the ex-slaves.

The change took place gradually or incrementally over a very long period. It culminated in major strides towards democratic parliamentary rule in the post-World War II period. It was supervised by the British Colonial Office who defined the rules within which the changes occurred. In place of a state dominated by rural planter interests, what has been established is a state controlled by middle class professionals, technocrats, and entrepreneurs who govern on behalf of the masses.

In order to comprehend the nature and magnitude of the political change involved, we first have to identify the characteristics of the traditional "aristocratic state" that existed between the seventeenth and early twentieth centuries. This traditional aristocratic state is characterized by the following main features:

1. Political power and privileges were restricted to the economically dominant white and racially mixed property-owning interests.
2. Governmental administration was minimal so as not to encroach upon the private domain or power of the land-owning interests.
3. Tight limits were consequently placed on the capacity of the state to raise revenue to finance public services.
4. The size and scope of government remained very limited and any proposal to expand it was seen as threatening to the freedoms and power of the landed interests.
5. The idea of the public interest was relatively undeveloped as the dominant ideology saw the interests of the political community as being defined by what favored the interests of the powerful land-owning class.

Libertarian notions of freedom and free enterprise were dominant among the powerful land-owning class but democracy was feared as a formula to give power to the illiterate and threatening black population. The white plantocracy sought not only to maintain its control over the black slave and ex-slave population at varying periods but also to resist competition for power from the property-owning brown or colored racial interests. This had the effect of weakening the unity of class interests among the racially stratified and divided property-owning groups and assisted later efforts by the blacks to undermine the power structure.

The colonial nature of this state system meant that the presence of imperial interests would exercise some influence in mediating and resolving conflicts between these racial-class interests as well as on the direction and pace of political change. As a strong imperial power with both the military and administrative capability to effectively govern this small island colony, the British were able to exercise a decisive influence over the decolonization process. The British colonial office strongly supported gradual democratic reforms.

The democratic reforms demanded in the decolonization movement sought to achieve the following main goals and objectives:

1. Full articulation and development of the idea of the public interest by attempting to develop an array of public policies which would address the interests of majorities classes or social groupings.
2. An expansionist view of the role of the state which led to efforts at substantially increasing revenue raising, taxation, and financing of governmental activity and rapid rates of increase in public spending.
3. The development of a more active governmental administration that would create over time a strong domain of public power that would challenge the domain of private power controlled by property owners by bringing these class interests within the control of public policy.
4. The creation of a state bureaucracy, technocrats, and policy-making and implementing institutions that would rapidly bureaucratize the exercise of power.
5. The development of reform ideologies that would seek to define how to maximize the public interest and the emergence of political factions with strong commitment to particular reform ideologies.

These essentially social democratic reforms required a dismantling of the traditional aristocratic state.

Parliamentary government based on political pluralism, electoral politics, competitive parties, and liberal notions of individual freedoms was seen by the emergent political leaders in the decolonization movement as the most desirable direction for changing the traditional aristocratic state. This national consensus, supported by British colonial influences, guaranteed the dismantling of the aristocratic state controlled by landed interests. These political reforms posed many problems for a society coming out of a slave plantation tradition with a rigid racial-class, caste-like social structure. The bargaining politics of liberal democracy can only work and survive if the main social interests that make up the political community have a sense of common destiny that limits how far they are inclined to undermine the public interest in the pursuit of private gain. It requires that there be a sufficiently common set of values to achieve the accommodations and compromises necessary to make the system work. It requires also a minimal level of broadly based class supports for public policies that impose costs on specific social interests. Finally all the major social interests in the political community have to feel assured that although public policy measures may impose costs on them, no attempt will be made to either eliminate the interests they represent or to emasculate their bargaining power within the political community. The rapid social changes that undermined and overturned the rigid racial-class plantation society in the postwar period established the social foundations on which these political accommodations were built.

These conditions for the successful operation of parliamentary democracy limit and constrain the level of radical public policy measures that are feasible without unraveling the assumptions which make the system workable. On the other hand, this inherent conservatism guarantees government by consent, anchored on a strong basis of legitimacy in contrast to authoritarian and communist regimes which require a larger measure of coercion to maintain effective political management.

THE OLD ORDER

An exclusive and aristocratic form of parliamentary rule under colonialism was established in Jamaica in the Early Representative System over the 1661 to 1886 period. It was based on the claim by the white plantocracy to be accorded the rights of a settler colony that included political rights similar to those enjoyed by the citizens of England. On this basis the planters were represented in an Assembly "chosen as the commons in England" by ballot and exercising legislative and financial powers and functions limited only by the colonial character of the state. The planters were also represented in the Governor's Council which had advisory, judicial and legislative functions. The planters also controlled local government, the lower levels of the judiciary, civil defense, the police, and the official church, the Church of England.

This aristocratic parliamentary system (like the restricted parliamentary institutions of feudal Europe) was based on a very small electorate representing planters, a small number of ex-slaves who owned freehold of a minimal value, and the salaried middle class. In the late 1830s after the emancipation of slaves, that electorate barely exceeded 1,000 voters of a population of over 400,000. By 1884 there were only 9,000 voters of a population of 600,000 and by 1901 when the population had grown to over 750,000 there were only 16,000 voters. The whole system of representation was even further removed from democracy by the fact that only a small proportion of eligible voters bothered to cast a vote in elections for the Assembly (usually between 10% and 20%)[3] and many assemblymen were elected unopposed.

Throughout the nineteenth century white planters dominated representation in the Assembly. However, the small settler voters[4] provided a basis on which a few black and even more brown or colored candidates challenged the white planters in elections and established a minority presence in the Assembly. After the 1850s successful efforts by the white planters (increasingly supported by brown land owners and middle class leaders) reduced the small settler vote from its majority strength in the electorate to less than 30 percent by restricting the eligibility to vote and by increasing access to the vote by taxpayers and salaried persons.

A minor uprising occurred in 1865 in which protest action by ex-slaves over access to land and the manipulation of the courts system by the planters led first to extreme repression by the colonial governor and later a return to Crown Colony government. This change relieved the Assembly of much of its powers and concentrated them in the hands of the governor. Between 1866 and 1884 Crown Colony government permitted the beginnings of administrative reforms under the initiative of progressive governors. These reform reorganized the administrative system, health and education services, the police force, and local government and promoted expanded public works programs and land settlement schemes for the benefit of the ex-slaves.

The Old Representative system effectively gave to the planter interests legislative and fiscal power to restrict taxation, limit the growth of the governmental administration, and block the expansion of public services or policies benefiting the black majority. The more basic changes of the colonial state apparatus could only occur under circumstances in which the majority representation was accorded to the blacks or in which the while planters surrendered their effective veto power to a modernizing colonial bureaucracy. The Morant Bay rebellion generated great planter fears about further social and political unrest and demands for radical democratic political changes, although the uprising was entirely local and was addressed to a very limited agenda of protest issues. By surrendering their power to the colonial bureaucracy with the return of Crown Colony government, the stage was set for some preliminary reforms of the aristocratic state.

When a limited return to Representative Government occurred over the 1884 to 1944 period, the resricted planter-dominated system of political representation continued with the obstructionist legislative assembly continuing to restrict the growth of social services, the administrative services and the revenue base for public spending. The intention was to block social policies likely to improve the life chances of the black majority. In the latter half of this period, however, the planter presence in the Assembly was diluted as the expanding middle class of independent small farmers and urban mechants and professionals became the largest social groupings represented in the Assembly due to the decline of the plantation economy and the growing urbanization of the main centers of economic activity around commerce, services, and small scale manufacturing industry. However, the conservative ideological climate developed during the period of planter political ascendancy continued unchanged, except for some limited and modest expressions of demands for liberal-democratic reforms.

Throughout the period between the emancipation of slaves in 1834 and the twentieth century, the white planters, the colored or brown land owners and professionals, the white Jewish, Chinese, and brown merchants and the expanding racially mixed middle class feared the potential political power of the black majority, although factions within these more privileged groupings cultivated black political support at the polls. What was feared was the prospect of the blacks developing an independent political voice under conditions in which they gained democratic rights such as those that were being extended to the working class in Western Europe in the late nineteenth and early twentieth centuries.

These fears were rationalized by claims that the blacks were both too illiterate and unsophisticated to be granted such extensive democratic rights. At the root of these rationalizations were deep fears that the unpredictable black population would use these newly won powers to overturn the system of white and brown privilege and power in much the same way as the planters used their political power under the Old Representative System and the partially representative system (after the decline of Crown Colony government) to block social and economic reforms benefiting the blacks.

The British imperial interests in this early period shared the local consensus among land owners and the brown urban middle class that the blacks were not ready for democratic advances. The underlying reasons for the British position had more to do with racist notions about the childlike simplicity of blacks and their lack of civilization than with the fears of instability that concerned the planters. The example of Haiti, where a black revolution led to the dismantling of the plantation system, the rapid deterioration of agriculture and a retreat into subsistence peasant farming reinforced these fears. As one governor wrote in a despatch to the secretary of state for the colonies, "it is scarcely necessary to point out that the Negro is a creature of impulse and imitation, easily misled, very excitable and a perfect fiend when under the influence of an excitement which stirs up all the evil passions of a race little removed in many respects from absolute savages."[5]

In the view of the British colonial administrators, the culturally backward black population needed to be led by responsible interests among the middle class and the privileged. The central task of engineering stable political change was seen as cultivating, encouraging, and promoting such responsible leadership. Democratic development in the colony therefore lagged behind developments in Europe and was not promoted by the British administration in this early period in contrast to the policy of actively supporting broadly based democratic politics based on a mass suffrage in white colonies such as New Zealand, Australia, and Canada.

The capacity for democratic politics in post-emancipation Jamaica was grossly underestimated by the British colonial administration and the fears of the planters and other privileged interests that a black majority vote would lead to political and social instability were equally without foundation. Adult literacy is, of course, an important factor contributing to a political community's capacity to assume the responsibility of adult suffrage. Census data indicates that by 1911, 47 percent of the population (ten years and over) was able to read and write. Neither did the level of literacy change fundamentally between the early twentieth century and that time when universal adult suffrage was eventually granted (1944). The ex-slaves consisted mainly of small settler and peasant households who were absorbed in Christianity, had a great respect for private property and embraced conservative social values. They were likely to support any leadership that promised public policies that addressed their social needs. They were attached to the system but wished to see it reformed and achieve a greater measure of social justice for the poor. They were therefore likely to rally behind the kind of reformist social democratic politics that had emerged dominant in European democracy.

The lag between the administrative reform of the aristocratic colonial state in Jamaica and its eventual democratization in 1944 with the granting of universal adult suffrage disguises the fact that the black majority was ready for democratic politics from the early twentieth century or late nineteenth century. The fears and anxieties that blocked this development were only removed by the colonial regime after political protests. The cumulative buildup of resentment of the apparent injustice of the political order combined with heightened levels of political consciousness generated mass protests against the deteriorating social conditions of the 1930s. These culminated in the riots and labor disturbances of 1938[6] and prompted the British to accelerate changes toward democratic politics.

THE DEMOCRATIC CHALLENGE

The political protest movement of the late 1930s was characterized by many varied issues. The peasants and small settlers were demanding more land in a country where they controlled 8 percent of the agricultural land while representing 84 percent of the farming population and the big planters owned and controlled 60 percent of the land. Workers were seeking jobs, trade union rights, and better wages and working conditions in a period of great unemployment, declining living standards, and increasing poverty caused by the Great Depression. The rapidly growing middle class of brown and black professionals, middle farmers, and property owners increasingly resented Crown Colony government, the monopolizing of top administrative jobs by British expatriates and the continued pre-eminent position of the white planters in the political community. From this class emerged the new leadership, which articulated both the need for democratic change and advances toward self-government based on a growing feeling of nationalism. The period leading up to the disturbances witnessed a significant growth in political capacity through new leadership, political organization, and a ferment of reformist doctrines and nationalist sentiments. The United Negro Improvement Association led by Marcus Garvey advocated racial pride, black solidarity, economic and social reform, and the appropriation of political power by the black masses. A significant number of citizens associations emerged, making demands on the state for improved social services. In Agriculture, a new generation of rural middle-class leaders spearheaded the creation of new farm organizations. Political clubs, study groups, debating societies, and new political parties were formed to give expression to this new wave of political consciousness.

The buildup of progress towards democratic politics took place against the background of a decline in the political and economic ascendancy of the planters who represented the most formidable obstacle to democratic political change. Their decline, therefore, facilitated these changes.

As a result of the overall cyclical decline in the profitability of sugar and the rate of return to large and medium-sized family-owned estates, the economic base of the planter's political dominance was substantially reduced between 1911 and 1940. Estates were sold. Large debts were incurred. Traditional sources of finance dried up. A large proportion of these family-owned estates were sold to merchants and foreign corporations such as Tate and Lyle and the United Fruit Company.

Sections of the peasantry were traditionally dependent on the planter class for working capital, loans, and employment. The decline of the family-owned estates weakened these ties of class dependency. The decline of these traditional family plantations opened up opportunities for ownership by an expanding rural middle class of independent farmers who emerged as a major leadership factor in the new politics of the period. The British-owned corporate estates in sugar (Tate and Lyle), and the U.S.-owned corporate enterprise in banana production (United Fruit Company) rapidly replaced the traditional planter families as the main owners of large-scale estate land. These larger corporate agricultural operations increased the proletarianization of rural workers in opening up employment in large impersonal production units where workers acquired an increased sense of worker collective identity. This in turn accelerated the development of trade unionism, as sugar and banana workers were in the vanguard of the struggle for workers rights.

The decline of sugar and the emergence of banana as the main export crop thrust the U.S.-owned United Fruit Company into the position of being the largest owner of land holdings in the colony by 1938. The company established control over large sections of the small peasantry and the middle farmers as well as some members of the traditional plantocracy through credit, crop liens, banana supply contracts, agency- and produce-dealing relationships, and manipulation of the local legislature. The effect was to divide the planter class into one sector allied with United Fruit and another sector that adopted a nationalist posture of opposition to United Fruit's growing dominance in the farm sector of the economy.

Finally, the growing divergence of economic interests between imperial Britain and the colony resulted in the latter pursuing trading policies inimical to the interrests of the mainly white local planter class. The effect was to demoralize the planters who depended on British paternalism and support as a prop in the face of their fears and anxieties about the growing worker-peasant populations of blacks. This weakening of the colonial economic links called into question the planter class assumptions regarding the future viability of Jamaican society and challenged their self-confidence as a ruling class. For example, in discussing the need for British assistance to keep the sugar industry viable, the following statements were made by two leading planters and were greeted with loud applause by a large gathering of planters and merchants at the 1936 annual meeting of the Jamaica Imperial Association, the most vocal and powerful ruling class lobby.

Mr. H. Lindo: What is going to happen in my district if I have thousands of people around me not having anything to do? They will literally starve and that is more important than the question of more increase in output. Then they will burn my fields and knock down my factory. . . . On Monday morning when I have to face 500 people who have come out to work and can only take 100 and send away 400, the position is serious.

Mr. A. Nathan: This is the Jamaican Imperial Association. I have
heard a lot of most excellent things with regard to
Jamaica, things that are most necessary, but I have
heard nothing imperial about the whole thing. We
do want to be linked up as much as we possibly
can with the Mother Country; cheaper cables, a direct air service and a fast line of steamers. If we lose
touch with the Mother country and they lose interest in Jamaica, all your ideas, all your cooperative movements, all your sugar will not be worth
a thing. (*J.I.A. Report* no. 9 [1936]: 31–33.)

These comments by two leading planter spokesmen bring very
sharply into relief the sense of both class and national impotence that
pervaded the planter class during this period as well as their fear of
worker–peasant antagonism in the face of mounting economic hardships.
The consequence of all of this was that the planters were now willing
to sell land; to support programs for the expansion of the small and middle peasantry; to support economic and social reform and to concede
greater power and influence to other strata as well as more pronounced
state initiatives in the cause of economic growth and mass welfare.

For example, in 1936 Sir Arthur Farquharson, the most influential
member of the planter class in that period and the president of the
Jamaica Imperial Association, advanced the view that:

The association has again and again emphasized the fact that the future
of the island depends on our small settlers. . . they must have suitable
land alloted them—a good deal has been done during the last ten years
and a great deal more should be done. . . education along proper
lines. . . facilities for credit. . . proper markets for their produce. (*J.I.A.
Report* no. 9 [1936]: p. 24.)

The leadership among the planter class was at last ready to support
some moves towards social reforms. Labor unrest on the waterfront, on
the sugar estates, and on the banana farms added to peasant demands
for land and protests from the unemployed for jobs all hastened the
agenda of reform by pushing the political system towards crisis.

These militant and violent expressions of mass discontent provided
the basis on which emergent party and trade union leaders secured from
the British colonial power structure universal adult suffrage, representative government, and welfare-oriented social policies as well as substantial outlays of aid from the Imperial government in the form of

Colonial Development and Welfare Funds for a variety of social and economic projects.

The full transition to democratic government was, however, a rather slow process and moved along the following timetable of stages and changes:

Stage 1. Elected majority in legislature and universal
           adult suffrage   1944
Stage 2. Ministerial system with elected representatives
           controlling the administration
           and appointment of chief minister   1953
Stage 3. Cabinet government and full internal self-
           government   1959
Stage 4. Independence from Britain   1962

The main idea behind this incremental process of advance to full democracy was the insistence by the British on having the emergent local leadership serve an apprenticeship in parliamentary government to ensure that they ran the system for some time under British supervision with a view to ensuring conformity to the rules of the game of British parliamentary democracy.

To be sure, the timetable for political change was slowed down by the occurrence of World War II which shifted the local political agenda away from domestic conflicts and cleavages and towards full support for Britain's fight against German fascism. Indeed, the war itself became an occasion for an outpouring of proempire sentiments concretized by the many Jamaican volunteers who eagerly offered themselves to fight in the war in defense of empire and freedom from fascist dictatorship.

Although the period gave rise to some expressions of nationalist sentiment, the majority of the Jamaican people were neither opposed to the British Imperial connection nor interested in severing it. If anything, the main sentiment was to seek more assistance from the mother country to promote more development of the economy and social services. More importantly, there were strong proempire sentiments in that period. The alienated and discontented workers and peasants more often than not looked to the assumed benevolent paternalism of the Metropolitan government in Britain to administer justice and respond to their grievances in the context of what was perceived as a hostile planter class and privileged minorities who were opposed to the progress of the black majority. All of this legitimized the role the British sought to play in guiding and directing this slow incremental process of advance to full democracy.

THE NEW ORDER

The decline of the planters left a political vacuum that was filled by a new breed of middle-class and lower-middle-class leaders in labor movement and the mass parties that were formed out of the political ferment of the 1930s. This resulted in important changes in the social composition of elected representatives. In the nineteenth and early twentieth centuries the legislature was made up mainly of planters and a minority of professionals and persons drawn from the middle class (merchants, middle farmers, and so on). In that earlier period usually between a third to one half of the elected representatives consisted of persons who were born in the United Kingdom and were part of that white property-owning class that moved intermittently between the colony and the mother country. By the 1930s, the balance shifted gradually in favor of a majority of persons from the middle class (professionals, middle farmers, merchants) and a minority of representatives from the planter class. At this juncture the overwhelming majority of elected representatives were Jamaican born and whites were in the minority compared to the earlier period when there was a dominant white planter presence.

With the development of universal adult suffrage and the domination of the vote by the two mass parties (The Jamaica Labour Party and the Peoples National Party), led respectively by labor leader Alexander Bustamante and lawyer Norman Manley, a large number of persons of relatively humble lower-middle-class social status were elected to the legislature. These primary school teachers, trade unionists, clerks and small businessmen, and middle farmers actually outnumbered the elected representatives from the established middle-class professions and middle-class businessmen and wealthy farmers.

This new balance of majority lower-middle-class representatives in the legislature was, however, rather short-lived. Between 1944 and the post-independence period in the 1960s middle-class professionals and businessmen assumed predominance in both the JLP and the PNP as both the political party machines and the voters gave preference to elite qualifications that seemed to better equip persons from this social strata for the demands of representing constituencies and managing ministries and cabinet posts.

As was the case with the transition from the feudal patrionial state to liberal democracy in Western Europe, the prior development of parliamentary forms under the aristocratic state set the framework within which demands for democratization were made by those classes that were excluded from that restricted political system. The aristocratic state legitimized parliamentary representation and those classes and interests that were excluded sought after political rights that gave them a voice within this institutional framework. Leaders and followers alike within the movements representing the disenfranchised sought after the vote, parliamentary seats, and to establish political parties and factions that could compete for power within the parliamentary system.

It is, therefore, absurd for anyone to suggest that parliamentary rule represented some sort of alien British institution imposed on colonies such as Jamaica. In the Jamaican case, the white settlers had in fact established aristocratic parliamentary representation. The long period of colonization stretching over the period between the seventeenth and twentieth centuries ingrained British notions of democracy both among the emergent elite who led the mass movements of the postwar twentieth century period as well as among the workers and peasants. The latter saw British-type democracy and the vote it gave them as increasing their leverage to bargain for more benefits and greater social justice within this colonial society. The fact that the political forms derived from British traditions gave them added respectability in a society where British culture was respected at every class level during that formative colonial era. Additionally, the fact that British-type parliamentary democracy was advocated by the new political leaders in whom the masses invested great faith to create a new social order meant that for all these reasons no one, even the most radical, raised any questions about the appropriateness of parliamentary government for Jamaica. It has only been in the late post-independent period that minority Marxist-Leninist world political tendencies among radical intelligentsia have raised questions about the appropriateness of parliamentary democracy for Jamaica.

In a real sense, therefore, there has been a remarkable continuity in institutional forms between the early aristocratic state and the later reformed democratic state that has developed along the lines of British parliamentary government. But while these historical factors explain the development of parliamentary democracy in Jamaica, one still has to account for its survival, persistence, and seeming stability and maturation over the four decades between 1944 and 1984. To analyze this question it will be necessary to examine how the various classes have been incorporated into the political system, how these class and political accommodations are reflected in and influenced by the pattern of economic change in the period since 1944 and how the formal and informal management of power impacts on those who make up the political community in Jamaica.

A number of important issues have to be put on the agenda of enquiry to fully understand how parliamentary democracy has taken root in this political community. Historically, parliamentary democracy has worked best in advanced capitalist societies where the middle class and the lower middle class have grown into the numerically predominant classes and mass affluence as well as significant movements towards income equality and equality of opportunity are thought to have facilitated class accommodation, political consensus, and class bargaining. In Jamaica in spite of the decline of the plantation economy, a rapid growth of a black middle class, and significant upward social mobility, an entrenched pattern of income inequality has persisted over the 1944 to 1984 period between the very rich and the very poor. Poverty remains widespread, although at a considerably reduced level compared to the earlier postwar or prewar years. Equality of opportunity has improved compared to the earlier colonial period but the poorer classes of peasants, low wage workers, and low income petty traders and artisans constitute the numerically preponderant class groupings. The welfare state in core capitalist economies cushions the blows from economic fluctuations while industrial advancement keeps unemployment at modest levels except in periods of prolonged recession. In contrast, unemployment has been very high in semi-peripheral economies like Jamaica for most of the 1944 to 1984 period and only modest welfare benefits are available from the state for the very poor. Yet paradoxically, there is more emotionally intense support for party leaders, political parties, and the political forces they represent than is to be found in most industralized Western parliamentary democracies. The factors that contribute to this paradox need to be carefully examined.

Central to an understanding of these issues of inequality and democracy must be an analysis of the postwar Jamaican political economy, the specific class and class fractions it has given birth to over that period and how they relate to each other and to the state. Equally important is the need to comprehend the changing pattern of political consciousness and political behavior among the various classes and especially the majority classes in order to come to grips with the nature of Jamaica's political culture and the underlying factors that shape it.

The transition to democracy in Jamaica over the long period of colonialism in which an essentially aristocratic state system was gradually converted into a reformed democratic state sets the background against which these more detailed features of the anatomy of Jamaican democracy can be examined.

The Jamaican political system has had to cope with many crises in the post-independence period. Notable among these is the severe economic crisis of the 1970s and 1980s and the sharp internal political conflicts and cleavages that were the products of that crisis. This pattern of crisis management by successive governments has left indelible traces and influences on the character of Jamaican democracy. How this crisis management coped with the stresses and the precise aftereffects have to be examined carefully. Most importantly, the decade of the 1970s witnessed Jamaica's high profile involvement in regional and global international politics which continued into the 1980s but with a somewhat different content. The degree of foreign penetration of the Jamaican political system and the increasing weight of foreign affairs, external ties, and foreign policy in determining domestic political outcomes are matters that need detailed analysis if one is to understand the limits and degrees of freedom that are enjoyed by the local political directorate.

Most important is the need to understand how the masses view the political system, its leaders and main channels for political expression, and how their political development has been shaped by the growth of mass media and the forces for social change in the political community (migration, urbanization, literacy, income growth, labor force, changes, and so on).

One of the most far-reaching changes that took place in the transition from an aristocratic colonial state towards parliamentary democracy was the shift in the locus of power from country to town. The decline of the planter class left a political vacuum that was filled by a new coalition of urban-based interests. The urban professional middle class moved into a controlling position behind the levers of power in the new political arena that was being built on democratic foundations. Economic power also followed this route by shifting rapidly in the postwar period from country to town as a newly formed merchant–manufacturing economic elite emerged to establish effective control over capital, investment, and ownership in the commanding heights of the economy alongside the big foreign corporations.

The relocation of economic and political power from the declining plantation sectors in the rural hinterland to the urban metropolitan area of Kingston and St. Andrew was to have a major impact on how the economy was managed in the postwar period and how the political management of the country was conducted. The changing pattern of relationships between these two arms of the new urban power elite (the middle class urban professional–politician and the merchant–manufacturing urban bourgeoisie) set the stage for many of the power struggles that were to take place in the post-independence period.

To understand the management of power in Jamaican democracy, how it has evolved, and the competing interests·and factions involved in these coalitions and contestations for power, it is first necessary to come to grips with an analysis of the Jamaican political economy.

NOTES

1. For a comprehensive treatment of constitutional development in Jamaica, see Lloyd G. Barnett, *The Constitutional Laws of Jamaica*, Oxford: Oxford University Press, 1977.

2. See Raymond D. Gastil, *Freedom in the World-Political Rights and Civil Liberties*, Westport, Conn.: Greenwood Press, 1982.

3. See Carl Stone, *Decolonization and Political Change in Jamaica and Trinidad*, Beverly Hills: Sage Publications, 1971, p. 310–37.

4. The important role of small settlers in many nineteenth century elections held under a restricted franchise is documented in some path-breaking research on nineteenth century Jamaican elections by Gad Helman. This work seriously challenges other historical interpretations that defined the aristocratic state as totally excluding blacks from political participation. See Gad Helman, "The struggle for the settler vote: Politics and the franchise in post-emancipation Jamaica," in *Peasants, Plantations and Rural Communities in the Caribbean*, eds. M. Cross and A. Marks, London: Royal Institute of Linguistics and Anthropology, 1979, p. 2–25.

5. Written by Governor Eyre in Despatch no. C.O. 137/396 to the Secretary of State for the colonies.

6. Perhaps the most detailed historical account of these disturbances is to be found in the invaluable work of Ken Post on this period. See Ken Post, *Strike the Iron*, vols. I and II, The Hague: Humanities Press, 1981, and *Arise Ye Starvelings*, The Hague: Institute of Social Studies, 1978.

3

THE POLITICAL ECONOMY

THE STRUCTURE OF PRODUCTION

In the almost two decades between universal adult suffrage in 1944 and the granting of independence in 1962, the Jamaican economy had undergone some very profound changes. These changes affected the structure of production, the character and composition of the labor force, the accumulation of capital, the distribution of wealth, and the nature of the capitalist class as well as the size and scope of government and its role in economic management. The direction of these changes was accelerated in the 1970s and provides the framework of policy issues, class interests, and economic strategies that have shaped the character of post-independence Jamaican politics.

Some important factors set the stage for the changes that occurred in the Jamaican economy between the 1940s and the 1960s. First of all, the Western capitalist economies experienced a major upturn in the post-World War II period that witnessed significant expansion in world trade, real incomes in the industrial economies, and large-scale investment by multinational corporations in the Third World. Jamaica benefited from these developments by increased demand for exports, the availability of mass-produced cheap imports, and significant inflows of foreign investment in crucial areas such as bauxite mining, tourism, and manufacturing. These increased foreign exchange earnings enlarged the revenue base of the economy and expanded employment both directly and indirectly. These favorable external developments set the stage for a modernizing of sections of the Jamaican economy, the rapid growth of local entrepreneurial activity and the demand for new jobs in various sectors of the production of goods and services.

Perhaps the most profound impact was that the gloom and pessimism that pervaded the collapsing of the plantation economy was replaced by a revitalized optimism as new sources of wealth generation and expanded opportunities for employment changed the horizon of options and opportunities between the late 1930s and the 1950s.

The prewar Jamaican plantation economy centered around sugar and other agricultural exports, merchandise trading, real estate, and small farming. The traditional export crops earned the foreign exchange that permitted the many merchants, commission agents, and shopkeepers to import most of the consumer goods needs of the rich, the middle class, and some of the consumer needs of the poor (food and clothing especially). This was therefore a very structurally dependent economy with great reliance on trade.

In the slavery period exports tended to exceed 40 percent of estimated GDP indicating the dominance of sugar in the economy. Between the emancipation of slavery and the World War II period export levels declined by some 50 percent down to the more modest levels of 20 to 24 percent of GDP while imports dropped from a pre-emancipation level of above 30 percent to slightly above 20 percent, except for the 1930s when import levels returned to where they were in the slavery period, as local production declined.

In the increased and diversified economic activity of the postwar years, trade dependency[1] increased indicating higher levels of foreign exchange earnings and the use of those increased earnings to expand the range and volume of consumer goods as well as the quantum of capital and intermediary goods imported to increase the economy's productive capacity. Exports exceeded 30 percent of GDP in the 1950s and surpassed 40 percent of GDP in the 1960s. Imports similarly exceeded 40 percent by the end of the decade of the 1950s and surpassed 50 percent of GDP by the end of the 1960s. Indeed, as the economy experienced gains from the postwar era of Western capitalist growth and prosperity, the living standards and productive capacity of the economy came to depend even more on trade than in the heyday of the plantation slavery period. Typical of small island economies, increased prosperity resulted in higher levels of trade dependence as living standards improved for all classes and the productive base of the economy grew and diversified.

The structure of production as shown in Table 3.1 reflected this change in the declining relative importance of agriculture and the rapid growth of manufacturing, bauxite mining, tourism, services, and the public sector[2]. These primarily urban-centered activities that became the new commanding heights of the economy moved capital and entrepreneurial economic power from the rural plantation areas to urban centers and especially to the metropolitan areas of Kingston, St. Andrew, and urban St. Catherine.

Table 3.1 The Changing Structure of Production— Percent Contribution to GDP over the Period 1938–83

	Agriculture	Bauxite Mining	Manufacturing	Ownership of Dwellings	Government Services	Trade and Commerce	Other Services
1938	36	0	6	10	6	24	12
1950	31	0	11	6	6	15	12
1957	14	9	14	3	6	17	13
1968	10	10	15	n.a.	9	13	16
1980	8	14	16	n.a.	14	19	17
1983	7	4	19	n.a.	15	20	21

Note: n.a. = not available

Sources: Abstract of Statistics, Department of Statistics, 1950–1968; Economic and Social Survey, Planning Agency, 1970–1983.

While continuing to employ a large proportion of the labor force (especially in small-scale peasant farming and traditional export crops), agriculture has declined dramatically in the postwar period in terms of its contribution to production. The manufacturing sector, government services, and other private sector services (including tourism) have expanded rapidly while agriculture declined. Bauxite mining developed at a rapid rate but has declined in the 1980s due to the world recession and the market conditions of oversupply relative to demand.

Wealth in the prewar era was controlled by sugar and banana planters, the big merchants who controlled the import of goods into the economy, and the internal distributive trade, and to a lesser extent by ownership of real estate. The professional class was very small and the demand for its services very limited. Business opportunities were very restricted and the sons of rich white and brown planters and merchants tended to become either civil servants or independent professionals (lawyers, doctors, and so on).

Among the majority of poor blacks, small farming, domestic service employment (as maids or gardeners), unskilled laboring jobs, and petty trading and artisan production provided the main means of earning income. The majority of the black poor were therefore either surviving in the petty commodity sectors (small farming, trading, artisan production) or in household labor. Only about 26 percent of the black poor could be classified as being located within the mainstream working class in sugar manufacturing, factory production, construction, and highly organized service jobs. The remainder were in the diverse subproletariat of casual laborers, household labor, and self-employed petty commodity producers.

THE PATTERN OF OWNERSHIP

As the economy became more urban centered and more diverse, this pattern among the rich and the poor underwent drastic change. With the entry of foreign capital in the postwar period on a big scale, the opportunities for local manufacturing production during the war years when imports were restricted, and the increased purchasing power and import capacity of the boom years of the postwar era, there was a dramatic expansion of private sector entrepreneurial activity. Traditional and established wealth among the merchant–capitalist segment of the rich moved rapidly into new manufacturing, services, and expanded trading activities. The sons of the rich abandoned the civil service for lucrative entrepreneurial opportunities in this expanding economy. Jews, Syrians, Lebanese, Chinese, light-skinned (or brown) families joined some of the more successful white planter families in establishing a more broadly based entrepreneurial class over the period between 1938 and independence in 1962. New wealth generated by aggressive business activity combined with old wealth grasping new opportunities created a dynamic and vibrant private sector environment that was unmatched in the Caribbean in the postwar period between the war years and the mid-1960s.

Large and powerful family controlled business empires were established over this period alongside a number of smaller enterprises that provided lucrative incomes for an expanded middle and small business class. Wealth and income were, however, heavily concentrated in the hands of the very rich (both old and new wealth). Tax data for 1952[3] indicates that 59 enterprises (or 10%) earned some 73 percent of the gross incomes earned by all business enterprises paying company taxes. By 1960 some 165 companies (or 19%) were earning 91 percent of the total gross incomes for companies paying company taxes. Between 1952 and 1960 the top 20 percent of biggest companies paying corporate taxes increased their share of gross earnings among all corporate taxpayers from 84 percent to 94 percent indicating the degree to which concentration of wealth and income was accelerating as the economy grew and diversified.

By 1964, 91 percent of the income of the very rich 220 income taxpayers came from profits and professional fees in urban-based activities while only 3 percent was derived from agricultural earnings. The average taxpayer earning rent and interest accrued six times the average income of 1964 taxpayers earning wages and salary. Those individuals earning profits from agriculture earned 16 times the earnings of taxpayers earning wages and salary. Those entrepreneurs and wealthy self-employed professionals (lawyers, among others) earned as much as 61 times the average earnings of taxpayers whose earnings were based on wages and salary. All of this confirms the pattern by which the concentrations of wealth and income moved from agriculture to urban-based economic activities. Typical of the expanding capitalist economy, wealth and income were increasingly concentrated in the control of a small number of entrepreneurs. Although urban entrepreneurs and business-connected professionals represented only 11 percent of the 1964 taxpayers, they earned 42 percent of the gross incomes accruing to all taxpayers. Those taxpayers who earned wages and salary constituted 85 percent of the 1964 taxpayers but earned only 48 percent of the gross assessed earnings for all taxpayers. The economy had shifted from a rural to an urban center and was being rapidly diversified but there was a continuity of minority control of wealth and economic power.

The expansion of the public sector and the withdrawal of the rich families from civil service jobs created increased opportunities for the black and brown families to find scope for economic advancement in the public sector. A dual racial division of labor developed in which the more affluent racial minorities dominated the private sector and the ambitious upwardly mobile black and brown families were able to establish dominance in the command positions of power in the public bureaucracy after the white Englishmen left the scene as the civil service was rapidly decolonized. Expansion of the economy meant increased demand for public and private services and much of the professional skills to man these new and growing areas of activity came from these black and brown families who used the expanding education system to acquire professional training. A significant imbalance developed between higher levels of education and formal training among the top levels of the civil service and the tendency for many successful business families to disregard the need for postsecondary education and to place little value on technical, scientific, and advanced education at the tertiary levels.[4]

LABOR

The development of urban manufacturing, services, tourism, and public sector services as well as the rapid growth of construction and transportation and public utilities to facilitate these major changes in the structure of production meant an enlarged market for labor and wider opportunities for employment. The mainstream working class in construction, manufacturing, services, and public utilities and transport grew very rapidly in the postwar period. Among persons earning a regular income the mainstream working class increased from 26 percent in 1938 to 40 percent in 1982. The expansion of the mainstream working class provided the basis for a powerful trade union movement. But the limits on the growth of the mainstream working class after the 1960s has meant that the self-employed petty commodity sector has been the fastest growing segment of the labor force since the 1970s, when severe economic crises gripped the Jamaican economy. The subproletariat of household labor, unskilled manual labor, and casual workers has significantly diminished and has enlarged the ranks of the unemployed which has grown even faster than the petty commodity sector since the 1970s.

The major changes in the gainfully employed labor force shown in Table 3.2 reflect the overall trends in the Jamaican economy. Between the early 1940s and 1970, skilled and semi-skilled production workers reflected the most accelerated growth, while farm workers, service workers, and casual workers declined as a proportion of the employed labor force. This trend reflected the modernizaton of the economy over the period. Between 1970 and the 1980s some of these trends are in fact reversed as the economy experienced a deep crisis in production, foreign exchange earnings, capital outflows, investment declines, and sharp increases in unemployment. Production workers declined as did the proportion of clerical workers, while service and farm workers increased modestly.

As more workers were thrown among the ranks of the unemployed

Table 3.2 Labor Force Distribution of the Gainfully Employed
1943, 1960, 1970, 1982 (in percent)

	1943	1960	1970	1982
Professionals, technical and administrative	2	4	7	11
Clerical and sales	11	11	15	12
Service	19	20	16	20
Farmers and farm workers	44	41	30	33
Production workers	13	20	26	19
Casual workers and laborers	11	4	6	5
	100	100	100	100
Percent unemployed	25	13	19	28
Self-employed as percent of labor force	31	31	26	41

Source: Census Reports, Department of Statistics, 1943, 1960, 1970. Labor Force Surveys, Department of Statistics 1968–1982.

over this period and as access to new jobs became extremely difficult for most segments of the labor force, more and more persons sought a livelihood in self-employed petty trading and artisan small-scale production. Unemployment increased from 19 percent to 28 percent over the period while the level of own-account workers expanded from 26 to 41 percent.

Significantly, there was an appreciable growth of highly paid professional, technical, and administrative personnel over this period due to the expansion of public and private sector services over this era of crisis when the productive sectors were on the decline. Bureaucrats, paper pushers, and the managerial elite expanded rapidly, while the jobs that sustained the productive base of the economy declined.

One of the effects of this change in the balance of occupations in the labor force was to accelerate the trend towards a concentration of income among the more highly paid within the work force. Paralleling the concentration of income in the control of a small number of wealthy entrepreneurs, there is also a pattern of high concentration of wage income in the hands of the better paid wage and salary earners in the economy. It is estimated[5] that in 1972 the top 20 percent of salary earners accrued some 53 percent of the total wage and salary earnings in the economy. By 1979, the share of total wages accruing to this top 20 percent was increased to 60 percent, reflecting the deepening pattern of wage inequality during this period of crisis.

For most of the postwar period Jamaica suffered from high levels of open unemployment. Indeed, the drop in unemployment levels between the early 1950s and 1960 is due not so much to job creation as to increased levels of emigration to Britain over that period. Table 3.3 presents

Table 3.3 Changes in the Numbers of Gainfully Employed (1943–1980)

Year	Numbers of Gainfully Employed
1943	505,000
1960	566,000
1968	592,000
1980	737,000

Source: Census Report 1943, Department of Statistics. Labor Force Survey 1968–80.

data on the number of persons gainfully employed in the economy over the 1943 to 1980 period. The classification of gainfully employed includes both self-employed and wage and salary earners. A number of trends are apparent from these figures. The rate of increase in gainfully employed persons was 3.58 thousand per annum between 1943 and 1960 and 3.25 thousand per annum between 1960 and 1968.

Although the rate of job ceation was slow, unemployment dropped from 25 percent in 1943 to 13 percent in 1960. Between 1943 and 1960 there was a net addition of 61,000 to the ranks of the gainfully employed or self-employed. Between 1953 and 1961, 153,364 persons had migrated to Britain. This emigration factor removed 2.5 times as many persons from the labor force as the number of net additions to the gainfully employed between 1943 and 1960.

Paradoxically, the highest rate of increase in gainfully employed persons takes place in the 1970s when the annual rate of increase climbs to 12,000 per annum, due mainly to the expansion of the public sector and the rate of growth of the self-employed petty traders.

Although emigration continued to account for a considerable leakage from the labor force in the 1960s, it is noteworthy that open unemployment levels did not fall between 1960 and 1970. Instead open unemployment levels increased over the period. This was due to the capital intensive nature of the areas of economic expansion that occurred in the 1960s. Additionally, some of this economic expansion involved replacement of smaller labor intensive enterprises by larger capital intensive enterprises producing no net gain in labor employed and often generating a net loss in the labor employed relative to the output of goods and services.

This concentration of ownership displaced many smaller and more labor intensive firms with larger, more capital intensive enterprises in many areas of the economy.

THE SUBSECTORS

In the early period of this postwar economic growth, the Jamaican economy showed a very high GDP growth rate of 8.1 percent per annum between 1950 and 1960, reflecting the developments taking place in bauxite and alumina production, tourism, manufacturing, and services. This very high growth rate slowed down somewhat between 1962 and 1972 to a growth level of 5.8 percent. In the crisis period between 1973 and 1980 the economy declined at a rate of −2.3 percent per annum. In the early period of the 1980s positive growth was restored at a rather modest level of 1.7 percent per annum. The first sign of major crisis in the economy was the coexistence of positive GDP growth in the 1960s with high and increasing levels of open unemployment.

The net effect of these economic trends was to create a political economy separated into clearly demarcated segments controlled by different social classes and with distinctly unequal social and economic power. A powerful corporate sector of larger enterprises controlling most of the income and profits generated in the economy had clearly emerged. It was divided between some branch plants of foreign multinationals and those enterprises owned and controlled by the wealthy urban bourgeoisie. Secondly there was a large, if somewhat fluctuating and unstable medium and small scale business sector consisting of enterprises employing very small numbers of persons but representing a large proportion of the enterprises in the economy. These enterprises are controlled and owned partly by the Jamaican middle class and partly by relatively lower income petty business interests employing very cheap labor.

Thirdly, there is the petty commodity sector run by self-employed persons with very little capital and employing no labor. This petty commodity sector represents the ingrained capitalism among the poor and reflects their aggressive survival strategies of creating self-employment in petty trading, farming, artisan production and services in the face of an economy that since 1960 has displayed a very low propensity to create enough jobs to meet the social needs of a rapidly growing population.

These three layers of capitalism: the rich, the middle class and small business sector, and the petty commodity sector complicate the task of economic management as their management and business practices vary considerably while governments are seeking to establish some comon set of procedures and regulations to guide the business transactions and policies in all three sectors.

These three subsectors of the political economy differ with respect to the areas in the economy where they cluster or concentrate. The petty commodity sector has a dual concentration on small scale agriculture (58%) and petty trading or higgling (32%). The small and medium scale business sector is mainly engaged in services (61%) including commercial trading 27 percent and other services 35 percent. Some 6 percent of these smaller enterprises employing labor are in farming and 25 percent are in manufacturing, construction, and electricity. Among the big business enterprises, the largest concentration (42%) is in manufacturing, construction, and electricity. Services represent 34 percent of these larger enterprises including commercial trading 14 percent and other services 20 percent. Farm enterprises represent 15 percent of these larger enterprises which is more than twice the proportion among the small and medium scale business sector.

The economic subsectors differ also in terms of the racial and social composition of the owners. The petty commodity sector is made up almost entirely of poor blacks. The small and medium scale business sector is made up of a minority of middle income persons with brown or light skin racial type, and a substantial majority of persons of black complexion as well as a small minority of Asian Indians and Chinese. The big business sector consists of owners drawn from the privileged racial minorities of Jews, Syrians, Lebanese, and whites, and a small minority of brown complexion. The foreign-owned enterprises of this big business sector are managed increasingly by a multiracial mixture of whites, blacks, Asian Indians, Chinese, and persons of brown complexion.

If we define these subsectors of the economy in terms of the petty commodity sector, including enterprises where there is only family labor or the labor power of the owner, the small business sector (including medium scale enterprises) as being those that employ between one person and 49 on a regular basis, and the big business sector as enterprises with 50 or more employees, the 1982 distribution of these non-governmental sectors would be as follows:

	number of enterprises	private sector percent of labor force
petty commodity sector	300,000	46
small business sector (including medium scale enterprises)	49,800	31
big business sector	969	23

Source: Data Records Of Housing Trust and National Insurance Contributions and Labor Force Surveys (1980–82).

The small business sector is in fact larger than the big business sector as regards numbers of enterprises, and labor force employed. Its 50,000 enterprises in the Jamaican economy can be therefore classified with the traditional capitalist sector which employs wage labor in contrast to the majority which is involved in petty commodity activities where labor and capital are undifferentiated and class conflicts between these interests, therefore, do not arise.

In this sense, the economy can be seen to mirror a fundamental duality between petty commodity activity on the one hand, and traditional capitalism, on the other. Equally important is the fact that in the traditional capitalist sector the majority of the labor force outside of the public sector is employed by very small enterprises. To the extent that we can characterize the traditional capitalist segment of the Jamaican economy it clearly has to be seen as a predominantly small business economy.

Within the big business sector there are only 65 enterprises employing more than 500 workers and 250 enterprises employing 200 or more workers. Fifty percent of these larger enterprises have between 50 and 99 workers while 26 percent have 200 or more employees and 74 percent between 50 and 199 workers.

The degree of dualism in the Jamaican economy is reflected in the fact that the traditional capitalist sectors (including the big and small business subsectors) contributes 74 percent of the economy's production of goods and services with 46 percent of the total public and private sector labor force while the petty commodity sector with 40 percent of the labor force contributes a mere 10 percent. The remaining 16 percent is contributed from the public sector where 14 percent of the labor force is engaged in traditional government and administrative services. The vast income and productivity gaps between the petty commodity sector and the capitalist sector contribute considerably to the inequality of incomes within the Jamaican economy.

THE BOURGEOISIE

In the transition from a plantation-dominated economy in which there was an ascendant white rural planter class to a more diversified urban-centered economy there has emerged a powerful grouping of urban-based wealthy families of mainly Jewish and Arab ethnic origin. This newly emergent capitalist network of rich families traces its social origins back to the merchant class families of the late nineteenth and early twentieth century. Although in the expected course of capital accumulation most of these families acquired land and moved into agriculture as their family holdings expanded, they represent a small section of the earlier merchant class families that have used merchant capital as the base from which to create large and diverse family economic empires. They have both penetrated and dominated many areas of the Jamaican economy. A few surviving families with origins in the traditional planter class[6] are to be found among these wealthy families but they represent a dsitinct minority.

Included among these are the following 15 families who are perhaps the most powerful, active, and influential families in the economic and political power domains of the country and they represent an important segment of the effective class leadership among the rich capitalists in Jamaica:

Powerful business families

Matalon, Ashenheim, Hendrickson, Facey, Mahfood, Issa, Hart, Henriques, Desnoes, Geddes, deLisser, Clarke, Rousseau, Stewart, Kennedy.

Only two of these powerful family interests have planter class ties (Clark, deLisser). Another three (Desnoes, Geddes, Hendrickson) represent early pioneering food manufacturing interests with no link to either planters or merchant capital. Two others (Rousseau, Stewart) represent new wealth acquired in the postwar period and with no connection with the earlier traditional business interests. The remaining eight family interests that are the wealthiest within this grouping all trace their class origins back to merchant families engaging in buying and selling imported consumer goods in the early twentieth century and late nineteenth century. Most of these families emerged as successful business interests by the first decade of the twentieth century. The Ashenheims and the Henriques were the first among them to diversify into areas outside of commerce in the prewar period. They all expanded and diversified on a massive scale in the postwar period, with the Matalon family emerging as the preeminent and most wealthy family interest in the economy.

In contrast to the rich family interests with planter or early manufacturing family connections, the families with merchant capital origins have been considerably more expansionist, more aggressive in buying into new enterprises and moving into new areas of the economy and have added considerably more to the stock of family wealth. The most aggressive, expansionist and successful among these family interests in the postwar period have been the Matalons whose massive holding company, Industrial Commercial Developments, Limited, controls a large number of subsidiary enterprises that turned over more than $250 million in sales and in 1983 accumulated approximately $19 million in pretax profits.

The rich capitalist families in Jamaica have maintained a close relationship with foreign business interests. Their beginning as commercial importers and commission agents of foreign companies created the basis for viewing themselves as having a natural alliance with foreign capitalist interests. That background engendered a view of the Jamaican economy as benefiting from a strong link with entrepreneurial interests in Europe and North America. In the period of postwar economic diversification, these ties were cemented by joint ventures, especially in manufacturing production and heavy dependencè on foreign borrowing, import credits, technology, and technical assistance.

THE MIDDLE CLASS

With the extensive penetration of the economy by foreign companies in tourism, bauxite, manufacturing production, and financial services and with the growth of an increased number of larger Jamaican owned enterprises in manufacturing and services as well as large government-owned public enterprises, a distinct professional managerial grouping has emerged in the public and private corporate sector in the Jamaican economy over the postwar period. Enlarged opportunities for higher education in technical fields and areas related to management and the social sciences (both overseas and in Jamaica at the Mona campus of the University of the West Indies) have allowed a cross section of middle class individuals from varying black, brown, Chinese, Indian, white, Jewish, and Arab ethnic backgrounds to enter important leadership positions in the economy. Large scale migration of lighter skinned ethnic minorities from Jamaica in the 1970s opened up wider opportunities for black middle class Jamaicans to be recruited into the ranks of the professional managers. This trend has diluted the earlier pattern in which the educated black middle class was located entirely in public sector jobs while the management of the private sector was monopolized by the ethnic minorities. Especially after the mid-1960s and increasingly so in the 1970s, racial barriers to middle and top level positions in the private sector that blocked the upward mobility of the middle class blacks in the 1950s and early 1960s were progressively removed as the black middle class expanded and became a more influential force within the political community.

In contrast to the highly trained professional managers who predominate in the larger private and public enterprises, the small business sector is run by owner-managers. These enterprises tend to be undercapitalized and to be dependent on large financial inputs of bank loans compared to relatively small outlays of equity financing. They are therefore burdened with large financial costs and the owners are not inclined to reinvest earnings or profits in the business, preferring instead to rely heavily on bank loans. The owner-managers tend to maintain artificially high life-styles that are a drain on the financial viability of these enterprises. A high propensity to consume imported luxury goods financed by income and excessive bank borrowing have produced a very Americanized pattern of middle class luxury living that is both a burden on the country's limited foreign exchange earnings and a source of enlarging the visible economic inequalities in the country.

The small business owner-managers who run a significant area of the economy are a militant source of ultra-conservatism in the Jamaican political community opposing radical social reform, resisting efforts by the state to regulate private sector activities and constantly complaining about threats posed to private initiative and free enterprise by big government and state control of key areas of the national economy. While approximately 25 percent of the big private sector-owned enterprises are foreign-owned or local and foreign joint ventures, the small business sector is entirely Jamaican-owned. These owner managers do not have a traditionally strong relationship with foreign capital and even where their line of business depends on links with foreign capital, they are inclined to fear or to be suspicious about foreign investments crowding them out of the Jamaican economy. Although they tend to be politically conservative, their precarious economic base leads them to use nationalism and a promotion of Jamaican ownership as a means of defending their class self-interests. While they therefore complain about big government, they have relied heavily on state protection from competition from overseas producers. Their essential ambivalence is also manifest in their high propensity to divert foreign exchange to overseas accounts to maintain their artificially high life-styles, while often expressing strong sentiments of economic nationalism supporting greater Jamaican ownership of the various sectors of the economy.

Some of the small business owner-manager class often fear the big business class, resent its dominance over sectors of the economy and will often identify with populist political stirrings directed by party leaders and activists against the very rich racial minorities. Moreso than the big business class, these small business owner managers are dependent on favors from politicians to survive in business and often get entangled in patron-client relationships with prominent power brokers and leaders in the major political parties. Because they lack the social and political influence of the rich capitalists, they get more actively involved in private sector interest groups and lobbies and are more inclined to join the ranks of the professional politicians by running for public office. The big business class, on the other hand, is more inclined to operate behind the scenes because it has the resources to influence the key policy makers. Where the latter get close to the public domains of power, they tend to serve more as confidants, consultants, and advisers to the dominant political leaders rather than by offering themselves for elected public office. Beyond this, the members of the rich business families also serve politicians and their own private business interests by accepting key[7] positions on statutory bodies, regulatory agencies, and state-owned public enterprises.

THE STATE SECTOR

While the private domain of economic power was expanding in the postwar years, the public sector was also growing at a fast rate although the momentum of public sector expansion only accelerated after independence. This significant public sector expansion is reflected in the growth of public spending as a percentage of national income, the enlarged share of the public sector within the labor force and as a percentage of the total economy's wage bill, and in the public sector's increased contribution to GDP for public and administrative service.

In 1943 there were 4.5 thousand public sector employees in local and central government. By 1968 this number had expanded to 57,000, and by 1980 it had grown even further to the level of 110,000. Public expenditure as a share of GDP was 13 percent in 1950 and increased to 17 percent by independence in 1962. By 1967 it had climbed to 21 percent and increased to 42 percent by 1977. The contribution of government services to GDP stabilized at 6 to 7 percent between 1938 and 1957. It increased to 9 percent in the 1960s and accelerated to 16 percent by 1982.

Two factors account for this growth of the public sector in the economy. These include the enlarged revenue base generated by the expansion and diversification of the private sector (including big and small enterprises) which gave the government more resources to spend and the momentum of political and social pressures which stimulated efforts at expanding and enlarging the scope and provisions of public economic and social services and the bureaucratic apparatus through which these services were manned.

But the growth of the state sector not only fed on the enlarged private sector but itself stimulated private sector growth. By creating a large grouping of middle and lower middle income employees the expanded public services influenced the generation of increased demand for middle income consumer goods, consumer durables, housing, and services. By the mid-1970s for example the public sector workers constituted the largest contribution to the economy's wage bill over and above any other sector with a 27 percent share of that aggregate wage bill and with the manufacturing sector (14%) and the construction and distribution sectors (12%) showing much smaller total wage and salary payments.

Equally important, public sector spending included both large wage payments as well as large purchases of goods and services bought directly from the private sector. By the late 1970s, 26 percent of total public expenditure was consumed by salaries and wages while another 32 percent was spent on procuring goods and services from the private sector. Many private enterprises, therefore thrived as the public sector grew larger and some developed a vested interest in servicing public sector needs to a point where the government emerged as their main market for selling goods and services. Securing access to this government business, of course, inevitably creates alliances, patron client relationships, and close collaboration between elected members of the political directorate and the key decision makers in the public bureaucracy, on the one hand, and networks of private sector family and business interests, on the other.

FOREIGN LINKAGES

An important factor in the broad sweep of change in the postwar period was the disengagement from the economy's close external links with Britain and their replacement with close external ties with the U.S. economy. Paralleling the growth of primarily U.S. foreign corporate investments in the Jamaican economy in the postwar period was a matching pattern of increasing trade dependence on U.S. imports and on the U.S. market as the main outlet for exports and hard currency earnings.

In the period of the early plantation economy in Jamaica trade with the United Kingdom dominated exports and imports. In 1850, 78 percent of export trade and 60 percent of imports were with Britain. With the entry of U.S. capital in the economy via United Fruit Company and banana exports, the United States emerged second to Britain in the ties between the Jamaican economy and other economies. By 1938 21 percent of imports were from the United States and 33 percent from Britain. By 1968 U.S. imports reached 39 percent and British imports fell to 20 percent. By 1978 trade with the United States represented 37 percent of the total value of exports and imports while trade with Britain was at a much lower 17 percent level. This accelerated trend towards U.S. economic ties was strengthened by the predominance of U.S. capital in sectors of the economy (bauxite and tourism, among others).

These trade and investment links were further reinforced by the shift in migration patterns from Britain to the United States between the 1960s and the 1970s. Between 1970 and 1980 an estimated 180,000 Jamaicans migrated to the United States compared to 17,000 migrating to Britain. The United States also replaced Britain as the main destination for students going overseas for higher education.

A further link to the United States has been forged through the billion dollar per annum marijuana drug traffic between Jamaica and the United States that has provided large lucrative incomes for middle class persons as well as small farmers in certain rural communities. This drug traffic has facilitated the penetration of Jamaican society by U.S. mafia interests and has funded a large informal shadow economy that operates outside of the reach of state control. This drug connection and the large incomes it generates have provided a source of prosperity and capital accumulation for a small section of the established middle class and have facilitated a certain amount of upward mobility into middle class incomes and life-styles by some peasants and working class hustlers who have earned large incomes from the trade.

All of these factors added to access to the United States through the mass media, the large inflow of U.S. tourists, constant travel between the United States and Jamaica by Jamaican residents and their U.S.-based relatives and friends have amounted to a significant level of U.S. influences on Jamaican life-styles. Consumer habits and tastes, drug use, social and political ideologies (including a major impact due to U.S. conservative Christian evangelists), and the desire for consumer durables and the creature comforts of modern living by all classes are just some of the evident manifestations of this U.S. influence. Perhaps the most damaging of these U.S. influences is the ease of access to high-powered submachine guns channeled partly through the drug trade. This has considerably strengthened the social power of urban criminal gangs and increased their leverage to influence the country's politics by hiring out their services to political parties and other interests needing the enforcement services of gunmen.

Drugs and guns have, therefore, emerged as an avenue of escape for the more adventurous among the urban poor from the vicious circle of high unemployment, limited horizons of social opportunity, and the trap of persistent poverty. These mercenaries who have a footing in this growing shadow economy of drugs have become a major social force in urban ghetto communities where they exercise leadership roles and are courted by the political parties for support. The overall impact on the society includes an extremely high crime and homicide rate and the projection of romanticized images of machismo and violence. They influence the youth in urban ghetto areas and expand the destructive pattern of drug use and abuse at this level of the society. The net effect is to increase the propensity for lawlessness and anarchy which generates strong popular suport for harsh law and order measures and the conferring of wider powers on the police and the army to pacify the society, often at the price of diminishing human rights.

POLITICAL CONSEQUENCES

This broad outline of the structure and patterns of change in the Jamaican political economy provides a basis on which to identify the major social forces operating in the political community and the agenda of issues that dominates attempts to represent those interests. Perhaps the most fundamental fact is that the final stages of the transition to democracy in the postwar period was accompanied by a rapid growth and diversification of the economy that created new sources of wealth, expanded the political and social space for the various classes, and therefore assisted the process of political accommodation and interest bargaining so central to liberal democracy. The transition to democracy was a relatively smooth one partly because it was achieved iñ an economic climate in which hope and optimism rather than pessimism were uppermost in the environment. The new political arrangements therefore were positively associated with a period in which the life chances of most members of the political community seemed either to be getting much better or to have the prospect of experiencing considerable improvement.

Secondly, the shift of economic power from country to town was paralleled by the shift in the nerve center of political power from rural to urban Jamaica. Highly organized urban class interests emerged to represent both labor and capital but in so doing crowded out the rural interests from either access to the corridors of power or access to the effective channels of interest representation and communication. This urban-rural imbalance in the political community in which a clear separation was drawn between urban interest groups and classes and those interests linked to agriculture and the small rural communities had major implications for how the political institutions functioned.

A number of specific class interests have been identified and linked to distinct areas of the economy. Many of the struggles for political power and influence have therefore centered on clashes between these interests. These include the 192,000 unionized working class; the approximately 106 very wealthy members of the big capitalist class; the larger body of some 10,000 middle class, smaller capitalist interests; the 40,000 small business class; the 300,000 strong petty commodity sector divided between petty traders and small farmers; and the 275,000 rural and urban unemployed.

Given the poverty and inequalities in the society and the economy's lack of a large enough income base to sustain a welfare state (such as exists in Western European and North American liberal democratic systems) some way had to be found to develop 'welfare politics' that channelled material benefits to the poor on a scale that is affordable. The development of a network of political[8] patronage and patron–client linkages emerged as a central domain of power. Party-based patronage was manipulated by the governing factions drawn mainly from the ranks of the urban middle class professionals who led the parties. They control the poorer classes who provide political support in exchange for the promise of receiving such welfare benefits. Underlying this is the crucial role of high levels of open unemployment guaranteeing the political party machines a constant over-supply of potential recruits willing to do the party's bidding for the prospect of some benefits.

The inherent weaknesses within this mainly small capitalist economy and its low propensity to either accumulate investment capital or retain foreign exchange earnings, combined with the social pressures on the political directorate to expand the productive base of the economy mean that much of post-independence public policy making has centered on efforts to find appropriate economic strategies that can advance the country in spite of these constraints. Crisis management of an economy slowed down by weak small business interests and the often risk-averse insecure big capitalists interests (in the 1970s) clearly brought sharply into relief areas of conflict and contention between political managers impatient to get the economy moving and the private sector. These conflicts have affected both JLP and PNP administrations between the 1970s and the 1980s.

Economies tend like humans to go through periods of growth, maturation, and aging. Unlike humans, however, who die, economies must be rejuvenated after the aging process sets in so as to enter a new cycle. That rejuvenation process becomes increasingly complex because for so many economies (especially in the Third World) the parameters that govern their options are set by the world economy. A great capacity for understanding those external factors and manipulating them to facilitate economic rebirth is central to the political management that can chart such a successful course. The Jamaican political economy was aging in the prewar period. Postwar growth and diversification revived it. That process of regeneration was partial, as reflected in the dual character of the economy divided between two capitalist subsectors and a large petty commodity sector. The modernization of the economy was therefore far from complete before the process of maturation and premature aging set in during the latter part of the 1960s. In contrast to other small dynamic economies in the region such as that of Barbados, the Jamaican economy has stagnated over most of the 15 years between 1968 and 1983. The search for domestic and foreign policy options by the political managers over this period represents a so far futile endeavor to find the levers of policy that can stimulate this regeneration and rebirth. How the democratic political process installed in the postwar period copes with this ongoing economic crisis and what have been the short-term and long-term effects on the character of democracy in the country are a central issue in the analysis of capitalism and democracy in Jamaica.

NOTES

1. This tendency of trade dependence to grow as small Third World economies modernize and shift their position in the international division of labor is a reality often ignored by those who analyze development from the perspective of dependency theory. See Carl

Stone, "Patterns of insertion into the world economy: Historical profile and contemporary options," *Social and Economic Studies*, 32 (1983).

2. For a detailed outline of the structure of the Jamaican economy, see Owen Jefferson, *The Post-War Economic Development of Jamaica*, Kingston, Jamaica: Institute of Social and Economic Research, 1972.

3. These tax data derive from the collector of taxes' reports, 1952, 1960, and 1964.

4. This point applies especially to some of the families controlling new wealth in the postwar period. Families with traditional wealth tended to have a practice of sending bright sons to British universities.

5. See Compton Bourne, "Economic recession and labor income inequality in less developed countries: A Jamaican case study, forthcoming in *Social and Economic Studies*.

6. The link between the old planter class and the new bourgeoisie is extremely weak in that the latter emerged out of the merchant class. This fact is misrepresented in a popular work on the subject by Stanley Reid, "An introductory approach to the concentration of power in the Jamaican corporate economy and notes on its origin," in Carl Stone and Aggrey Brown, eds., Essays on Power and Change in Jamaica, Kingston: Jamaica Publishing House, 1977.

7. A good example is the case of Mr. John Issa, chairman of the Jamaican Tourist Board whose family interests in tourism were able to take over the first two hotels that were divested to local hoteliers.

8. For a thorough discussion of the role of clientelism in Jamaican politics, see Carl Stone, *Democracy and clientelism in Jamaica*, New Brunswick, N.J.: Transaction Books, 1980.

4

THE POLITICAL CULTURE

The tradition of politics in any country is shaped not only by the institutional structures such as parliamentary government but also by the values, beliefs, myths, ideas, behavior patterns, and underlying attitudes that are shared by those who make up the political community. These factors we can broadly define as constituting a political culture that is passed on from generation to generation by the main agencies of political socialization (family, peer groups, community, church, political parties, and so on).

In the Jamaican case, the basic parliamentary forms of government were inherited through the British colonial connection, but it is the local political culture that has determined how these institutions worked and how various social grouping relates to them. We can separate the political culture into two main elements: the first concerns the beliefs members of the political community have about how power and influence are exercised within it; the second concerns the actual relationships that govern political interactions of power, influence, and authority within the political community. Indeed, it is often the case that subjective beliefs around which political faith and loyalties are built are at a variance with the reality of power relationships and commitment to a political system is sustained by myths and mistaken beliefs about the realities of power. Support for democracy in Jamaica is sustained both by a body of myths and mistaken notions about the reality of power as well as by the nature of the power relations within the political community.

THE PARTIES

When asked about what things Jamaicans can be proud of in a national survey[1] carried out by the author in 1981, a majority of those who identified something to be proud of referred to the Jamaican citizens' right to vote. The right to choose political leaders periodically and to exercise choice regarding which faction of leaders should govern has been invested not only with feelings of pride but has become valued as a means by which ordinary citizens exercise real power over the political community. In contrast to intellectual cynics who portray the Jamaican two party system as offering no meaningful choices for voters and other minority critics who see the majority classes as being manipulated by powerful minorities, the majority of Jamaican citizens derive a real sense of political efficacy from having the power to decide who should represent them in parliament and which party and party leader should control the executive. This belief is an important factor in sustaining high levels of voter turnout which achieved 72 percent and 80 percent turnout, respectively, of the estimated population eligible to vote in the 1976 and 1980 parliamentary elections.

Not only is voter turnout very high in Jamaican elections, surveys have consistently shown that in an electorate of slightly more than 1 million eligible voters the two major political parties have an activist and easily mobilizable following between them of 250,000 persons. These represent the party hard core that can be relied on to do party work, attend party meetings and conferences, and disseminate the party line and party propaganda throughout the various rural and urban communities in the country. The activist core of committed followers fluctuates over time in that when either of the two parties loses an election, the hard core support falls while that of the winning party increases. Also, when a party in power begins to lose popularity, the opposition party garners increased hard core support while the party in power experiences a loss of committed followership. This hard core support for the Jamaica Labour Party and the Peoples National Party, therefore, fluctuates between an estimated bottom line of 90,000 to 110,000 and grows as large as 150,000 to 160,000 when the party's fortunes are on the ascendancy.

This hard core party support is characterized by great intensity of feeling, emotional loyalties, and aggressive and combative sentiments of support. It is sustained by a number of factors that mirror the role of democratic organs in the Jamaican society. It has to be understood as a response to the need for power on the part of the majority classes (workers, peasants, unemployed, and petty traders and artisans). Unlike other political cultures in the Western industrial countries where middle class and middle income persons are overrepresented in activist party membership[2] compared to less educated, lower socioeconomic groups, the reverse is the case in Jamaica. Hard core party membership of both the Jamaica Labor Party and the Peoples National Party underrepresents the middle class and overrepresents the poorer classes (both urban and rural). The middle class professionals and owner-managers added to the labor aristocracy and the clerical and white collar workers who make up approximately 25 percent of the adult population constitute only about 2 percent of the hard core activist and reliable membership of the two major political parties. In contrast, the bottom 40 percent of income earners make up some 75 percent of the two parties' hard core membership, with 23 percent from the middle 40 percent of income earners and 2 percent from the top 20 percent of income earners. In terms of the social composition of their membership, the two major parties draw disproportionately large support from the poorest of the poor and can be said to be poor people's parties.

A number of factors account for this social composition of the mainstream political parties in Jamaica. Economic power continues to be highly concentrated among a small minority of rich and privileged families. These interests together with foreign capital dominate the economy. The middle class while not having that level of power are able to use their location in key institutions and their networks of intraclass contacts to influence decisions and secure their interests. Middle class and bourgeois interests are represented by a wide range of economic interest groups, professional associations, and special issue lobbies. The trade unions tend to draw most of their support from the middle 40 percent of income earners, which leaves entirely unrepresented the poor and powerless who fall in the bottom 40 percent. The trade unions, moreover, tend to confine their concerns to collective bargaining issues and matters relating to industrial relations. The workers they represent are concentrated mainly in the public sector and the big corporate sector of the privately owned enterprises. Their interests are somewhat different from those of the large army of unemployed youth and women in the very poor communities, the petty traders and higglers, the small farmers, and the extremely poorly paid subproletariat in small business enterprises. These poorer socioeconomic groupings have neither resources, leadership, nor motivation to organize themselves on a community or other collective basis. The subculture of poverty in which they are trapped generates survival strategies that focus the individuals' energies on coping with personal problems on a very individualistic basis or in mutual aid relationships with small face-to-face neighborhood networks. They therefore lack the political capacity and resources for either community or interest group organization on a scale that could give them bargaining power in the political system. This lack of organizational capacity, combined with their deep sense of alienation in a social system in which power is controlled by a few and only the privileged and the middle class have access to the levers of decision making, creates a political vacuum that has been filled by the major political parties since the early 1940s. How well they have filled that vacuum remains to be evaluated. What is beyond dispute is the fact that these political parties provide a channel by which the very poor and powerless can have some access to the levers of decision making and can have their interests represented through the machinery of the political party that seeks their votes, their loyalty, their commitment, and their enthusiasm in being part of a coalition of interests that compete for control over the state or the public domain of power.

These political parties therefore serve a powerful combination of functions in Jamaican democracy. They first of all aggregate and bring together a variety of class interests that unite in the cause of taking power through elections. In the process of this aggregation of interests, party loyalty rather than class loyalties assumes dominance in the individual's political socialization. The shopkeeper, the farmer, the unemployed youth, the low income household helper, the highly paid wage worker in bauxite or a large food-processing factory, the higgler, and the middle class professional all come together on the basis of promoting and defending the cause of the party with almost evangelical fervor. Because the poor and socially disadvantaged are in the majority, it is their cultural style and emotional and social needs that shape the style of the political party's internal life. For them the party is their road to power and social opportunity and is therefore deserving of total commitment and great sacrifices in defending its interests. The party confers dignity, status, respectability and recognition through the membership's vicarious identification with party leaders and the party's power. While the party addresses class needs and interests in its public policies, the party superimposes party loyalties over class loyalties and obliterates them as a frame of reference for political action.

By providing the most alienated and socially disadvantaged with a frame of reference for collective identification and collective action, the political parties guarantee political stability and a minimal level of support for the middle class professionals who control these parties and their leadership. By overrepresenting the interests of the poor in their internal social composition, the parties get converted into instruments of populism which irritate the rich, the privileged, and the middle class and increase the class commitment of the very poor to the cause of the party. By overrepresenting the poorest of the poor in organizations controlled by small minorities drawn from the mainstream professional middle class (most of whom live in fear of the poor), the parties help to bridge the class gap in a class-stratified society and provide a direct channel of communication that sensitizes these leaders to the expectations, aspirations and world view of the very poor.

The political leaders and the parties inevitably get caught in the cross fire of class conflicts in socially divided Jamaica. Two main types of populist leaders emerge from this political culture. There is first of all the paternalist populist leader who projects a sort of godfather figure. He does things for the poor quietly and systematically. He uses his levers of power to channel resources toward meeting poor people's needs, opens up access to public resources and puts pressure on the privileged to accommodate and deal with the needs of the poor. JLP leader Edward Seaga who emerged to prominence representing a poor urban ghetto community is typical of this type of leader. The other type of populist leader is the militant who attempts to do all things which the paternalist type of populist leader seeks to achieve but he goes about it with a somewhat different style. Whereas the paternalist type of populist leader avoids open confrontation with the rich and the privileged, the militant tries to generate political energy by engaging in mock battles with the powerful classes that have no real revolutionary intent but are designed to intimidate the powerful into being more amenable to making concessions on behalf of policies addressed to poor people's needs. The militant bargains with the rich by arousing the anger of the poor while the paternalist relies on persuasion and arm twisting behind the scenes, thereby keeping the antagonistic interests as far apart as possible, and seeks to muzzle the expressions of anger from the poor that the militant thrives in arousing. The militant attracts more hostility from the rich, the privileged and the middle class but neither type of populist leader is trusted by them. Not only do the rich and the middle class generally treat these leaders with great skepticism, but they tend to see party politics as a crude, vulgar, and dirty game with poor people that is corrupted and contaminated by the subculture of the poor. It is seen as a dangerous game that they prefer to view from a safe distance.

In the same way that the brown property owners and urban middle class in the old plantation society feared the prospect of blacks gaining power in the political arena, the black and brown middle class feel intimidated by the way the political parties accommodate to poor people's interests. The rich tend to echo the political views of the old planter class in seeing democracy as inevitably corrupting the society by giving power and influence to the ignorant and unenlightened, the uncivilized and the uneducated. The political parties, populist leaders, and the alliance between middle class professional party leaders and hard core support from the bottom 40 percent of income earners come under constant criticism and attack in the newspaper, the *Daily Gleaner*, owned and influenced by rich capitalist families, and from articulate spokesmen[3] in the mass media who express the class biases of the rich and the middle class.

The real difference between the middle class professionals who enter party politics as leaders and the middle class from which they originate or the privileged brown strata in the old plantation society is that the former are part of a small minority within the ranks of the socially privileged who do not fear the poor and are influenced by political and social beliefs that motivate them to make common cause with the poor and therefore to develop a capacity for leadership. What is often forgotten by critics who characterize these political parties as being middle class parties because of their middle class leadership is the fact that these middle class party leaders are atypical and unrepresentative minorities within their class of origin and that their populist leadership is viewed by the middle class as a betrayal[4] of their class origins.

The populist leadership generated by this political culture is authoritarian. The social need for a sense of power that lies at the root of the political impulse in the society dictates that leaders should be strong authority figures defining a path to be followed by the party hard core with unambiguous loyalty. The party leader is invested with ultimate authority and becomes a sort of transcendental, larger-than-life figure who must not be criticized nor questioned. Since the hard core derive psychological satisfaction and self-fulfillment from a vicarious identification with the power, stature, and authority of the party leader, the stronger and more decisive and dominating is that leader, the greater the fanatical loyalty his leadership style generates. This leaves little room for party leaders who are mere consensus builders and who simply echo the views of the factions who make up the party. The political culture encourages leaders who pronounce solutions but do very little listening and pursue their own larger than life prophetic visions for public policy that the hard core party enthusiasts will echo with great fervor. The free exchange of ideas, the give and take of internal self-criticisms, and the critical evaluation of party direction that strong internal democracy demands in a political party are just not compatible with this type of transcendental leadership where hard core followers are content to merely echo the lead of the party's maximum leader. To criticize such a leader openly is equivalent to an expression of party disloyalty. Disagreements, debates, and honest competition between divergent ideas about party direction can only take place in private and in small groups of like-minded individuals. The rank and file are carefully insulated from such internal political dissonance.

Although party membership may satisfy the need for a sense of power on the part of the Jamaican poor that fact should not obscure the reality that the thin layer of middle class professional leaders guard very jealously their positions of power at the national level and exercise tight control over many aspects of internal party life, such as policy formulation, ideology, overall political strategy, party finances, and national leadership recruitment. Moreover, as I have documented elsewhere,[5] the party's top leader tends to be invested with extraordinarily wide powers of personal control over these matters. However, the relative absence of internal party democracy is not an issue with the rank and file membership of either of the main political parties. The party rank and file concedes to its leadership monopoly of power at the national level, but at the local constituency and community levels the national party leadership has to permit considerable local autonomy in matters such as the allocation of scarce benefits (jobs, housing contracts, and so on), campaign strategies and tactics, the recruitment of local leadership, and the day-to-day handling of conflicts and party internal matters at these levels. Indeed, there is a real sense in which these parties are not tightly controlled centralized hierarchies but are built on a principle of stratarchy that defines boundaries of national and local power domains and allows local level activists considerable say in the management of party affairs at these lower levels. What these parties therefore do is to give opportunities for a considerable number of ordinary citizens to assume local level leadership roles and a feeling of being very important within the local communities.

A more central issue for party rank and file relates to how well the parties take care of the economic and social needs of the party faithful. The Jamaican economy lacks the resources to create a welfare state such as exists in Western Europe and North America. What has therefore evolved is welfare politics based on the use of state power to allocate benefits to the party faithful. These benefits include employment on government projects, contracts to carry out government projects in the building of economic infrastructure such as roads, bridges, markets and water supplies, and access to facilities such as housing in housing schemes, and highly sought after opportunities for overseas employment in contract labor schemes in the United States.

The members of parliament and local government councillors are the main channels through which these scarce benefits are made available on a constituency basis but there is usually a considerable level of local community leadership pressure and inputs in these decisions as to who gets what. Benefits available in any constituency are seen as the exclusive preserve of party faithful in that geographical area and norms governing their allocation do not permit party faithful from other areas to receive those benefits. There are usually more needs to be taken care of than scarce benefits available and some of the local community leaders often try to channel a disproportionate share of these opportunities for their own benefit. There is also constant competition and seeking after such scarce benefits and this often becomes an issue over which a great deal of local conflicts have to be sorted out. Conflicts invariably arise between the party leadership at the national level and local party faithful when any local benefit perceived as having great patronage value is allocated for national reasons along nonparty lines. In such cases it is not unusual for violence to be used as an instrument of protest against the bureaucrats who have responsibility for making the allocations. A typical case was the granting of a contract for land preparation by the National Sugar Industry Authority to a contractor from another parish on the grounds that the work required someone with specialized knowledge and no such contractor was available locally. The local member of parliament (MP) under pressure from angry constituents led a demonstration against the contract award. The contractor was refused entry to the property and threatened with violence. The head of the sugar authority who was someone of national stature in the governing party and the brother-in-law of the prime minister and party leader was forced to negotiate with the MP on the site where he was surrounded by a large and angry gathering of local party faithful who insisted that he could not leave until the contract was reawarded to someone within the constituency, who, of course, would hire local labor. The outcome was victory for the locals.

At another level, national party leaders from time to time seek to reduce the quantum of scarce benefits that are allocated along partisan lines. This is usually done to appease nonpartisan national opinion which is very critical of party patronage. Invariably, such policy initiatives are rejected at the local level and become incapable of being implemented. Where major employment projects occur in the urban metropolitan area local pressures have been generated by party faithful in more than one constituency for a sharing of the benefits between adjacent constituencies. Where this is not done considerable and violent conflicts can arise as was the case in the building of the International Seabed Authority building in downtown Kingston. The building site was located in the constituency of an opposition member of parliament. Most of the construction jobs were allocated to party faithful from the constituency represented by the prime minister which is the constituency that is immediately adjacent to the one in which the building site was located. Party faithful in a nearby government-controlled constituency made efforts through their MP to obtain a proportion of the jobs but they were not successful. Hostilities between these two constituencies led eventually to a feud and political violence in which several persons were killed.[6]

A great deal of violence that occurs between party faithful supporting the rival political parties centers around scarce benefits. Deep resentments build up over the fact that most benefits go to constituencies represented by governing party MPs and those benefiting tend to be overwhelmingly the party faithful of the party in power. Invariably when there is a change of governing parties, houses are burnt out and party faithful supporting the losing party are chased out of communities or are on the receiving end of violence out of resentment against scarce benefits allocation in their favor and out of desire to take revenge now that these party faithful no longer have the protection of state power. The extensive allocation of scarce benefits to party faithful give the latter a sense of having a real stake in the fortunes of his or her party that often justifies extreme and militant actions against persons supporting the opposing party. Even where no benefits are actually received, the hope of obtaining benefits among the desperately poor and socially disadvantaged who make up a disproportionate number of the party faithful often becomes sufficient reason to militantly identify with the most extreme action (violent or otherwise) that is likely to assist the party's chances of winning an election.

PARTY VIOLENCE

In a real sense, anger and social frustration as well as deep feelings of hostility and alienation that develop among the very poor are harnessed by this interparty antagonism to generate much of the extreme fanaticism, intolerance, and violence that characterizes electoral contests between the Jamaican political parties. This anger which might otherwise have been directed at the rich and the privileged is displaced onto targets who become persons from the same class of impoverished and socially disadvantaged but have the misfortune of supporting the wrong party. By providing an outlet for discharging or working off the anger and hostilities of the frustrated poor, the political parties reduce the prospects for class conflicts between the rich and the poor and propertied and the propertyless.

To sustain these antagonistic relations between lower class party faithful, there is an emotionally charged image that is internalized by the party faithful and projects the members of the opposing party in stereotypes representing the ultimate in evil and deviltry. The parties develop through strong intraparty socialization (in the family, at the community level, and within the peer groups) a whole demonology characterizing the evil qualities of those who support the opposing party. The stereotypes include qualities such as dishonesty, uncleanliness, opportunism, love of violence, mental under-development and stupidity, selfishness, arrogance, ungodliness, mean and inhumane behavior patterns, and lack of commitment to the national interest. These stereotypes fan the flames of interparty hostility antagonisms, and violence and make it extremely difficult to achieve political tolerance, peaceful and violence-free political disagreements or dialogue at the local community level, intracommunity co-operation between party factions within the same community or peaceful, co-operative relations between adjacent JLP or PNP communities. This process of socialization provides incentive and motivation for those who carry out the most extreme acts of aggression against the enemy and reinforces these actions by feelings of satisfaction that justify them.

The deep animosities and hostility between the party faithful supporting opposing political parties create an opportunity for the armed gangs of ghetto youth to play a key role in defending party territory or communities in the inner city slum areas and low income government housing sites or tenement areas. The gunmen often engage each other in extended gun battles and shootouts and place the lives of political activists at risk by frequent attempts at political assassinations of local level party organizers. They operate under the cover of community support in those areas where their role is to defend the party's territory from external attack or political infiltration. They serve further as enforcers who keep the dissidents and troublemakers in the community in line by methods varying from banishment, beatings, and threats to actual murder. The political gangs operate freely in at least eight of the 15 constituencies[7] in the capital city of Kingston, and St. Andrew. These constituencies have the heaviest concentrations of urban poor and many of their communities provide the hard core militants willing to risk life and limb in defense of the party and willing to carry out daring physical attacks on the party's real or imagined enemies. Some of these communities were formed out of government housing projects where residents were carefully selected by the party in power. In others, residents who were perceived as not supporting the dominant party were either burnt out or chased out at gunpoint, leaving relatively homogeneous communities giving preponderant support to one party. Entry and exit to and from these communities are controlled by the so-called "top ranking" gang leaders who have close relationships with the constituency MP, get preferential access to contracts and jobs, and function as a key element of the local level community political leadership in both parties in these inner city poor areas. These constituencies are made up preponderantly of these "garrison communities" where organized political gangs with high powered M-16 and A.K. 47 assault rifles and submachine guns control clearly defined political boundaries and territories where political protection insulates them from the reach of the security forces.

The degree of violence and the extent of property damage occurring during intense periods of political territorial wars between JLP and PNP gangs in the inner city imposes an extremely heavy cost on ghetto dwellers. Between July and December 1980 in the period leading up to that election there were an estimated 510 fatalities due to political violence. Studies by a political geographer, Dr. Alan Eyre[8] have established that 77 percent of those deaths occurred in the Kingston and St. Andrew area which has 36 percent of the island's population. Eyre's data also confirm that 31 percent of those political deaths occurred in the Kingston area with 8 percent of the country's population and 15 percent occurred in a western Kingston-Lower St. Andrew political war zone where JLP garrison communities confront PNP garrison communities and where some 1 percent of the population is to be found. In this area it was discovered that between 1976 and 1982 some 3,000 buildings housing citizens were destroyed in political gang warfare in heavily tenemented areas while another 1,000 dwellings were destroyed over the period in high-rise multi-story government housing projects. Between 1976 and 1982 some 40 percent of the population in this area had to vacate due to intense political warfare.

This violence has an appreciably destabilizing impact on the political community in that its occurrence intimidates the middle class and the rich and creates a feeling of anarchy among the majority of the poor who feel defenseless against the political gangs with their high-powered weapons and often get caught in the political cross fire. The gunmen undermine the process of law and order and the state's role as a guarantor of personal security. The gangs are often more equipped with sophisticated weapons than the police. Even when their members are caught, citizens are too terrified to give evidence against them in court. The gangs obtain their weapons both from the drug trade, in which some members are deeply involved, and through political party officials[9] who engage their services as political enforcers and mercenaries.

The party faithful, however, are a minority within the political community as a whole and within the body of persons who constitute the poorest 40 percent of the society. The power they have and that of the political leaders they follow at the national and constituency levels is often resented by persons who vote but don't share the intense loyalties of the hard core party members. This is especially so with those independent voters who have no long-term party loyalty and no strong sense of attachment to any political leaders. Like the hard core party faithful, however, the loyal party voters feel deep reverence for party top leaders, look to them for guidance on national political issues and are generally supportive of the role the leaders and parties play in the political community.

NONPARTY INFLUENCES

Outside of the two major political parties who have both strong national and community-level organizations, the only other organizations with broadly based membership and support among the majority classes of poorer citizens are the church, the trade unions, and to a lesser extent the various farm organizations representing small and medium scale farmers. None of these nonparty organizations reach a majority of the electorate. The churches represent a combined strength of some 32 percent of the electorate in terms of regular church attendance and committed church membership. The trade unions reach only 28 percent of the electorate, representing the combined organized support behind the labor movement. The agricultural associations speak for only approximately 10 percent of the electorate. Although hard core party membership is only about 25 percent of the electorate, if we add the loyal party voters who look to the party leaders for guidance and give strong emotional support to the policies and programs their parties promote, the level of party impact in the electorate and the extent of the reach of the main political parties is 60 percent of persons likely to vote in a high turnout election or 51 percent of the electorate. This represents a more extensive reach of socialization influences than that generated by the nonparty organizations. Because of organizational membership overlap, when we take this factor into account some 42 percent of the electorate is in fact not incorporated in the membership of these main political and nonpolitical organizations. The main limits to the domination of the political community by the mainstream political parties, the JLP and the PNP, are, the existence of strong nonpolitical organizations that exercise some influence over the political community and the large number of persons especially among the poorer socioeconomic groupings who are not reached by either of these organizational influences.

The main strategy of the dominant political parties has been to try to co-opt all forms of nonparty organizations to harness their support on national issues, for national and local political leaders, and to use them to provide a supply of activists, leaders, and financial and other resources at the national and local levels. Although the church has only been sporadically active in the party political arena, its intervention has been manipulated by the major political parties at varying political periods. In the period leading up to the 1972 elections in which the opposition PNP successfully challenged the governing JLP, a strategic alliance between the Jamaica Council of Churches and the PNP leadership challenged the JLP over the operation of a National Lottery,[10] insisting that its existence was an affront to the nation's moral standing. The author's postelection survey confirmed that the issue helped to galvanize support for the PNP by adding to a long list of anti-JLP issues around which new voters and disgruntled independent voters rallied against the governing party. After the PNP won the election the National Lottery was abolished. But social pressures over the loss of employment with the closure of the lottery, led the PNP to abandon its morally puritanical posture on gambling and to authorize the setting up of a new area of national gambling in the form of racing pools.

The Jamaica Council of Churches represents the established churches with a large concentration of middle class membership in the Roman Catholic Church and in the many protestant denominations whose histories go back to the slavery period. This church faction is distinct from the evangelical churches, on the one hand, that are strongly influenced by U.S. evangelism and the revivalist and Rastafarian churches, on the other, that represent strong African and folk traditions. The nationalist sentiments within the leadership of the Council of Churches gives them a somewhat ideological affinity with the perceived nationalist leadership of the PNP.

The PNP-Council of Churches alliance revived in 1984 over the JLP government's proposal to introduce casino gambling[11] in Jamaica. PNP supporters and hard core church activists generated considerable opposition to the proposal. This opposition forced the JLP government to proceed very cautiously in approaching the introduction of the casino gambling proposal. The effect has been to delay the introduction of a measure which the government sought to utilize as a major foreign exchange earner and as a means of increasing the inflow of tourists in Jamaica.

Beyond these specific issues, the Council of Churches generally provides strategic support for the PNP on many national issues where the PNP has attempted to challenge the JLP. The other church factions representing the evangelists have tended to provide strategic support for the JLP. The central supportive issue has been the opposition to leftist and communist influences in the political community which loomed large in the 1980 elections and assisted the JLP to win a larger share of the popular vote. Here the PNP, with its local communist ally[12] the WPJ, and its international and regional communist ally, Cuba, fell victim to a strong anticommunist attack from the JLP and the evangelists. The JLP, however, has run into problems with most of the evangelists on the question of casino gambling, as this faction of the organized church lobby joined forces with the Council of Churches in opposing casinos.

At the local community level both political parties seek to co-opt and induce support from influential church leaders. Where the local church insists on remaining politically neutral that position is usually respected. This is in contrast to other nonparty organizations that are usually subjected to continuous pressure from efforts to co-opt and absorb them into one of the local party factions. Indeed, attempts at nonparty community organization are usually perceived as a threat to the dominant local party fiefdom and harassment of the persons involved is not an unusual response to any resistance to the co-optation overtures. Where the membership cannot be won over to the party fold, the dominant party faction will at least be satisfied with being able to co-opt or exercise influence over key leaders.

Essentially, the dominant parties seek to monopolize or co-opt all forms of nonparty organization that they perceive as likely to have widespread community influence. In the past both parties have been relatively successful at leadership co-optation of rural and urban nonparty organizational leaders, by offering them middle and lower level positions of leadership within the party. For most of the early postwar years, the PNP's expansion in the rural parishes was facilitated by the co-optation and leadership recruitment of leaders in the Jamaica Agricultural Society and the Jamaica Teachers Association. Much of the early PNP rural majority support in parishes such as St. Ann, and Manchester was based on the impact of supportive political action by JAS leaders in these parishes. The Teachers Association played a similar role in broadening the base of PNP support nationally in rural communities where they exerted considerable political influence.

Two problems are constantly on the agenda for the local branch plants of the major political parties. The first is that political representation and access to local government and parliamentary representatives are constantly a problem for persons who do not belong to the ranks of the party faithful. Access to these party representatives tends to be monopolized by party activists and these representatives in turn allocate most of their time and energy to dealing with internal party matters. The result is that inadequate contact or communication is maintained with the majority of communities and individuals in the respective constituencies. Further, consituents usually find that there is no one available to deal with citizens' problems when they arise and that the local constituency office is neither staffed with personnel able to give much assistance in sorting out community problems nor is it usually disposed to deal with nonpartisan issues.

SCARCE BENEFITS ALLOCATIONS

On the other hand, scarce benefits allocations bypass a large number of deserving persons who are either nonpartisan or attached to the wrong party. This generates considerable resentment over the privileges of the supporters of the party in power and results in a buildup of anti-governing party alienation by opposition supporters as well as by independent voters and nonvoters, who together usually consititute a majority when compared to the citizens supporting the governing party at the constituency level. For this reason, no matter how generous the scarce benefits a party has to dole out to supporters, the long-term impact is never sufficient to sustain majority support as the political judgements of the majority of voters are based on visible indicators of success of government policies and programs since the majority never receives any direct allocation of scarce benefits and has no real hope of receiving any such party favors.

The generous handouts of political patronage are, therefore, never adequate to influence the national vote to significantly enhance a party's chances of re-election. It is the main thrust of social and economic policies and the benefits they seem to be generating within the society as a whole that is crucial to maintaining a party's credibility. Parties who sacrifice credible and effective national policies in order to service the patronage needs of the party faithful usually find that they pay a heavy cost in terms of loss of national support from voters with weak party identification or from those who see themselves as being independent of partisan loyalties.

INTEREST REPRESENTATION

The party leaders therefore have two related problems arising from this. They spend most of their working hours in the company of the party faithful as regards representational contact in the various constituencies. The political culture is divided between highly partisan minorities and their leaders who are invested with wide ranging power and control over national resources, on the one hand, and another almost 50 percent of the political community where party sentiments are weak. The elected representative has real problems dealing with these two quite separate constituents, especially since the political system is party dominant and the nonparty citizens resent the power of those with direct access to the levers of public power and decision making. A serious crisis exists with respect to the representative function of MPs because the typical MP (with rare exception) becomes encapsulated within the partisan political networks and loses touch with and fails to adequately represent those many citizens who operate at a great distance from those party linkages at the local or national level.

A related issue is that while real and objective group interests exist in the communities (groups of farmers, petty traders, mini-bus operators, shopkeepers, consumers, small manufacturers, and so on), the parties lack any internal system of group representation that gives recognition to these objective economic interests. The result is that the internal channels for dealing with the problems of the party faithful or party activists treat with individual problems and turn them into personalized political favors rather than provide an opportunity for treating with the wider class or group interests or the problem involved.

There is need both for a diversification of nonparty organizations representing especially those constituents who are outside of the grouping of party faithful as well as some clear internal differentiation of interests inside the party organizations so that economic interests rather than mere geographical location becomes an acceptable basis on which to group party membership, mobilize their support and elicit their inputs into the process of thinking out public policies. If women, unemployed youth, unionized workers, professionals, farmers, petty traders, small business manufacturing interests, shopkeepers and merchants, students, and a variety of other such interest categories formed the basis of internal group representation within the political parties, it would improve the party's capacity for representation and increase the capacity of party members to make coherent inputs into the party's policy thinking. While the consituency basis of grouping local level membership is unavoidable, within each constituency the dominant social formations should be given recognition within the consitituency party. This means that in a sugar estate area there should obviously be a grouping within the party representing sugar workers. Such a development would increase the policy content of local party deliberations and activities, by diversifying them beyond electioneering and scarce benefit allocation. Its impact would improve the party's efforts at political education at the local level. Finally, it would provide the parties with a more organic link to nonparty organizations representing those interests recognized within the party. It would also appreciably improve the local party's representational effectiveness by providing better channels of communication between local interest and the MPs and local party officials.

An alternate approach could involve the creation of bipartisan community councils in most areas in each constituency. These councils could be involved in project implementation by providing an auditing role on behalf of the community and in providing a channel of direct communication between politician, bureaucrats, and citizens that is now more often than not absent at the local level. To avoid party polarization such councils could also include representation from nonparty organizations such as citizens associations, service clubs, churches, farm organizations, and small business association branches.

The economic power in the hands of the big capitalists and the foreign corporations guarantees these interests access to the public policy decision makers through various channels of influence. A number of these interests make campaign contributions to the political parties. These contributions are secret and therefore run no risk of public embarrassment or exposure. Some make consistent contributions to only one party while others play it safe by contributing to both, varying the size of the contribution to fit their political preference. Since the mid-1970s the largest share of capitalist political contributions have gone to the pro-private enterprise JLP while the pro-socialist PNP has had problems raising funds from this source. Enterprises that depend on the patronage of politicians to secure contracts and sell goods and services to the state tend to be forced to make financial contributions to the party in power. The opposition party invariably is able to garner some financial support from enterprises that have been adversely affected by the policies of the party in power.

These financial contributions do not guarantee that the donors will be able to exercise great influence over government policy. It is not unusual for some such enterprise to be adversely affected by policies developed by the very party they have helped to finance. Very often expectations for certain policy emphases end in disappointment as party leaders change their minds about how to proceed after they come to power and discover constraints and options that were not so obvious from the innocence of opposition. For example, many private sector interests had expected the JLP under Seaga's leadership to dismantle the State Trading Corporation which was set up by the Manley government to take over the importation of basic foods and drugs from the private sector merchants. Once the JLP came to power and discovered that the Corporation was having the effect of keeping down consumer prices, the JLP abandoned its earlier "opposition" antagonism to the corporation and simply proceeded to change its name to the Jamaica Commodity Trading Corporation. Some big capitalist interests involved in financing the JLP campaign have been upset over the tight financial measures introduced by Prime Minister Seaga to curb currency racketeering and capital flight. In a surprise move, the JLP government pressed charges in 1983 against a businessman who had been exporting U.S. dollars on behalf of many big companies, some of which had supported the JLP into power with generous financial contributions. The businessman and his wife were given stiff prison sentences, much to the dismay and disapproval of most of the rich capitalist interests. The accused attempted to plea bargain by threatening to cite details of which enterprises he served as a courier but that did not deter the Seaga government from making an example of him to stop the extensive export of currency that was taking place in the economy.

Although Prime Minister Seaga came to power with heavy financial backing from these big companies, the leading voices among the big capitalist class have been constantly complaining about insufficient access to the prime minister, about his not listening to their points of view and about their sharp disagreements over many of his policies. The simplistic notion that business interests who finance party campaigns are assured both full access to policy makers and wide avenues for influencing the policies that are promoted by the governing party they finance is self-evidently refuted by the experience of the Jamaican big business class and the Seaga government.

Faced with the management of an economy on the edge of collapse, Prime Minister Seaga has had to rely heavily on international support from Washington, the World Bank, the IMF, and the donor countries in the Western capitalist bloc. His policy emphases have therefore been tailored to fit the economic strategies and prescriptions favored by Washington and the World Bank. Opening up the economy to competition, setting a realistic rate of exchange to promote export expansion by devaluation, restricting credit, scaling down public spending, forcing local enterprises to move into export production to survive, and bringing foreign investors and armies of expatriate advisors into the country are just some of the economic measures introduced by the Seaga government that have been opposed and criticized by vocal capitalist and middle class spokesmen. Big business interests that earned easy profits in protected markets promoting import substitution resented Seaga's attempt to introduce *World Bank* type structural adjustment policies in the 1980s and had to be dragged against their inclinations into this new approach to economic strategies. A simplistic interpretation of policy making in Jamaica as merely reflecting the perceived interests of the capitalist class would have some difficulty explaining the Seaga regime's effort to dismantle the import substitution model of industrial production inherited from the 1950s.

Essentially what is achieved from funding political parties is not the ability to influence government policy but preferential treatment in the award of contracts and concessions or licenses that private sector interests seek from the state. Secondly, businessmen with the inclination to enter public service get access to board chairmanships and board membership of statutory corporations and quasi-government bodies that enhance their status and give them opportunities that derive business gains. The top leaders in both political parties have tended over the 1970s and 1980s to have strong and well defined notions about domestic and foreign economic, political, and social policies and there is very little room for even the more influential big business personalities to seriously change or modify these policy preferences no matter how much funding they provide for the party campaign coffers. To be sure, a few big business personalities manage to get very close to the party leaders, and this will often mean that special party favors can be obtained in securing their business interests in any dealings with government. But this influence usually does not extend to broad policy matters unless they are part of the government, as in the case of Senator Hugh Hart in Prime Minister Seaga's JLP cabinet in the 1980s or Mr. Eli Matalon, who served as a member of the Manley PNP cabinet in the early 1970s.

Two other main channels of influence on policy makers are available to big business interests. These include the interest group lobbies represented by manufacturing, export, and commerce associational interests and the informal personal network influences in which family ties or friendship groups open up opportunities of access to party leaders and key public officials in a small society characterized by tightly knit upper and upper-middle classes. But as in the case of other channels of political influence, these points of access to decision makers can protect or maximize one's business interest or gain special favors but are not likely to open up opportunities to influence broad policy directions.

The small size of the society and the extent to which the business and professional elite all know each other create a context in which party leaders are careful to keep policy information as secretive as possible to avoid information dissemination to the media, to the opposing party, and to interests that might be adversely affected by some new policy. The result is that political leaders do not usually open up dialogue on policy matters except with expert advisors, political colleagues, or persons who are operating from inside their parties. Moreover, the contemporary political directorates in both political parties have a common view about the limited policy and economic knowledge of most of the Jamaican private sector and their strong proclivity to be concerned about very little beyond their own personal business fortunes. That perception does not lend itself to relying on big business personalities for policy advice.

The business lobbies such as the Chamber of Commerce, the Manufacturers Association, the Exporters Association, and the umbrella Private Sector Organisation are very active and vocal on national and policy issues. They frequently challenge the direction of government policies and engage in policy debates with the policy makers. While they are sometimes able to get adjustments, modifications, and revisions of policy measures, they are largely excluded from the process of policy formulation. Virtually all of their policy statements represent reactions to policy decisions regarding which the policy makers in the public domain of power are extremely reluctant to change direction.

These private sector organizations are, however, quite influential in placing policy issues on the agenda of public discussion by their ease of access to the mass media. This invariably forces policy makers to react by issuing statements, revealing policy information, and by attempting to persuade public opinion about the validity and soundness of their public policies. Where the private sector lobby is able to provide important feedback about the negative effects of policies or the lack of policies, they are often successful in prodding governments into devising new policy measures. Examples of this are revelations from the private sector about illicit imports, corrupt practices in government agencies, unrealistic pricing of goods under price control, shortages of factors needed to sustain production, inefficient or unreliable public services, and problems of accessing sources of credit financing. Most of these types of issues relate to problems in policy implementation rather than basic policy direction. Where the private sector lobbies attack basic policy direction they are treated as being anti-government and the reactions tend to be antagonistic and leave no room for any accommodation or policy adjustments. Essentially, the political directorate guards very jealously its policy-formulating role and does not easily yield to pressures for policy changes from influential private sector interests or organizations.

The greatest opening for policy influence arises where private sector interests come out in support of government policy or policies, and offer assistance in implementation in exchange for which the political directorate will usually take their policy advice into account in adjusting and modifying the policy measures. In effect, the decision makers in the public domain of power feel most comfortable and are willing to make most concessions with a compliant and supportive private sector. Where, of course, there is agreement on some broad policy objective such as increasing the price of a price-controlled item, or extending a government subsidy to some group of producers, the policy makers in the government are amenable to negotiation with private sector interests. Such negotiations can be conducted with individual enterprises affected or sectoral interests represented by these interest groups. Where the private sector interests support the overall policy direction, there is considerable room for those interests to obtain concessions and favorable terms in any such negotiations.

In effect, what has evolved in Jamaica is a political system in which the public domain of power controlled by elected party leaders has asserted a strong sense of autonomy in its relationships with the private domain of power based on ownership of the means of production. While influential private sector interests have liberal opportunities to negotiate for policy concessions and for policy benefits, the opportunity for such interests to have great inputs on policy formation or to block or fundamentally change government policy is very restricted because of this strong sense of policy autonomy and the extreme privacy observed in information management in the making in public policies by both PNP and JLP governments in the post-independence period.

POLITICAL VALUES

The Jamaican democratic political system is held together partly by a common core of political values that cut across class and political party affiliations. The political values relate to the centrality of private property as an expression of personal freedom, the fundamental virtue and value of religion and religious beliefs and practices to ensure the moral health of the political community, the importance of individual personal freedoms and the rights associated with voting and joining political organizations, and the central role of the state in ministering to the needs of the weaker and more socially disadvantaged classes.

In the escape from slave labor and the establishment of 'free village' peasant communities with the help of Christian missionaries, the black population attached great importance to ownership of land as a basis of their newly embraced freedom, as a sign or symbol of their independence and manhood to survive outside of the dominating plantation system, and as the means by which to accumulate wealth on a modest scale to improve the life chances of their children. The rapid expansion of the small peasantry between the late nineteenth and the mid-twentieth century is itself eloquent testimony to the eagerness with which the exslaves established themselves as small holders with a great attachment to the land and the freedoms associated with owning property.

In the absence of welfare institutions based on public resources to cater to the poor and needy on a large enough scale, the church has tended over the centuries to play that role in society. Both the established churches and the revivalist folk religions, as well as the evangelists, have not only ministered to spiritual needs but have attempted to cater to social needs. In the settlement of exslaves the church missions played a critical role in assisting with the financial and administrative problems of the small settlers. In the more recent period, the church has been a major source of welfare assistance to the poor, especially the aged and the very young. Most importantly, the church has been a prime developer of educational institutions at all levels in those periods when the aristocratic colonial state system dragged its feet in providing educational and other social institutions for the black majority.

Liberal notions about individual rights and freedoms are an accepted part of the consensus around political values that have provided a basis for the survival and continued viability of Jamaican democracy although political violence and combative and intolerant approaches to political campaigning often violate the citizens' capacity to enjoy these rights. What is beyond dispute is the broad acceptance of their value and importance. Similarly the concept of a reformist state imbued with responsibility to oversee the area of social rights that involves some responsibility for providing social services (housing, health, and so on) for the very poor has become part of that national political consensus, although views sharply differ regarding the magnitude and level that should be reached for in that welfare function.

A national survey[13] carried out by the author in December 1981 asked citizens to identify which of a short list of factors helped to promote progress among the poorer classes. These factors included freedom of speech, the right to own property, politicians helping the poor, and state ownership of production. The findings set out in Table 4.1 are broken down by party affiliation in order to assess the degree of interparty consensus that exists on these issues, given the sharply diverging ideologies between the prosocialist PNP and the procapitalist JLP at the leadership level. The survey findings report the results for the 18 and over segment of the national sample which had included 1,000 such adults and 500 youth aged 14 to 17. The findings were also broken down by class to identify the levels of class differences in these attitudes.

The majority view from all political tendencies and classes identifies freedom of speech as having aided poor people's struggles through the association with democratic political rights and the degree to which these

Table 4.1 Which Factors Have Helped to Promote Progress by the Poorer Classes in Jamaica (in percent)

	Freedom of Speech	Right to Own Property	Politicians Helping Small People	Government Ownership of Business
JLP supporters (410)	74	59	56	14
PNP supporters (340)	70	42	67	32
Independents (250)	71	45	34	21
Middle class (100)	52	31	48	7
Farmers and petty traders (312)	61	81	33	5
Wage workers (402)	75	58	60	29

Source: Author's December 1981 Political Survey.

rights have increased the bargaining position of the poor in the political community. A majority of the petty commodity sector (farmers and traders) as well as wage workers associate owning private property with poor people's progress in Jamaica, while a substantial minority of PNP followers, independent voters, and the middle class subscribe to that view. Ideological differences between the PNP and the JLP account for these political divergencies. The middle class view is influenced by a realistic sense that most poor people don't own property, in contrast to the views of the poorer classes who aspire to own property and therefore see more of a positive connection between property owning and poor people's progress.

A majority of the PNP adherents, the JLP adherents, and most wage workers see politicians helping poor people as something that has been positive, while only a minority of the more independent farmers and higglers, the independent voters, and the middle class share that view. State ownership is not associated with the progress of poor people, although close to a third of the PNP supporters and the wage workers endorse that positive connection between poor people's advancement and state ownership. Clearly this view on state ownership was heavily influenced by reactions to the impact of state ownership under the Manley-led government in the 1970s.

Implicit in these findings is a dual commitment to political freedoms and social justice and a faith that these two aspects of political values are not only mutually compatible but capable of being achieved in the Jamaican political community.

CONCLUSION

The major political parties dominate public life and are perceived as the main vechile for protection and advancement of political freedoms and social justice. The poorer classes give strong support to the political system on the assumption that the parties and their leaders have the capacity to deliver a minimum of both freedom and social justice. The political parties therefore have become the main channel of political expression among the poor, notwithstanding whatever weaknesses and deficiencies they clearly have in the area of political representation.

On the other hand, the powerful, the rich, and the middle class rely mainly on nonparty channels of political expression, viewing the political parties as being alliances between their middle class professional leaders and the masses. A variety of promotional, professional, economic interest and sectoral organizations and associations represent the rich and the middle class in the political system. Because of their relative detachment from party politics in spite of efforts at party co-optation, they have a significant capacity to influence nonpartisan public opinion that the politician needs to govern and to win elections. These organizations, therefore, play a key role in the issue debates and public opinion reactions to politicians, their policies, and trends within the political community. They have no great power given the strong sense of autonomy in policy making observed by the political directorate but their political influence via the mass media is considerable.

In essence, what emerges from this treatment of the Jamaican political culture is a picture of a highly competitive political system where there is open and often extreme confrontation for power but where the middle class professional leaders who control the party-dominant political system have effective control over both policy making and the machinery of political power, the mass party. The strength of the political system lies in the degree to which the political parties have become an instrument of political expression by the poorer classes while serving the vital unifying function of intergrating a cross section of class interests that come together in the political parties to compete for power.

Three fundamental weaknesses and areas of potential stress have been identified. The first is the relative detachment of large sections of the middle class and the rich from party politics which could aggravate and intensify conflicts between the public and private sectors over policy. Secondly, continued mass support for the political system requires a minimum level of performance and results in the form of tangible achievements of social gains by the poor. Thirdly, the intensity of combative and violent forms of contention for power added to the inadequate representational role of the parties and their MPs threatens to reduce support for the political system from the large numbers of citizens who operate at a distance from the party machines and have no strong partisan loyalties.

NOTES

1. See Carl Stone, *Baseline Survey on Political Education*, 1981, a research report prepared for the JLP.

2. The sources for these data on party support are, of course, the political polls conducted by the author over the 1976-84 period.

3. The chief spokesman for this point of view is journalist Wilmot Perkins who is considered to be the number one public affairs commentator by the bourgeoisie whose views he often reflects on controversial political and social issues. Perkins has established a reputation as the most virulent, articulate and consistent critic in the country of democratic socialist tendencies.

4. These leaders are often the subjects of vicious jokes and rumors originating among the middle class.

5. See Carl Stone, *Democracy and Clientelism*, New Brunswick, N.J.: Transaction Books, 1980.

6. These violent episodes took place between Tivoli Gardens (the prime minister's constituency) and Rema. High-powered weapons allegedly used by Tivoli gunmen silenced the vocal opposition from Rema. In one major invasion of the Rema community some seven persons were shot dead and buildings were burned in 1984.

7. These constituencies are located in Kingston and lower St. Andrew.

8. See Alan Eyre, "Effects of political violence on the population and urban environment of Kingston, Jamaica," forthcoming in *Geographical Review*.

9. Large illegal importations of high-powered weapons are believed to be connected to the two major political parties.

10. See Carl Stone, *Electoral behaviour and public opinion in Jamaica*, Kingston, Jamaica: Institute of Social and Economic Research, 1974.

11. The surveys carried out on the subject by the author reveal the influence both of church membership and PNP party affiliation on strong anticasino sentiments in the electorate.

12. After the 1980 election defeat, the PNP severed this alliance with the WPJ.

13. See Stone, *Baseline Survey on Political Education*.

5

MANAGING PUBLIC POLICY

A very difficult task of institution building has taken place in Jamaica in the postwar period toward the development of a public sector policy management. This process of institution building has been incomplete and still reflects major weaknesses but important changes have taken place in the scope of government, the degree of involvement by the state in the economy, the management tasks entrusted to the public sector, the machinery for decision making, and the problem-solving capacity of the state in the areas of responsibility assumed.

EXPANDING THE ROLE OF GOVERNMENT

In terms of the development of a public policy capability, there were three distinct periods of the postwar era prior to the 1980s. The 1980s period has to be seen as the beginning of an entirely new era with a different set of constraints and parameters determining the state's policy capability. The first period covered the decade of the 1940s and 1950s when the aristocratic colonial state was in the first phase of being converted into a democratic state. This involved the expanding and diversification of state services to meet more adequately the needs of the majority classes. The central areas of focus concentrated on improving health and educational services and developing a capability to deliver technical, credit, and extension facilities to the numerically large small peasant farmer population.

Once the machinery for delivering these social and economic services was put in place, the latter were expanded considerably in the second and third periods of administrative development. In agriculture, for example, the major policy developments were increased investment in rural infrastructural developments, an expanded land settlement scheme, the development of marketing services for agriculture, and the extension of credit to small peasant farmers. Between 1954 and 1960 some 150,000 acres of land were allocated to establish 28,000 farm holdings under the expanded land settlement scheme. As a result of this and other factors between 1943 and 1958 the percentage of small farmers owning land increased appreciably from 60 percent to 77 percent. The political impact was to consolidate small settler land tenure, especially among the better-off rich or middle peasants. Between 1946 and 1968, $56 million was allocated mainly to small peasants and middle peasants in the form of credit and subsidies. The growth of technical expertise in agriculture over the period was most impressive in the public sector.[1] In the period between 1929 and 1970 the Department of Agriculture was transformed from a small servicing agency for planter interests in export agriculture with limited technical expertise into a large department with highly developed specialized skills relevant to most phases of domestic agriculture. Between 1929 and 1949 the clerical and administrative staff expanded from ten to 60 and by 1969 it had expanded further to 351. The technical staff increased from 45 in 1929 to 93 in 1949, and achieved a size of 676 staff members by 1969. Between 1929 and 1949, agricultural expenditure grew from 2 percent of the recurrent budget to 6 percent, and from 3 percent of the government's capital budget to 29 percent over that period.

In 1929 the areas of departmental specialization in agriculture included public gardens, animal and plant disease, and research and experimental stations. By 1969 this had expanded to encompass agronomy, agricultural chemistry, plant protection, fisheries, livestock, veterinary services, extension work, land valuation, planning, agricultural engineering, land use and development, and information services. The creation of regional land authorities, and increased government marketing of agricultural crops added to increased expenditure on rural roadways; water supplies and other facilities improved the economic environment for the small peasant farmer. These developments were taking place at a time when agriculture was lagging behind the rapid growth taking place in the rest of the economy and was not able effectively to compete with other sectors of the economy for labor, capital, entrepreneurial and technical skills, and other critical factors needed to expand production. As a result, the impact of increased governmental support was not quite as large as might otherwise have been the case because the income and rate of return to agricultural investments were not competitive with what was happening in the more fast-moving nonagricultural areas of the economy. As a result, total land in farm production declined 19 percent between 1943 and 1968. This new state policy thrust in agriculture which took shape mainly in the 1940s and 1950s and expanded in later periods, represented an increasing role for the state in agriculture. Credit and cash flow support for small farmers formerly supplied by shopkeepers, produce dealers, and planters were replaced by the state's provision of a steady flow of credit, technical services, loans, and overall services from the newly reformed administrative state machinery.

A major thrust of the social reforms engineered by the new administrative machinery of the state centered on improved health care and health services through expanded hospitals and health centers and an expanded education system to provide larger enrollment at primary and secondary levels of that system. As a result, literacy levels improved and all health indicators reflected dramatic changes in the quality of life of the population as this was reflected in health indicators. As can be seen from Table 5.1, there has been a steady decline in infant mortality levels during the postwar period, indicating the clear improvement in levels of health for the majority of the population. Life expectancy levels are also shown to have increased considerably, reflecting changed patterns of mortality and morbidity within the population as a whole.

Impressive improvements were recorded in the official statistics on literacy but the more recent measures of adult literacy inflate the real level of functional literacy. These official data suggest that literacy rates increased from 77 percent in 1951 to 91 percent in 1970, but a more realistic estimate of functional literacy indicates that over this period the magnitude of change was more likely in the region of a 55 to 65 percent increase in literacy levels. This improvement in literacy was linked to increased expenditure in education and expanded educational facilities.

Comparative levels of national expenditure in the region on health and education[2] and other comparative data on school age population per teacher, school enrollment, and share of population with access to safe water supplies all indicate that, relative to its per capita income, Jamaica has developed an above average level of commitment to health and educational services and an above average level of advancement in social services within the Latin American and Caribbean region as a whole.

Table 5.1 Changes in life expectancy & infant mortality in Jamaica

	1950	1960	1970	
Life expectancy at age one	61	67	70	
	1938	1950	1960	1970
Infant deaths per 1,000 live births	119	81	63	36

Source: Department of Statistics, Statistical Digest and Annual Reports (1951, 1962, 1971).

Table 5.2 gives health and educational expenditure data for 18 developing countries in the region. Jamaica ranks tenth in per capita income but sixth in both areas of per capita expenditure. Jamaica ranks fourth after Barbados, Trinidad and Tobago, and Uruguay as regards the percentage of its population that has access to safe water among these 18 countries. In terms of 1978 data, Jamaica ranks first with the lowest rate of infant deaths per 1,000 live births. Clearly a progressive record of social policy reforms and priorities have accompanied the transition to democracy in Jamaica in the postwar period. Both the attempt to serve small farmer interests in agriculture and the concerted effort at improved social services in the immediate aftermath of universal adult suffrage indicate the impact of this democratic change in inducing new public policy directions and an effort to establish policy capability that reaches out to the majority classes.

These areas of improvement in the quality of life of the majority classes represented the commitment of the newly emergent political leaders in the JLP and the PNP to use the expanded resources of the state to remove the extreme effects of poverty and inequality in the society. These social policies implied a broad consensus between these party leaders on social democratic goals to reduce social inequality, guarantee

Table 5.2 Per Capita Public Expenditure in Health and Education and Ranking (1978) in $U.S.

Per capita income		Country	Education		Health	
2933	(1)	Trinidad	140	(3)	63	(3)
2822	(2)	Venezuela	149	(2)	83	(1)
2194	(3)	Argentina	54	(8)	11	(11)
1861	(4)	Barbados	158	(1)	70	(2)
1707	(5)	Uruguay	32	(10)	20	(8)
1606	(6)	Costa Rica	99	(4)	19	(9)
1474	(7)	Chile	50	(9)	34	(6)
1270	(8)	Cuba	82	(5)	41	(5)
1237	(9)	Panama	65	(7)	60	(4)
1160	(10)	Jamaica	79	(6)	34	(6)
934	(11)	Guatemala	14	(16)	7	(16)
934	(12)	Colombia	20	(12)	11	(11)
846	(13)	Dominican Republic	18	(13)	12	(10)
817	(14)	Paraguay	13	(17)	3	(17)
673	(15)	El Savador	23	(11)	9	(14)
633	(16)	Peru	13	(17)	3	(17)
494	(17)	Honduras	18	(13)	10	(13)
183	(18)	Haiti	2	(18)	1	(18)

Source: Ruth Sivard, World Military and Social Expenditures, Leesburg, VA: Priorities, 1981, p. 28-29.

citizens minimal access to social services and facilities, and develop the state's administrative capability to minister to these needs through an enlarged base of revenue support. They demanded an expanded governmental administrative machinery. These policies initiated the drift toward big government.

The change toward greater government intervention in social policy and economic management (in the agricultural sector) was relatively painless because it took place against the background of a significant growth in the productive and income base of the economy. Instead of resistance from the bourgeoisie, these policies were seen by the economically privileged as a real positive investment in a more unified and stable society. Broad national consensus, therefore, served to legitimize these new policy directions toward social democratic goals.

The political impact on the working class and peasants was equivalent to the effect of the welfare state in Western Europe. These state interventionist policies strengthened support for democracy and legitimized the democratic constitutional reforms that were seen by workers and small farmers as being decisive in making the state more responsive to their social needs. Equally important was the fact that these policies had the effect of reducing those gross inequalities[3] in the society that had their origins in the old plantation order.

DEVELOPING ECONOMIC POLICY CAPABILITY

The second phase in the development of increased public policy capacity by the reformist democratic state was in the area of trying to promote economic development by government policies designed to stimulate new investments, economic expansion, and more optimal use of resources for production. The initial thinking here was in two parallel directions. Firstly, it was held that given the weak business tradition in the colony, the state had to play a major role as a sort of policy midwife helping the private sector to give birth to new investment initiatives by a variety of policy measures. These included tax holidays, protection for infant industries, broad investment incentives to attract foreign capital, and efforts to provide much of the infrastructure for production by developing industrial estates under a planned industrial development program. Additionally, the state attempted to establish a number of state run enterprises whose main function would be to assist in the development of entrepreneurship from local or private sources or to give guidance and assistance in crucial areas that could bring investment ideas to the stage of project implementation and production.

This investment and business promotion initiative was developed around certain key institutions such as the Jamaica Industrial Development Corporation, a public enterprise that did much of the pioneer work setting up and promoting import-substitution manufacturing enterprises[4] in the economy in the period between the early 1950s and the mid-1960s. Other such public enterprises include the Jamaica Development Bank which borrowed long-term money from international lending institutions and made long-term development money available for investment locally. Also included are the Central Planning Unit which was developed to provide a framework for medium- and short-term indicative planning based on detailed studies of economic trends so as to guide the private sector initiatives. The centrality of foreign exchange in the growth and development equation of a small trade-dependent economy meant that there was need for the early setting up of a Central Bank to oversee the economy's finances while managing foreign exchange. The need for urban planning and infrastructural development also led to the creation of an Urban Development Corporation.

Beginning cautiously in the 1950s but increasing in importance as the central thrust of government policy making, the growth of a policy capability related to economic development became the central activity of the political executive. The policy leadership in this area was shared between the ministerial portfolios of Finance, Development and Planning, Industry and Trade, and the office of prime minister. This policy capability developed only gradually for a number of reasons.

First of all, the civil service was lacking in trained personnel with expertise in the field of economics. The resource persons used to provide the policy thinking and technical knowledge on how to proceed came partly from overseas technical assistance made available through the British government and by drawing on the more knowledgeable members of the local entrepreneurial class. As a result, many of the key development institutions, like the Jamaica Industrial Development Corporation, were established as public enterprises or corporations outside of the regular civil service.

In 1944 an Economic Policy Committee[5] was established by the colonial governor to "conduct a systematic economic survey" and to "report on the economic prospects of Jamaica" with particular reference to the achievement of full employment and guidelines to govern the directions "future economic policy should follow." This committee can be regarded as the first major move towards developing a local perspective on economic development strategies and policies. The composition of the committee provides an interesting indicator of the dominant class interests within the country's ruling groups at that early period. The Committee was chaired by British Economist Dr. F.C. Benham. Its other members consisted of a Jamaican civil servant who was a high school graduate, three leading members of the planter class (H.V. Lindo, G.G.R. Sharp, and Alexander Gordon), the social worker wife of a leading planter, an urban based entrepreneur who was both a big planter as well as a pioneer in industry and construction (O.K. Henriques), and an expatriate engineer.

Clearly, the urban merchant class hadn't the social status, power, nor influence to gain representation on this committee, indicating the degree to which the planters were still influential in the 1940s in spite of their declining political and economic power. Only one member of that committee represented the point of view of the emergent urban entrepreneur with stakes in manufacturing production which was to become a major center on the economic development strategies of the 1950s and 1960s. Not surprisingly, the committee was opposed to providing tariff or other protection to stimulate local industrial development. While conceding the need to protect existing local industry from dumping (which was a thinly veiled reference to Japanese imports), the committee dismissed industrial development as a real economic option by which to generate employment expansion and economic diversification in Jamaica. Its thinking reflected the biases of the British government which saw colonial economies like Jamaica as markets for British industrial exports. Such markets would be lost if local industrialization was encouraged. Its biases also reflected the point of view of the majority of the merchant class who functioned as commission agents for foreign companies and the planters who saw the country's future as continuing to be dominated by agriculture and especially export agriculture.

Between 1944 and the mid-1950s this policy perspective on economic strategies changed radically as elected politicians came into full control of domestic economic policy. The effect was to encourage a less colonial approach to economic policy development which saw industrial manufacturing as a key element in the modernization of the Jamaican economy. A new alliance between the emergent manufacturing urban entrepreneur and the middle class politician representing the political and policy ascendancy of urban middle class interests over that of the planters forged a whole new direction in industrial policy thinking. A key figure in this development was a black Jamaican (Robert Lightbourne) who had established himself as an industrialist in Birmingham in Britain and was brought back to Jamaica by JLP leader Bustamante to establish and develop the Jamaica Industrial Development Corporation which he directed between 1951 and 1955. Also important were the more enterprising minority among the merchant class who saw the prospect of business expansion and diversification in industry, tourism and service areas of the economy. These more enterprising urban capitalists were not satisfied with being commission agents and had an impulse to move into new areas of entrepreneurial activity and to expand their role in the economy. They increasingly were able to convince the leading middle class urban politicians that the economy could be diversified around new industries.

The Matalons, the Ashenheims, Abe Issa, the Henriques, and a number of other such expansionist family interests and business personalities who had contact with both JLP and PNP leaders played a key role in changing the traditional colonial thinking on industrial development in Jamaica. The effect of the war years in inducing strategies of greater economic self-reliance (in the face of declining British imports) gave a boost to local manufacturing expansion and set the climate within which such a change in policy thinking was likely to emerge.

The colonial bias against local manufacturing industries was only removed in the 1950s in which period both Cabinet government and control over the domestic policy making by elected political leaders came into effect. The Jamaica Industrial Development Corporation was established in 1951–52 to "stimulate, facilitate, and undertake the development of industry." It was charged with developing financial and technical services and the provision of factory space at moderate rentals with access to all utilities. Its initial role in the field of finance was later transferred to the Jamaica Development Bank and its role in infrastructural development also passed on to the Urban Development Corporation. The two main instruments of legislation around which the new industrial policies were developed were the Industrial Incentives Law and the Export Industry Encouragement Law, both passed in 1956 when the PNP was in power, following the lead given by the JLP government in setting up the Industrial Development Corporation. Although the industrial policy had a dual focus of encouraging import-substitution and export industries it was the import substitution focus which emerged dominant.[6] Both local and foreign capital were encouraged by generous tax incentives to pioneer industrial development in Jamaica in diverse areas of production. The state, therefore, came to play a key role in the modernization of the postwar Jamaican economy in close partnership and collaboration with local and foreign entrepreneurial interests, using resources available to the state to subsidize the costs of new investment and to minimize the risks involved. The state, in effect, became an instrument of the development of modern capitalism in Jamaica, replacing the dominance of the economy by planter interests.

The period of industrial expansion between 1956 and 1967 when production in furniture, metal products, chemicals, cement, food processing, garments, footwear, and many other areas expanded rapidly coincides with the parallel economic expansion in bauxite, tourism and other service industries which gave birth to a vibrant, new, and increasingly wealthy and politically influential urban entrepreneurial class. The political directorate treated the class interests of the new entrepreneurs as equal to the interests of the economy as a whole as the future seemed to hinge on their continued expansion. The class had easy access to the corridors of power. Their policy advice was eagerly sought after by the relatively policy inexperienced political directorate. They effectively replaced the planters as the dominant owning interests that influenced the public policies of the government. While some of the more powerful members traced their origins to early merchant families of modest levels of wealth and middle class social rank, most of those who emerged in this new urban entrepreneurial class represented interests that did not inherit wealth and were the first generation of newly created wealth protected by facilitating government policies (incentives, tariff barriers, and so on). The experience of this period gave the newly emerging urban capitalists a sense both of their immense power to influence policy and politicians as well as of the way in which public policy and the state bent over backwards to facilitate their interests.

PUBLIC SECTOR POLICY LEADERSHIP

The third period of policy development by the state began in the mid to late 1960s when the economic boom of the postwar years leveled off, unemployment was on the increase, and private sector power affluence and conspicuous consumption began to be seen as sharply contrasting with the poverty of the majority. The development of the University of the West Indies produced a new radical and nationalistic intelligentsia who challenged the status quo.[7] The black middle and lower middle classes became a large middle sector sandwiched between the poor majority and the rich white, brown and light-skinned capitalists and wealthy professionals (lawyers, doctors, and so on) and were increasingly resentful of the evident social inequalities in Jamaica. Racialist ideologies and black power, religious protest movements, such as the Rastafarian, and populist political currents in party politics began to stir the militant political consciousness of the urban ghetto youth and the more politicized among the new middle class intelligentsia. All of this set the stage for a new perspective on public policy.

Both Prime Minister Seaga and opposition leader Michael Manley achieved prominence in Jamaican politics during this period and their initial political images were colored with the new populist perspectives that had set in as a consequence of increasing disillusionment with the failure of the development objectives in the area of employment, economic and social opportunity for the majority, and greater national control over an economy dominated by foreign enterprises in bauxite, banking, tourism, and certain areas of services and manufacturing. Seaga emerged in the JLP as a militant critic of income inequality in Jamaica. His political ascendancy was dramatized by a carefully presented speech in the Senate attacking the PNP government for perpetuating social inequality.[8] Seaga was influenced in this period by U.W.I. economist

Lloyd Best. Manley was an established trade union leader in the National Workers Union, the trade union affiliate of the PNP. He emerged leader of the PNP in 1968 after his father retired as party leader. His political perspective was also influenced by U.W.I. social science radicalism, through close interpersonal contacts. He committed his leadership to decolonizing the Jamaican economy by challenging both dependency and the control of the economy by foreign corporate interests.

As Seaga got absorbed into the JLP leadership hierarchy as a bright young technocrat, his politics shifted in a conservative direction and he came to espouse a policy view prescribing private sector dominance but operating within the framework of policy leadership provided by the political directorate. Manley, in turn, moved to the left in the role as opposition leader between 1968 and 1972 as he became spokesman for increasingly critical attacks on the so-called neocolonial approach to development promoted by the JLP in which Seaga played a major role as minister of cultural development, development, and planning and as a finance minister over the long 1962-to-1972 period.

What both leaders had in common was a view of the state playing a dominant role in the economy by setting a framework of policy within which the private sector had to operate. Both therefore saw the state as having to regulate private sector behavior and having to regulate and manipulate the forces operating in the economic marketplace. Manley tended to see solutions in greater emphasis on income distribution, increasing national ownership and control of the economy's commanding heights, greater popular participation in the economy and in decision making and by the need to develop a clear set of ideological commitments around which efforts at changing the society should be organized. Initially his ideological framework was nationalist but between 1968 and 1974 it moved towards socialism. Seaga, on the other hand, placed great faith in the creative capacity of dynamic entrepreneurship. He saw foreign capital as an asset (not a deterrent) to development and supported the idea of the state helping the weaker classes (such as poor peasants) while using its resource base to promote dynamic local and foreign entrepreneurship. He believed in careful planning, the creation of strong development promoting institutions staffed with well trained technocrats and that answers to the country's economic and social problems could only be found by promoting diversified new investments in a climate of close private sector–public sector collaboration, but under the guiding hand of strong, purposeful government economic policies.

This third period, therefore, moved policy capability toward what we can call "political management" of the economy in which an infrastructure of public sector institutions and the political directorate established detailed economic policies and programs based on specific prescriptions, trade, fiscal and financial goals. These detailed policies were developed by cadres of experts, technocrats, advisors, and bureaucrats who gradually displaced the policy advisory role of the business class and provided a basis on which the political directorate could develop autonomy and strong leadership in the formulation of national economic policy. This development was facilitated by rapid increase in the supply of highly trained economists, planners, and technical experts in the public sector through overseas higher education, and the impact of the University of the West Indies as a major source of such trained personnel. It was also facilitated by the increased levels of formal education among the political directorate with more and more recruited persons who had university training. Both Seaga and Manley, for example, had university training. Seaga was a social science graduate of Harvard University and Manley read economics at the British London School of Economics.

The central point of departure between this third period of policy development and the second period was that the policy-making institutions in the public sector had now developed the institutional capacity to adequately formulate economic policies, research and monitor economic trends on a detailed basis to lay the foundation for establishing a framework for national economic policies into which private sector activity had to fit. Policy leadership effectively passed to the public sector and the relative autonomy of the policy-making institutions restricted and limited the avenues open to the private sector to influence the direction of national economic policy. Moreover, implied in this development was the need for the public sector policy makers to increasingly regulate private sector activities to maximize national development objectives as well as the creation of a strata of public sector technocrats and advisors who promoted specific policy priorities with the backing of the political directorate. The increasing policy consensus between the two major political parties between the mid-1950s and the beginning of this third period of policy development in the middle to late 1960s permitted the emergence of powerful technocrat–civil service advisors who played a key role in shaping the policy priorities of the JLP and PNP political directorates. These included personalities such as Arthur Brown, economist, financial secretary, and governor of the Central Bank; Horace Barber, economist, bank governor, and financial secretary; Don Mills, economist; Sir Egerton Richardson, financial secretary; and a number of others. Increasingly the private sector had to defer to the policy priorities of these public sector decision makers who reflected the point of view of bureaucrats and technocrats rather than businessmen but saw their role as trying to harmonize the interests of the business class with those of the nation.

Inevitably, therefore, sharp conflicts and tensions developed between the private sector and the public sector policy makers. Under the then Finance Minister Edward Seaga in the 1967–72 JLP government, a policy of insisting on minimal Jamaican equity ownership in financial institutions to further the objective of economic nationalism was opposed vigorously by the powerful interests in the private sector led by the vocal Ashenheim interests who, along with other leading rich business family spokesmen, appealed over Seaga's head to the intervention of Prime Minister Hugh Shearer, a trade unionist. Seaga's vigorous and successful efforts at increasing income tax collection in the revenue departments also earned him the wrath of the private sector and both these policy conflicts shifted large sums of campaign funds in the direction of the opposition PNP, assisting Manley to win the 1972 parliamentary elections.

When Manley came to power these public sector–private sector policy conflicts escalated to crisis proportions due to his party's political attacks on private sector interests from a socialist ideological perspective, increasing state takeover and ownership of enterprises formerly controlled by the private sector, and Manley's radical anti-imperalist and pro-Cuban foreign policy combined with his distancing from the traditionally close Jamaica–U.S. relationships. Indeed, the Manley regime took public sector leadership and dominance to an even further level by largely excluding private sector interests from the policy formulation process, weakening their political leverage to influence policy and political outcomes and by developing a retinue of party and personal advisors to the prime minister who became established in a sort of "White House" support staff in the prime minister's office. Although some of the advisors close to Manley were individuals with private sector connections (for example, O.K. Melhado of the Desnoes and Geddes family interests and Douglas Graham, a rich commercial farmer with controlling interests in the local movie entertainment sector), even these capitalist advisors tended to reflect radical nationalist-reformist approaches to policy making rather than narrow private sector perspectives.

The large buildup of a policy advisory staff around the prime minister made up mainly of social scientists, such as Richard Fletcher, economist, Professor M.G. Smith, anthropologist, Louis Lindsay, political scientist and Dr. Paul Robertson, political scientist, created a source of policy advice that supplemented and in some respects replaced the traditional policy advisory role of the civil service technocrats. Tensions inevitably developed between the two groups, with the "White House" staff supported by short term contract officers (placed in key posts) and a cadre of consultant-advisors (some paid and others unpaid) establishing their ascendancy over the traditional civil service in policy influence.

This development was shaped by three important new factors. The system of cabinet government was being transformed under Manley's leadership into a kind of prime ministerial system in which the prime minister was not just chairman or head of the governing cabinet but was now the effective center of power and source of key decision making to which the cabinet merely provided a rubber stamp endorsement function. The sweeping ideological and political changes that seemed imperative in the period of the 1970s, and the distrust of existing status-quo institutions, added to Manley's extraordinary personal charisma which was in itself a major source of authority in the eyes of voters between 1972 and 1975, all led to a rapid personalization of administrative authority around the prime minister of the day. This created the need for new advisory and support staff established in White House fashion in Jamaica House where the prime minister's office was located and the creation of an Economic Council which became the main forum for detailed policy discussions and deliberations. On that Council sat key ministers and government advisors and the Council effectively replaced the cabinet as the major policy-making body. Its internal workings were controlled by advisors and ministers close to the prime minister and by the prime minister himself.

Manley had brought some members of the radical intelligentsia right into the corridors of power and policy making and this upset both senior civil servant and private sector interests. The former eventually retired from the service in significant numbers from key posts and the latter increasingly became alienated from the policy-making process and the policies it generated. The widening gulf between the public and private sectors became a major problem since effective policy leadership from the public sector required cooperation and acceptance of that leadership role by the private sector. Political attacks[9] on that sector by militant socialist rhetoric and sharp ideological differences between the PNP and the private sector over economic and social policy widened the already large gulf between the two sectors in the 1970s.

When Seaga replaced Manley in 1980, power remained highly concentrated in the prime minister's office. Indeed, the trend towards centralization increased further under Seaga's JLP for a number of reasons. The fundamental divergence between the two regimes was that Manley retained a Jamaican team of advisors, unlike Seaga. Seaga, by contrast, relied heavily on foreign experts and highly paid foreign consultants rather than on Jamaican advisors. Manley attempted to provide policy leadership within the government, which meant that he often took responsibility for policy initiatives falling within the ministerial portfolio of other ministers, but Seaga went further by taking over large areas of subject matter project responsibility in several ministries not within his prime ministerial portfolio. Secondly, Seaga established a large prime ministerial portfolio that included for the first time in the country's history the responsibility of the finance minister with that of prime minister. He also assumed responsibility for matters relating to culture, industrial policy, and areas of agricultural policy.

Manley's concentration of decision making in the office of prime minister was based on his overall political direction of the change process which was assumed to be taking the country into socialism. As the main source of this ideological redirection he naturally took responsibility for major policy changes that were all dressed up in socialist ideological clothing. In the case of Seaga, he assumed a role of technocrat in chief taking on the task of bringing managerial effectiveness and expertise in policy design and implementation in carrying out what his party proclaimed as the returning of the country back from economic and political chaos towards stability and growth without the chaos of the Manley years. His role as controller of finances gave him virtually a dual power position of managing director and chief financial officer within the government. Some of the excessive concentration of decision making that has taken place under the JLP since 1980 mirrors Seaga's personality as a tough, no nonsense manager who prefers to monitor everything himself, to keep his cabinent colleagues under constant surveillance, and only reluctantly to permit key areas of policy making to be delegated to subordinates. Under Seaga the Economic Council has ceased to function as there is no room for that kind of large policy deliberating body, given the personalized control over all key decisions that Seaga exercises over the executive.

Between the second and third periods of policy development, the power, authority, and influence of ordinary cabinet members and traditional top civil service adivsors have been reduced by the process by which various advisors have been inserted into key policy-making roles. Under Manley in the 1970s these redefined policy-making roles brought in social scientists and technically qualified persons into a strong team of Jamaica House advisors. Under Seaga, this redefined policy-making system brought in large numbers of expensive foreign consultants and experts.

In this third phase of policy development in the public sector important new initiatives in policy-making capability were introduced by both Seaga and Manley. Seaga single-handedly developed the area of folk and popular culture as a basis for annual independence celebrations and as a mechanism for promoting and highlighting popular music, traditional dance and other forms of creative cultural expression. This area of state-promoted policy had a major political and social impact in challenging the Eurocentric and European dominant notions of artistic and cultural expression which prevailed among the older generation elite and middle class. It gave expression to a strong mood of cultural nationalism that was built around participation by communities and schools. It provided a symbolic outlet for some of the populist and nationalist political currents that had gathered strength in the society among the younger generation in the mid to late 1960s. State promotion of culture coincided with efforts to commercialize various expressions of popular music coming out of the urban ghetto (ska, reggae, among others). Alienated Rastafarian youth and ghetto militants found an outlet towards upward social mobility in the opportunities that were opened up for the outstanding artists to become national and international stars. Seaga in his private capacity played a key role in the promotion of commercialized 'pop' music expressing the subculture of urban ghetto society in Jamaica. An important ministry of culture was therefore added to the main policy areas of social services and economic management.

Manley attempted to develop social programs and policies[10] with a significant input of grass roots community participation. This took the form of community councils, community-based enterprises promoted by the state, cooperative and state farms, volunteer labor in community development, and the close involvement by party activists in the implementation of some public projects. This initiative ran into many difficulties and to a large extent there were far more failures than successes. The problems had to do mainly with the lack of organized political capacity and management capability within what was and is essentially an electoral party. Indiscipline was rampant, theft and corruption contributed to waste and project failure. Civil servants who tried to maintain proper management and financial accountability were threatened with violence and there was at least one case of assassination[11] and there were several instances of such persons being beaten up by party goons. Socialist people's participation in public projects dispensing large sums of money was seen as an opportunity to engage in plunder of the state's finances. Many who saw these jobs and assignments as reward for party work refused to give a day's work for the pay received. Paybills were often padded with lists of political gunmen who only turned up to collect pay but were never available to do any work. Neither production nor financially viable projects emerged from these initiatives and they turned out to be no more than massive waste of public funds disbursed to party activists and corrupt local level politicians.

What was conceived in lofty ideological terms as involving the people in development revealed starkly the limitations of electoral parties built on party patronage as vehicles for implementing public policy. The result was a nightmare of confusion and disorder in certain ministries and departments that demoralized many public servants and induced others to actively undermine government projects and policies by subtle acts of sabotage or sheer performance inertia and lack of concern about achieving policy results. The more the lethargic civil service dragged its feet, the more the PNP policy makers distrusted them and leaned heavily on a few partisans and on giving more of the party faithful access to program and policy implementation roles. It was a vicious circle that totally undermined administrative capacity to spend limited funds prudently, to complete projects, to get money's worth for funds allocated or to account for large expenditure on various projects in such ministries as Housing, Construction, Agriculture, Youth and Development, and Local Government.

Over this three-phased staging of policy development and expanded policy capability in the public sector, there were some important positive signs of increased public management capability. But there also were some clear signs of weaknesses, problems, and areas of incapacity. Although the educational level of top and middle level civil servants advanced to cope with the larger demands for policy formulation and project development and implementation, some of the effects of this greater professional training in technical scientific subjects, accounting, and the social sciences was negated by organizational weaknesses in the public sector.

BIG GOVERNMENT

The rapid expansion of public sector agencies and accelerated growth of the staff size of departments and ministries often exceed the capacity of the existing systems of financial and performance accountability to continue functioning with any efficiency. The rapid rate of growth is reflected in the share of gross domestic product (GDP) accounted for by government consumption expenditure. Table 5.3 gives the percentage level of GDP taken up in government consumption expenditure for certain years between 1950 and 1977.

It is worth noting that by 1977 only two developing countries in the region with noncommunist-type economies had higher levels of government consumption expenditure than Jamaica (Guyana and Suriname). Among the European and Western industrial countries only Sweden had a higher level of government consumption expenditure over GDP. In other words, the public sector had grown to quite exceptional dimensions, especially between 1970 and 1977 and the states' administrative and financial system was simply not able to cope with this sudden growth. The result was increased inefficiency, mismanagement, corruption, and lack of either accountability or control of either finances or pro-

Table 5.3 Levels of Government Consumption Expenditure as Percent of GDP (1950–1977) in Jamaica

	1955	1960	1965	1970	1977
Government consumption expenditure as percent of GDP	6.2	7.1	8.2	12.1	22.1

Source: World Bank Tables, 1980.

ject implementation. The virtual doubling of public sector workers and staff (central and local government and public enterprises) from 57,000 to 107,000 in the short five-year period between 1968 and 1973 is itself staggering testimony to this rate of expansion that entirely disrupted the system of administration. Beyond the problems entailed in the pace of growth, the actual size of some ministries grew far beyond what was amenable to effective management control and financial accountability. By the early 1980s, massive employment of temporary and special project staff who remained after projects were completed swelled the size of ministries such as the Agriculture Ministry to a staff size of an estimated 10,000. The rapid rate of recruitment added to highly political selection of temporary and special project staff often led to a serious lowering of standards and professionalism that negated the impact of improved levels of formal academic training at the upper and middle levels of the service.

Between low civil service salaries (compared to salary levels in the private sector) and the lure of migration, many of the most qualified and gifted members of the civil service and local government staff left these services during this period of rapid expansion. This added further to the fall in standards, the limited skill and management resources available to cope with the massively increasing burden of policy responsibility and the deteriorating level of performance in the public sector as the system moved from the second phase of policy development to the third stage. At the very period when political management of the economy become a reality and the burden of policy responsibility in the public sector grew to large proportions in the 1970s, the caliber of personnel in the public sector began to rapidly deteriorate.

The rapid expansion of the state's administrative apparatus and its capability to deliver economic and social services demanded larger and larger supplies of tax dollars to keep it going. Table 5.4 shows the steep rate of increase in the size of the Jamaican tax burden. Up to the early 1970s when inflation levels were relatively low, the tax burden was bearable.

By the end of the decade of the 1970s when inflation consistently exceeded 10 percent and was often more than 25 percent and pressure for

Table 5.4 Revenue as a percent of GDP

	1930	1950	1960	1965	1970	1974	1981
Total revenue over GDP	8	14	15	17	21	21	24

Source: Abstract of Statistics, Department of Statistics (1950–68) National Income and Product, 1970–82, National Planning Agency.

tax dollars induced governments not to fully adjust tax rates to fit the reduced value and purchasing power of the dollar, the Jamaican tax rates became one of the most burdensome within the Third World. Indeed, Table 5.5 shows that only one country among a list of 18 has higher or matching levels of tax rates on incomes than Jamaica for the year 1983. The rapid rate of expansion of the state in the 1970s was achieved at the price of both excessive external borrowing as well as the imposition of punitive levels of income taxation that excessively burdened wage and salary earners and constituted a major disincentive for investment.

One major hurdle before any effort to improve the public sector's administrative capability is the high level of corruption and the strong tendency toward illicit deals among both the private sector and public servants. This has been most evident in the areas of illegal currency transactions, the underinvoicing of exports and illegal imports. In an effort to disguise foreign exchange earnings and to permit some of those earnings to be held overseas rather than repatriated through the Central Bank, many exporters of agricultural products have been substantially underinvoicing exports. This practice was picked up by a comparison of U.S. Customs valuation of these commodities and the value entered on local documentation. In 1983 the discrepancies amounted to

Table 5.5 Comparative Tax Payments for Single Individual on Income of $U.S. 20,000

Country	Total Income Tax Paid (1983)
Chile	1,600
Guatemala	1,600
Honduras	1,800
Argentina	2,300
Peru	2,500
Singapore	2,800
Hong Kong	3,000
Taiwan	3,100
Puerto Rico	3,600
Brazil	3,900
South Korea	4,100
Panama	4,500
Mexico	4,700
Colombia	5,000
Barbados	5,700
Bolivia	7,000
Trinidad and Tobago	7,400
Jamaica	9,400
India	10,800

Source: Individual Taxes: A Worldwide Summary, New York: Price Waterhouse, 1983.

millions of dollars. In spite of efforts to tighten up on imports by complicated procedures governing import licenses and customs documentation, it is estimated that more than $800,000 worth of illegal imports came into the economy via the port of Kingston in 1983. In areas of the economy such as tourism hard currency earnings have been illegally exported in spite of complex procedures established by the Central Bank to monitor earnings.

The Jamaican private sector has been militantly opposed to government regulation of business transactions. When asked about governmental factors, which are important obstacles to business success in a survey[12] of managers of some 214 larger enterprises in the capital city carried out by the author in 1983, 84 percent mentioned slow and time-wasting government bureaucracy, 61 percent cited cumbersome customs procedures, and 34 percent identified excessive control of the private sector. Since the private sector has long lost the power to shape public policy, the tactic used in neutralizing policies that are seen as adverse to their interests is to influence the implementation of policy by bribing public officials to ignore existing regulations or to violate them. Given the modest salaries earned by most public sector officials and the absence of high levels of professionalism, such services can be easily bought. The implication is that business interests with enough money buy their way through or over government regulations and are beyond the reach of effective policy control. In addition to the big business enterprises and middle class capitalists who engage in these practices, a large area of illicit business transactions take place within the petty commodity sector among the traders who bring in large quantities of illegal imports and have often intimidated customs officials into compliance. Sporadic attempts to clean up the corruption tend to be short-lived and the practices return once the policy makers shift their attention to other matters. To be sure, some areas of these rule-breaking practices are encouraged by the very political directorate who will authorize the bypassing of regulations and procedures to facilitate their friends, thereby undermining the very system of transaction regulations that they set up.

As the regime of complex regulations of business transactions has gotten more onerous and tedious and as the red tape and complicated bureaucratic procedures grow larger, more and more ingenious methods are devised to get around them. Threats of severe penalties and punishment hardly help as the collusion between public official and private sector interests leaves little room for the uncovering of any evidence firm enough to bring any charges against the offenders or even to discover most of the corrupt practices that take place daily.

As the complex red tape and cumbersome procedures delay business transactions, what happens is that the businessman in a hurry is grateful to find some public servant willing to accept a bribe for cutting through the red tape. Complicated bureaucratic procedures create a demand for bribes and encourage corrupt practices to find ways around them.

The extensive efforts of both the PNP government in the 1970s and the JLP government in the 1980s to regulate currency transactions, imports, prices, and a whole range of other matters have not been effective and the experience points to clear limits beyond which the society will tolerate regimentation and regulatory devices without developing countersystem procedures that neutralize them.

More importantly, the tendency has been for the state to resort to the big stick of regulation in situations where its policies are not supported by the private sector. In those circumstances, private sector resistance manifests itself in skillful techniques in bypassing the rules or finding ways to get around them. The Jamaican private sector has been extremely resourceful in achieving this with the most draconian and watertight regulatory devices. Clearly, the public sector needs to work more closely with private sector interests in achieving consensus on policy measures and policy instruments or at least in eliciting sympathetic private sector support rather than to be constantly falling back on threats, administrative and legal fiats, and imposed rules that become ineffective because both public officials and private sector interests opposed to such measures will invariably neutralize their effect.

There is a very serious lack of communication that complicates public policy making and creates a lack of mutual understanding between private sector interests and public sector policy makers. If this were the only problem it could be sorted out without much difficulty. But it is compounded by two even more difficult problems: first, the private sector interests and the public policy makers do not share the same perspective on economic matters; secondly, the private sector interests tend with few exceptions to have very little real commitment to Jamaica and consequently have a high propensity to export capital and keep their financial holdings in overseas banks and to resist policies that are justified in the national interest if it imposes a price on them. The combined effect of these divisive factors is to increase the policy dissonance and distrust between the public and private sectors. This means that rather than periods of national crisis inducing more collaborative and cooperative relations between these two power domains the opposite tends to be the case. Prolonged crises lead to increased mutual antagonism as the private sector blames the government for being an obstacle to its development by its prescribed excess of red tape and regulation and the government blames the private sector for not responding to incentives and opportunities to move the economy. The PNP politicians maintained that line on the private sector in the 1970s and the JLP politicians have repeated those themes, albeit with less militancy and aggression in the 1980s.

One therefore has to examine both the subjective problems of conflicting perceptions and the nonsharing of information and points of view as well as the underlying objective structural weaknesses in both private sector entrepreneurial resources and capabilities, given the country's problems and the administrative and political incapacities of the public sector policy makers that are often covered over by glib rationalizations of policy failures.

The way the private sector views the economic problems of the country differs greatly from that of the public policy makers. The typical middle class owner-manager has no grasp of the macroeconomic levels of economic trends nor is there any effort to keep informed regarding how these macroeconomic factors operate. That typical owner-manager sees the economy entirely from the vantage point of the microproblems that face the enterprise he or she runs. This is not true of many of the professional managers in the larger corporate enterprises nor is it true of the more educated among the big business owners. But this level of low awareness of macroeconomic forces means that more often than not the logic, purpose, and rationale behind many of the economic policies formulated by the government are neither understood nor grasped by a large section of the smaller business operators. The public policy technocrats, on the other hand, often are able to grasp only the macro level trends but lose sight of how these impact on the individual enterprise because there is no corresponding reliable micro level data to assess. Both groups therefore are often unable fully to grasp the issues that are uppermost in each other's minds. The small businessman will often react by accusing the government technocrats of being impractical while the latter will in turn, accuse the businessman of being unenlightened. These divergent perspectives make effective communication difficult.

PRIVATE SECTOR WEAKNESSES

The private sector itself is inherently weak and many of the expectations about how it will respond to incentives, opportunities, and wide options for economic activity fail to appreciate some of the basic weaknesses in the Jamaican business class that inhibit them from moving the economy. In many respects, the Jamaican private sector is now deficient in many of the qualities that fueled its early growth and expansion in the postwar period. Some other serious limitations have arisen since that early period.

The first generaton of urban-based entrepreneurs who pioneered the postwar diversification of the Jamaican economy were aggressively clawing their way into new opportunities in an economy with limited options. Apart from the big plantations, the ,only other means of making big money was in trading or the commission agency business. They did not have the high status of the planters or the British colonial officials. They sought to move up the social ladder by the accumulation of wealth. To do that they had to break new ground in the economy. Their life-styles were simple and they were not caught up in the traditional status symbols that preoccupied the plantation society's elite. The money they made was not dissipated in luxury living. They reinvested and expanded, grasping every opportunity to move into new areas of the economy. A small minoritry of aggressive entrepreneurs coming mainly out of merchant class backgrounds managed to expand their family enterprises to form the initial foundations for the big Jamaican-owned corporate companies that now exist in various sectors of the diversified Jamaican economy.

Once that first generation built these family economic empires, the next generation that was born into wealth lost the drive, acquisitiveness, urge for expansion, and the sense of conquering new frontiers by seeking to build larger and larger economic empires. The next generation that inherited this wealth either got caught up in seeking respectability through the prestigious professions or was more concerned with carving out an exaggerated version of Americanized affluent life-styles to spend this inherited wealth rather than with tending the business and seeking after new sources of wealth accumulation. As the planter class receded into the background in the postwar period, the urban rich established themselves as the new elite. The status symbols of British accent and British education and landowning combined with a keen sense of appreciation of the refinements of European culture were replaced by the status symbol of big money and the affluent life-style it was used to acquire. The elite's frame of external reference shifted from Britain to the United States and U.S. materialism and affluent living became the core of the new set of high status symbols. Palatial residences, luxurious motor cars, expensive yachts, luxurious offices, and acquisition of all the latest modern consumer gadgets became the new status definers. Consumerism and lavish living replaced the dominant impulse to create wealth and new sources of wealth that preoccupied the first generation of postwar capitalists. These changes in values became pronounced in the postindependence period of the 1960s and 1970s.

The middle class capitalist with far less income tried to imitate and exceed the lavish life-styles of the rich. Expensive motor cars and luxurious dwellings were purchased before the business even indicated that it could sustain such a life-style. Loans could be easily had from banks through social network contacts to finance the business and finance the luxury living.

The new value system discouraged genuine capitalism. The new value system placed no great emphasis and importance on production or technological achievements. The businessman established his worth by driving the latest model of BMW motor cars or Mercedes Benz, or by the size and lavish outlay and fixtures of his dwelling. A norm of excessive consumerism and luxury living was set. The challenge of risk taking or breaking new ground was no longer important as the first generation of urban entrepreneurs failed to reproduce themselves.

But what was demanded was not just a reproduction of the old powerful motivations but the generation of a new breed of capitalist educated to master, experiment and tinker with new production technologies. Instead what was reproduced at both the big capitalist and small capitalist levels was a new generaton preoccupied with consuming luxury goods rather than with the transforming of production. The effect is that the productive technology in the economy stagnates and remains at a pre-1970 level in a world fast moving toward twenty-first century high technology.

Instead of being used to expand the wealth-generating base of the economy and thereby create more demand for employment, so much of the surplus or profits generated get siphoned out of the cycle of production and invesment. Instead of remaining in the economy to finance an increased level of domestic economic activity, much of that surplus is spirited away to overseas U.S. accounts and used to maintain the lavish life-style of the urban rich. Even large sums borrowed through the development bank ended up in this channel of leakage from the cycle of production and investment to the cycle of wasteful luxury living, hard currency exports, and capital flight. Under conditions of economic crisis such as has descended on the economy since the 1970s the response of the small business owner-managers or the younger generation of urban rich is to defend their lavish life-styles and oppose all austerity measures rather than to seek to take hold of the forces of production as they have been constantly urged to do by successive PNP and JLP regimes since the late 1960s.

To preserve and expand this lavish life-style the rich owners of the means of production and the middle class capitalists dodge responsibility for paying taxes. Apart from the larger corporate enterprises who have no option but to carry their responsibility for corporate income taxes, most of the smaller enterprises either avoid paying any tax or pay far less than they should. As a result the burden on salary and wage earners is out of proportion to the share of national income they earn. In the early 1950s close to 60 percent of direct taxes on income was paid by corporate enterprises owned by private interests and the remaining 40 to 44 percent was paid by wage and salary earners. By the late 1970s some two-thirds of the flow of direct taxes on incomes came from wages and salaries and only 30 to 35 percent from corporate taxes, although the business sector has grown much larger, bigger multimillion dollar enterprises have multiplied, and the private sector now has a stronger base of business profits from which to pay taxes.

The inherent weaknesses in the private sector and the limited capacity that sector has to revitalize the Jamaican economy lies at the root of many of the sharp differences between the public and private sector interests over economic policy. Invariably expectations of positive private sector performance are never matched by the sector's performance.

To be sure, there are minority groupings in the private sector that have the capacity to meet some of these challenges. Some among that minority belong to the first generation of urban rich who are much too old or set in their ways to pioneer new initiatives in the economy. Others belong to the small business class and have the drive, initiative and innovativeness to break new ground in the economy but are excluded from getting access to the quantum of financing they need because the existing economic elite monopolizes what money is available for business expansion and uses its corporate power to keep smaller enterprises from getting the financial and other support to grow larger and diversify into new areas. There are some enterprising businessmen among the younger generation of rich capitalists but they do not represent a large enough segment of the class to make a very big difference in macro terms. What is clearly needed is a government policy that can identify all the enterprising and potentially dynamic entrepreneurs and give them priority access to capital, state support and promotion, and international financial backing to lead the revitalization of the economy. No government to date has either had the foresight or the courage to challenge the business elite and the business lobbies by carving out an aggressive policy in directly supporting those entrepreneurs who together and as a strategic group could revitalize the prematurely aging Jamaican economy. By often proceeding on the false assumption that they are making economic policies for a dynamic and resourceful private sector, all governments since the 1970s world oil crisis have oversimplified the economic problems of Jamaica by believing that money and the right monetary, trade, and fiscal policies can solve the problems. There is a more basic difficulty of opening up opportunities so that the more resourceful and enterprising among the business class (big, small, white, black, and brown) can be given full state backing to move the Jamaican economy into new gear. Instead both the regimes of Prime Ministers Seaga and Manley have relied on simplistic ideological formulas that were not tailored to addressing some of the basic structural problems.

CONCLUSION

Despite these obstacles and problems in the path towards increasing the policy capability of the state, the positive growth factors were quite impressive. Increased training of public servants in the postwar years, the development of key policy-making institutions, a larger outlay of public resources, improved management capacity by a more educated political directorate, improved capacity to deliver social and economic services and more resourcefulness in the making of economic policies all strengthened the public sector's policy role between the early 1940s period and 1970. After those years the rapid growth of the state's policy responsibilities and its administrative machinery in the 1970s both overtaxed the country's financial resources as well as the public sector's management and financial systems of accountability. To further strengthen the public sector's policy capability to cope with the crisis management demands of the Jamaican economy, the public sector will have to be pruned, reorganized and drastically overhauled to ensure professionalism, accountability, fuller utilizaton of the service's skill, and trained manpower and better use of public expenditure in all areas of the public sector.

Beginning with the deepening of the economic crisis facing the country in the late 1970s and increasing financial dependence on friendly foreign governments, the IMF and the World Bank, it appears as if the country's policy development is entering a fourth phase. In this phase policy parameters are being set by foreign international agencies that are forcing the managers of the state to cut back expenditure in line with the declining economic base of production. These new directions threaten to dispense with some of the gains realized earlier in the development of effective social policies for health, education, and the development of economic services as all areas of public spending have received drastic budget cutbacks. Beyond this, the expansionist fiscal policies of most of the early postwar era have come under the austerity restrictions of International Monetary Fund fiscal prescriptions with severe political reactions from the majority classes who have benefited over the years from the state's advances in public policy capability, as well as from the lower middle class for whom the rapidly expanding public sector had almost become a sort of middle class welfare institution. But detailed analysis of these changes must await a more comprehensive discussion of the policy directions developed under Manley in the 1970s and Seaga in the 1980s. The balance of political support for big government is so great that in spite of these pressures to reduce expenditure, there are limits to which public expenditure can be effectively reduced. The policy objective of expenditure cut-back is to reduce the large 17 percent budget deficit. But even if this objective is achieved, the level of public spending will remain high as a percentage of national income.

Perhaps the clearest indicators of the growth of the state's administrative capacity is to be found in the mobilizaton of tax revenue. Income tax collection is known for its great problems in Third World economies with large numbers of self-employed persons. However, the rapid expansion in income tax payers from 36,000 in 1951 to 76,000 in 1964, represents a growth of appreciable proportions in the percentage of gainfully employed persons paying income taxes. From 7 percent of the labor force paying income tax in 1951, this increased to 13 percent in 1964.

But as the state has grown larger and mobilized more and more resources from a wider cross section of the political community, negative reactions to big government have set in. The problem is that public attitudes reflect deep ambivalence. The mass public sees the need for big government to provide an ever increasing flow of cheap or free public services. In areas such as health and hospital services Jamaica is one of the few countries in the Third World where such services have been made available from hospitals and clinics totally free of charge.[13] Such free public services cost a lot of money yet the public resents the increasing net of tax collection that has burdened captive P.A.Y.E. taxpayers and has begun to penetrate the self-employed sector on a big scale and affect even the big traders in marijuana, who in 1984 were called upon to pay over $100 million in income taxes by the Seaga government.

This ambivalence about big government among the majority classes creates a climate in which private sector capitalist and middle class interests who see big government as inherently threatening their freedom space can find ready allies and support on controversial issues in which the state's efforts to tax, regulate, control and direct private interests can be challenged with appreciable public opinion support.

Given the decisive influence being exerted by international lending agencies such as the World Bank and the IMF (with full support from Washington) to scale down big government in aid-dependent economies such as Jamaica, and the dependence of the poorer classes on aspects of big government, added to the state socialist orientation of the Peoples National Party, the 1980s are going to unfold an interesting political struggle between forces seeking to contract big government and forces seeking to expand it even further. Resources to finance public spending are going to be a major factor determining the outcome and the trend now seems poised towards a contraction of big government led by the JLP's acceptance of the IMF-World Bank position. How far a contraction is politically feasible or acceptable to the political community and how much the prosocialist PNP will make this into a major issue of capitalist conservative public management versus people-oriented or socialist public management remains to be seen. But this is surely going to be a major issue on the agenda of administrative–political change in the 1980s and 1990s.

NOTES

1. See Carl Stone, "Political aspects of postwar agricultural policies in Jamaica (1945-70)," *Social and Economic Studies*, 23 (1974).

2. These and other comparative social policy indicators are throughly analyzed for Cen-

tral America and the Caribbean in Carl Stone, *Profiles of Power in the Caribbean*, Philadelphia: ISHI, 1985.

3. As occurs in most reform situations, attempts to reduce inequality increase expectations for greater improvements and sharpen political awareness of the issue of inequality. For most of the later postwar period, expectations for reductions in economic and social inequality ran ahead of the actual changes occurring, often giving the false impression that the society was not changing. The reality is that inequality was significantly reduced over this period but several areas of social inequality persisted in a political climate in which left-leaning political currents sharpened popular demands for greater equality. By the end of the 1970s there were few traces of the rigid caste-like plantation social structure of the old order and more egalitarian social relations across class boundaries had become the norm.

4. For an excellent discussion of the development of industrial manufacturing in Jamaica, see Mahmood Ali Ayub, *Made in Jamaica*, Baltimore: Johns Hopkins University, 1981.

5. See, *Report of the Economic Policy Committee*, 1945.

6. These ideas about industrial strategies were heavily influenced by the writings of Nobel Prize-winning St. Lucian economist, Sir Arthur Lewis, who emphasized export manufacturing as the key to development in small island economies with surplus labor. In this respect Lewis' ideas envisioned the industrial transformation that occurred in the newly industrialized Asian economies.

7. These challenges of the status quo were led by the New World Movement under the leadership of economists Lloyd Best, George Beckford, Norman Girvan, C.Y. Thomas, and Havelock Brewster.

8. As a result of this "have and have not" speech, Seaga earned an early reputation of being a Marxist.

9. For a treatment of this public sector–private sector conflict in the 1970s, see Evelyn Stephens and John Stephens, "Democratic socialism and the capitalist class: An analysis of the relation between Jamaican business and the PNP government," Working Paper no. 8, Universidad Interamericana de Puerto Rico, 1983.

10. For a detailed discussion of these policies see Carl Stone, "Democracy and socialism in Jamaica, 1962–79," *The Journal of Commonwealth & Comparative Politics*, (July 1981).

11. A permanent secretary in the Ministry of Works, Mr. Ted O'Gilvie was assassinated after opening up investigations into construction racketeering in that ministry.

12. See unpublished survey by author, Carl Stone, "Survey of the business climate in Jamaica (1983)."

13. Under IMF pressures to cut the budget deficit, the JLP government introduced comprehensive hospital fees in 1984.

6

LABOR AND CAPITAL

In the attempt to dismantle the aristocratic colonial state, the impulse toward democratic changes and reforms was greatly influenced by the pressures from the working class to harness the vehicle of democracy towards achieving certain specific class objectives. These objectives included increasing workers' power to bargain with the owners of the means of production, establishing channels through which labor can influence the decision-making process, defining and securing workers' rights, and establishing the interest of labor as a major priority concern of the state and those who define state or public policies.

There were two main aspects to this use by labor of the reformed democratic state to enhance its position in the political community. The first was connected to the use of the political parties by organized labor to provide the means by which public policy could be influenced to the futherance of workers' economic, social, and political rights. During the first decade of party politics in the 1940s both political parties became captives of organized labor. The Jamaica Labor Party was little more than an executive committee of the affiliated Bustamante Industrial Trade Union, led by party and union leader Alexander Bustamante, the most popular and powerful of the early labor leaders. Promoting the welfare of labor became the central policy goal of the JLP under Bustamante's leadership. Indeed, it was not until in the mid-1950s that the JLP developed an organizational structure separate and apart from the BITU.[1] The Peoples National Party consisted of a strong middle class nationalist element combined with organized labor. This duality to the party's character and the dual elements in the party's leadership created deep internal divisions that were only resolved when the nationalist leadership expelled the radical labor leaders and their union and created a new trade union arm to replace that union and to challenge the BITU-JLP alliance. In appraising the impact of these political changes on the power of labor in the political system, one has to examine the changing relationship between organized labor and the political parties.

The second area of labor's political thrust concerns the development of a system of collective bargaining enabling workers both to increase their power at the workplace as well as to bargain for improved economic benefits from management and owner interests. Both areas of labor politics in Jamaica have gone through important changes and stages of development that have to be understood to comprehend the nature of power in contemporary Jamaican politics. In the early postwar period, the labor movement saw the two areas of labor politics as a unified whole or parts of an integrated struggle for workers' rights and freedoms. The transition to parliamentary government through consititutional changes was a simple and smooth process pushed by local political pressure groups and leaders and supported by a sympathetic imperial government in Britain. Labor's relationship with owner interests were far more problematic to bring within the framework of democratic changes parallel to the changes that had occurred in the transition from the feudal patrimonial state in Europe to liberal democracy. The values and power relationships that characterized the traditional Jamaican plantation society did not change simultaneously with the liberalizing of the constitution or the decline of the traditional family-owned plantations. A master-servant ideology, a rigid caste-like, color-class social hierarchy and an impassible social barrier and social distance between the privileged white and light skinned employers and the poor black working class did not make for easy recognition of workers' rights at the workplace in the early period of the labor movement in the 1940s. Employers fought union representation efforts bitterly, viewing the emergence of trade unions in their family-owned and run enterprises as a challenge to their prerogative rights as owners. The very idea of workers and union leaders exercising power at the workplace was seen as subverting the freedom of capital and the unfettered authority that they were socialized to believe ought to accompany the rights of ownership and management. Even when unions got a foot in the door of collective bargaining, the unionized workers were regarded as being disloyal to management and the union spokesmen were defined as an enemy presence in the plant. Unlike Western Europe, which for most of the early transition to capitalism was able to organize the accumulation of capital and the modernization of the economy without trade union pressures, capital had no such breathing space in the postwar modernization of the Jamaican economy. Owners and managers resented this attempt to constrain their freedom to hire and fire, to set work norms, pay, and working conditions for their employees or to use their authority at the workplace to reward loyal workers and punish those who undermined their interests.

Labor, in turn, resented the reactions of owners and managers to their pressures to achieve for labor the bargaining power at the workplace which was won by the European working class in Britain and other Western societies.

Labor relations were, therefore, extremely conflict prone and given to confrontation, violent strikes, lockouts, deadlocks over bargaining issues and unwillingness by both labor and capital to compromise in collective bargaining. The union leaders and labor came to recognize that to enhance their bargaining power they had to develop the weapon of extreme worker militancy as experience suggested that it was often the decisive factor in bringing management to the bargaining table or forcing employer interests to listen or make compromises with labor.

This tradition of adversary relations between trade unions and owner and management interests and the deep distrust between labor and capital that it reflects remain continuing features of labor relations in Jamaica. As a result, Jamaica has one of the highest[2] levels of strike incidence among countries with free labor bargaining.

The party-trade union alliance was intended to provide labor with policy and legistlative protection in their battles with employers. But the expectation did not materialize. Between 1944 and 1972 no major legislation designed to strengthen the bargaining power of labor was passed. Indeed, as elected party leaders came into more and more control of the levers of public policy making, their priority concern for labor was pushed into the background as they confronted larger questions of development policy and found themselves having to reconcile conflicts between a variety of social interests (farmers, merchants, manufacturers, professionals, public servants, petty traders, and wage workers). As the formulation of national development policy became the main focus of the elected party leaders by the mid-1950s, labor moved in three directions to protect its interest at the workplace.

First of all, the labor organizations developed a certain degree of institutional autonomy and a separate internal life of their own from that of political parties to which they were affiliated. While there continued to be overlapping leadership between parties and trade unions, the interests of the unions were no longer seen as identical with the interests of the party. This differentiation between party and union interests was even more sharply defined after the mid-1950s and especially in the late 1960s and early 1970s as the unions came to represent large numbers of public sector workers whose employers were the elected leaders of the respective political parties, and this generated sharp conflicts between the party-leadership policy role and the union role to represent labor. While important trade union leaders continued to play key leadership roles in party politics (Hugh Shearer, Michael Manley, Pearnell Charles, Errol Anderson, Carlyle Dunkley, and others), the high degree of institutional separation between trade union and political party has meant that some of the labor politicians have severed their trade union ties. Secondly, workers came increasingly to distrust[3] the union-party affiliation insofar as it was seen as a manipulation of workers and workplace issues by party politicians. To retain membership and attract new members, the party-affiliated unions had to project an image of relative independence of the party they were affiliated to. Thirdly, the trade unions have tended to abandon party politics as a main channel by which to secure power for labor and have concentrated, instead, on intensifying the focus on collective bargaining and the securing of rights through militant bargaining positions at the plant level. Paradoxically, the close political party-trade union linkages of the early postwar years gave way to a much looser alliance cemented more around labor and party leadership overlap and exchanges than through trade union-party solidarity among the working class. By the late 1960s and early 1970s union membership had no predictable impact on working class voting. BITU and NWU members tended to vote with the overall trends in the electorate rather than with the political preferences of union leaders. As this link became looser, union leaders had less and less ability to deliver trade union votes, which they were able to do in the 1940s.

As labor abandoned party politics as a major area for the achievement of working class goals, reliance on worker militancy as a key bargaining weapon in dealing both with employers and governments became the norm, thereby intensifying the incidence of industrial unrest and industrial conflicts. The continued rivalry between the party-affiliated trade unions and the many smaller unions without party ties added yet another source of conflict to an already conflict-prone and highly unstable climate of industrial relations.

The development of the labor movement must, therefore, be divided into two distinct periods. First, the 1938 to mid-1950s period in which the unions represented an integral and relatively undifferentiated part of the broader party alliances. Up to that period, the interests of organized labor were paramount and powerful in both major political parties. After the mid-1950s the power of labor within the party declined decisively. In the JLP, big business allies such as the Ashenheims emerged as major sources of policy advice and direction for the inexperienced elected JLP party leaders. The JLP, in fact, became a curious trade union big business alliance party held together by the enigmatic populism of Bustamante. The PNP, having jettisoned its radical trade union leaders in the affiliate Trades Union Congress, in 1952 also got into an alliance between big business interests such as the Matalons and the middle class nationalist intelligentsia that led the party. The new trade union arm of the PNP, the National Workers Union, accelerated the trend toward relatively autonomous trade unionism. Its power position in the PNP was never significant and its energies were concentrated on catching up with the enormous dominance enjoyed by the JLP's BITU in terms of its majority share of worker representation in that early 1950s period.

In effect, as the power of labor declined within both political parties, the influence of key members of the big business interests increased, similarly the influence of the growing middle class of professionals and owner managers expanded quite considerably in the determination of party policy. The decline of organized labor's policy and political influence in the political party power structures was carefully disguised by the continued high profile role of major trade union politicians in the top leadership of both parties. The paradox is that while union leaders like Hugh Shearer and Michael Manley took over leadership of the JLP and the PNP respectively in the 1967-1968 period, the political parties and their affiliate trade unions were drifting further and further apart due to the sharpening division of labor between the political parties and organized labor. Organized labor came more and more to represent the interests of the middle 40 percent of income earners while the political parties centered their membership on the poorest bottom 40 percent in the economy.

As the trade unions interest developed its relative autonomy from party politics, the trade union link became less and less useful to the parties. They could no longer deliver the vote and they provided little more than a good populist image for aspiring trade union politicians. But trade unionism ceased to be the most important road to political leadership. Neither could the union leader claim any more to speak for the majority of the poor. Indeed, for the most part, the centers of the greatest militancy in the labor movement were to be found among the ranks of the relatively privileged labor aristocracy in public utilities, bauxite, big manufacturing enterprises, and government public enterprises.

INDUSTRIAL CONFLICT

Between the earlier and later periods of trade union development, the pattern of industrial conflict escalated and trade union membership expanded. Table 6.1 gives the number of work stoppages occurring in the economy over the period between the 1940s and the late 1960s. There was, indeed, a steady increase in the number of work stoppages, which rose from 45 to 234 per year. However, the most pronounced period of work stoppage increases occurred between the 1960s and the 1970s, when the incidence of strikes doubled.

Instead of labor relations becoming less conflict prone as union representation widened in the economy, strike levels tended to increase as union membership grew. Clearly, a norm of adversary union-

Table 6.1 Number of Strikes (1948-1979)

Years	Number of Work Stoppages
1948-51	137
1952-55	113
1956-59	154
1960-63	250
1964-67	257
1968-71	316
1972-75	568
1976-79	702

Source: Digest of Statistics, Department of Statistics 1948-68. Social and Economic Survey, National Planning Agency, 1970-82.

management relations had become virtually institutionalized as strikes began to be used not as a weapon of last resort in deadlocked negotiations but a form of intimidatory early warning used to test management's position on issues in dispute. Invariably, the use of the strike weapon produced results in terms of management accommodation, compromises, or greater willingness to negotiate in good faith. The effect was that workers came to feel that only when the strike weapon was used could labor feel assured that the best possible bargaining position was achieved and that peaceful settlement of disputes was likely to yield less favorable settlements than where workers resorted to strike action. Trade union leaders were often under pressure to prove their loyalty to the workers' cause by supporting the most militant industrial action because of the deep distrust of union leaders that developed as labor became less a political movement with broadly defined national goals and more an expression of business unionism catering almost entirely to wage bargaining.

The steady increase in strikes over the 1948 to 1971 period reflected the rapid growth of union membership. As more workers came into the trade movement, the incidence of strikes increased, reflecting the greater capability of labor to initiate industrial action as more workers had the protection and power that union membership confers.

The accelerated rate of work stoppage increases that occurred in the 1970s was directly related to the unprecedented high rate of cost of living increases. Indeed, for the first time since World War II the trade unions were unable to achieve wage increases that matched the rate of increase in prices. As workers' living standards declined, the union movement became more militant and for the first time began to attract a large number of white collar supervisory, and middle management employees in a labor movement that prior to the 1970s was predominantly representing manual workers. Double-digit inflation levels pushed large sections of white collar workers into trade unions in this period, thereby adding to the movement workers with a greater propensity to challenge management on many nonwage issues. Indeed, by the end of the 1970s among the countries with free trade unions, only Britain, Australia, and France had strike levels per 10,000 wage workers that were as high as the strike incidence in Jamaica.

Although there is a high propensity to strike in the Jamaican labor relations system, this is compensated for by the fact that work stoppages tend to be of very short duration. Workers receive no strike pay and therefore have limited means to survive prolonged strike action. Secondly, the occurrence of work stoppages usually triggers negotiating positions that produce quick action toward dispute settlement.

UNION MEMBERSHIP

The growth of union membership[4] in the postwar period has been impressive as demonstrated in Table 6.2. This is in spite of the fact that the wage-earning labor force has grown very slowly. In the earlier years when the trade unions were more organizationally integrated with the political parties and the struggle was concentrated on overcoming employer resistance to trade unionism and extending the movement's membership beyond a core of sugar workers and wharf workers, the rate of growth of membership was extremely high. Beginning with 1000 members in 1938 the movement grew to 11,000 by 1941 and to 46,000 by 1944. By the end of the 1940s union membership had spread to government workers (38%), manufacturing (21%), utilities (26%), transportation (63%), construction (10%) and commerce (12%). Sugar and banana workers representing the core of the 30 percent level of unionization within agriculture and the wharf workers (90%) set the early pattern of high levels of worker militancy.

Between 1947 and 1960 the rate of growth was much slower but it accelerated again in the 1960s and 1970s as new larger enterprises were

Table 6.2 Growth in Union Membership

Year	Union Members	Percent of wage labor
1938	1,000	.4
1941	11,000	.4
1944	46,000	16
1947	64,000	21
1950	67,000	21
1960	78,000	18
1970	150,000	35
1982	192,000	43

Sources: Digest of Statistics, Department of Statistics 1947-68. Survey data from labor study in 1982.

established in both the public and private sectors in the 1960s due to the expansion of the economy. Cost of living pressures also diversified the membership in the 1970s, pulling in white collar and middle management workers in big enterprises.

The overwhelming majority of unionized members of the labor force are concentrated in the two big unions that are affiliated with the major political parties. Fifty-seven percent of the unionized workers are in the BITU (JLP), 31 percent in the NWU (PNP), and the remaining 12 percent spread between the TUC (6%) and a multiplicity of very small trade unions. Although they are constantly raiding each other's membership, the bigger trade unions have a broad alliance among them (BITU, NWU, TUC, JALGO). Their dominance of the union membership is resented by the smaller trade unions, thereby creating a sharp cleavage between the established unions and the smaller ones. Among the smaller unions the most active are the communist party affiliated UAWU; UTASP, which represents clerical, technical, and administrative workers; and JU-POPE, which represents government workers.

THE STRIKE PATTERN

A detailed analysis[5] of industrial disputes occurring in 1980 revealed that the smaller unions that are battling to increase their share of the membership (often at the expense of the bigger unions) are more active in work stoppages and industrial disputes than the bigger unions. Sixty-two percent of the incidence of industrial action involved the BITU and the NWU who together represent 88 percent of the union membership. The other unions that accounted for the remaining 38 percent of the conflicts, represent only 12 percent of organized labor.

Industrial conflict tends to occur most in the larger private sector and public sector enterprises. In 1980, for example, 58 percent of the work stoppages occurred in large private sector companies, and 34 percent in large public sector enterprises. Fifty-six percent of the public sector strikes were in enterprises with mainly white collar workers, while in the private sector only 9 percent occurred in mainly white collar organizations. The rapid growth of large manufacturing and service enterprises in the economy since the 1960s has therefore increased industrial unrest as there tends to be a rather high propensity to strike in these organizations. Whereas in the earlier years strike militancy was concentrated primarily among the sugar workers, construction, and transportation workers, in the more recent periods the main centers of industrial agitation are to be found in the much expanded larger manufacturing enterprises and in the larger public enterprises. Indeed, it is the higher paid labor aristocracy which enjoys job security that tends to exhibit the highest propensity towards industrial action and strikes while the more lowly paid workers are more quiescent. In the early 1980s period, the lowest levels of strikes are to be found among agricultural workers, workers in the distribution sector or commerce, and smaller manufacturing plants, especially those with predominantly female labor. As suggested in the earlier analysis, the propensity to strike relates to the organizational and power capability of groups of workers and not to the levels of relative economic deprivation between higher paid and lower paid workers.

In the earlier period of trade union development, work stoppages tended to focus mainly on wage issues and on the issue of worker representation. Since the 1970s both types of issues have been overtaken in importance by issues related to workers' rights. These tend to focus on disciplinary matters in which workers are fired or suspended or on other areas of management decisions that are viewed by workers as adversely affecting their rights. The democratic socialist ideological trends popularized by the PNP in the 1970s encouraged a climate in which workers sought to challenge more the prerogatives and authority of management. Active PNP support for the idea of industrial democracy sharpened labor's sense of the need for greater power at the workplace and generated greater questioning of management decisions. This broadened the agenda of issues that triggered industrial unrest.

There was, however, a certain element of futility about the whole pattern of heightened industrial action by labor in the 1970s. More and more, costs were being incurred by labor in the way of wages lost in strike action for less and less results as the wage gains for most workers fell considerably behind the cost of living increases in the second half of the decade of the 1970s. Big wage increases among organized labor in the early 1970s compensated for the sharp domestic price increases caused by the world oil crisis. But after the economy came under IMF restrictions in 1977, wage increases fell considerably behind price increases, particularly in years such as 1978 (49%) and 1984 (20% in first six months), when massive price increases followed the large IMF-induced devaluations of the Jamaican dollar under both PNP and JLP governments.

The conventional IMF policy of shifting the burden of structural adjustments on labor rather than on capital and in transferring real income from labor to capital had the effect in Jamaica of increasing social pressures on workers that could not be eased at the bargaining table. But not having developed a capacity to either mobilize their members around wider political, nonwage, and national policy issues and having abandoned any prospect of becoming a strong national policy lobby by retreating into business unionism and collective bargaining, the trade unions had no means of defending themselves against anti-labor policies that arose from the loan conditions laid down by the IMF over the

1977 to 1984 period. In addition, the deep party divisions within the labor movement paralyzed its capacity to act with internal unity on matters of economic policy that would bring the unions into a collision with a governing party.

The labor movement has been successful in securing certain important gains for the working class in the postwar period. In an economy with high levels of open unemployment, the strength of the trade unions has been important in ensuring a minimal level of job security for individual workers. Management is no longer free to exercise unfettered discretion or managerial prerogatives in dismissing workers. The likely reaction of unionized workers has to be taken into account and such extreme disiplinary measures are only adopted in severe cases of unlawful behavior.

LABOR'S GAINS

Unionized workers have been able to negotiate wage increases that have exceeded the rate of inflation for most of the postwar years. Problems have arisen in the post-1977 IMF period of economic policies but even here sections of unionized labor have been able to keep abreast of the cost-of-living increases for most years in spite of rigid wage guidelines in enterprises where the employer has the ability to pay.

The militancy of organized labor in larger private sector and public sector enterprises has had the effect of forcing management to weigh decisions carefully on matters likely to affect workers. These workers often exercise a sort of unofficial veto power over decisions affecting conditions of work. In some areas of the economy, labor-displacing technology has been delayed or blocked by governments responding to trade union pressure, as occurred in the sugar industry. A great deal depends on how accessible and responsive the prime minister is to the trade union leaders. In this respect, Hugh Shearer (JLP) and Michael Manley (PNP) as former union leaders have been more accommodating to trade union interests than Prime Minister Seaga (JLP).

The attempt by the Manley regime to promote worker participation[6] or industrial democracy failed to materialize on a large scale. The union leaders gave lip service support to the idea but refused to work fully for its realization out of fear that it could become a means of institutionalizing plant level worker leadership at considerable cost to the unions by reducing the need for the negotiating or advocacy roles they perform. The word was quietly spread among organized workers that worker participation was a management device designed to muzzle trade unions and limit their role in collective bargaining. The lack of support from organized labor combined with employer-management resistance destroyed any prospect of developing industrial democracy in Jamaica. The working class in the 1970s was too engrossed in the problems of day-to-day economic survival and wage-related issues to give active support to this proposal for restructuring power at the workplace. In any event, workers tended to see their power position in normal collective bargaining as having given them a power base from which to deal with management. Finally, the fact that some worker participation measures were introduced by management often tainted the idea with a management and consequently an anti-worker symbolism.

UNION DEMOCRACY

Like the political parties, the trade unions are controlled by the leaders and there is no significant element of internal union democracy that allows the working class any real say in how the unions are run, in the selection of leaders, or in the disbursement of union funds. To conclude[7], however, that workers have no control over the unions would be to completely misunderstand the nature of the relationship between the trade unions and the workers they represent.

To begin with, the unions operate as a bureaucratic agency the workers hire to be their advocates. If the union fails to represent their interests adequately, the workers' reaction is to seek out another trade union as there is rarely any sense of strong loyalty felt towards any single union. Indeed, the moment any group of workers begins to indicate strong dissent towards a union that represents them, a rival trade union will usually begin to show an interest and challenge the existing union for bargaining rights. This intense rivalry between unions in this very competitive union environment gives the workers a powerful lever of control and accountability over union leadership.

Secondly, workers are never reluctant to voice strong criticism of union representatives in situations where their motives or effectiveness seem in doubt. It is not unusual in some enterprises for workers to abuse or intimidate union representatives and there have even been some cases of workers using violence against union representatives.[8] The union leaders are, therefore, under constant pressure. Workers' distrust of management often forces unions to adopt an extremely adversarial style in public encounters with the latter to maintain credibility with workers. The increasing pattern in wage negotiations for example, is for workers to insist on a strong presence at negotiations taking place between trade union representatives and management. This often limits the negotiating flexibility of the union representatives. In spite of this, it is not unusual for workers to reject agreements made between union representatives and management.

In most situations of industrial conflicts leading to work stoppages, strikes are actually initiated by workers themselves rather than by the union leaders, except where strikes occur during wage negotiations. Alongside the union representatives and the elected worker delegates, there is usually a network of informal worker leaders who exert considerable influence over collective action by workers and they are usually the most militant and vocal workers. Workers, therefore, exercise considerable influence over labor relations generally and how trade unions operate at the plant level, although they have no control over the internal bureaucracy of the union. This high level of worker control over the unions does not make for rational or stable labor relations nor for strong unions able to guide workers or take firm positions on conflict issues. Additionally, the blanket structure of the unions means that the relatively small union bureaucracy in the larger unions is spread thin across large numbers of enterprises, which means that outside of wage negotiations the union leaders are not in close touch with plant level developments and are usually hostages to the sentiments of workers on many conflict issues with management. In the earlier period of close union party integration union leaders could control and direct workers through party loyalties and populist leadership. A strong labor leader like Alexander Bustamante in the 1940s and 1950s had effective control over workers he represented. That situation, however, changed fundamentally as the workers now distrust union leaders almost as much as they distrust management.

LABOR'S POWER

While the impact of organized labor has constrained management's control over workers to a point of weakening work discipline in some larger enterprises and making it difficult for management to hire and fire workers freely or to change working conditions unilaterally, trade unionism has given workers power over a narrow agenda of issues and areas of decision making at the workplace but has not fundamentally affected the economic power of owners. In any political economy, it is the interests who control capital and its accumulation who control the workplace environment. Only under conditions of advanced industrial democracy can workers begin to exercise real control over the work environment. Organized labor and the workers it represents have merely developed the means of blocking management decisions in specific areas of plant administration and of extracting concessions and compromises. But the unions and the workers react to management rather than initiate policy or issues, except in the area of wage bargaining.

The high levels of militancy and the high propensity to strike which are features of the informal power exercised by labor in the economy have generated adverse public opinion reactions to trade unions and strikes. In spite of the high level of union representation large sections of Jamaican public opinion are hostile to the unions, their methods, and their disruptive influence on the economy in the constant spate of short duration strikes they perpetuate across the economy and especially in essential services such as electricity. A national survey carried out by the author in February 1981 found that 45 percent of the persons interviewed agreed with the suggestion that trade unions cause too many strikes and serve to undermine production and the economy.

Thirty-five percent disagreed and took the view that unions strike mainly over just causes. Of course, 85 percent of the union members in the sample supported the view that unions strike over justifiable causes. Underlying the views of the 45 percent plurality who have an unfavorable view of the unions is a deep feeling that the country's labor relations system is chaotic and is in need of serious reform to minimize the frequent disruptive strikes that occur. All of this means that where a government adopts a hard line towards any union or group of workers in a strike situation, the government has the option of appealing to anti-union public opinion and thereby bringing pressure to bear on organized labor through the mass media. The majority of the self-employed and the unemployed who together outnumber wage workers make a sharp distinction between the narrow interests of workers and those of the nation as a whole. Anti-union middle class and capitalist opinion can, therefore, find strong allies among the majority classes in controversial labor conflicts and this tends to restrain union leaders and pressure them into seeking speedy settlement of conflict issues.

THE LABOR MARKET

Except for its constant advocacy in support of minimum wages and minimum wage adjustments for nonunionized poorer workers, the trade unions have shown little or no interest in the problems of the large subproletariat of poorer workers in the economy who look to political parties to secure their class interests. On the contrary, the impact of trade unionism accelerates wage and salary inequalities in the labor force, bids up the price of labor beyond its real market value in some sectors, and indirectly passes on higher living costs to the poorer bottom 40 percent in the labor force by large wage claims which result in higher prices.

In manufacturing, for example, unionized labor with similar skills usually earns between 3.5 to 4 times the wages of nonunionized workers. Extreme inequalities in earnings between sectors of the economy are influenced by the impact of trade unionism. Wage levels in manufacturing are 50 percent higher than wages in commerce because of the higher level of union representation in the former, although profit margins and the ability to pay are higher in commerce than in manufacturing.

The Jamaican labor market is extremely fragmented and can be divided into four main subsectors. First, there are the high status professional skills that are internationally marketable and earn large salaries that reflect their international demand. Second, there are the skills that are represented and protected by trade unionism. Third, there are the large body of nonunionized workers representing 57 percent of wage workers. Fourth, there are the large concentrations of labor in the petty commodity sector. Extreme inequalities in labor income are a consequence of this segmentation of the labor market in which each of these four sectors have very different bargaining power on the labor market.

Some important changes have occurred within the Jamaican labor market in the postwar period without any influences from organized labor. These include the important upward mobility by blacks into technical, managerial, and administrative jobs in the private sector in the postindependence period. Up to independence in 1962 such jobs in large private sector companies were the monopoly preserve of whites, Chinese, the light-skin-colored population, Jews, and Syrians, irrespective of formal education or training. A combination of social and political factors combined with an expansion of access to tertiary level education by middle class blacks has removed most of these racial barriers in employment. Racial biases still exist, however, in various top managerial jobs in some enterprises. Another important change has been the rapid upward mobility of women into middle and top management jobs in both the public and private sectors. In 1982, for example, women comprised 57 percent of the professional, technical, and administrative workers in the labor force.

WAGES AND PROFITS

In responding to trade union pressures for higher wages, employers have merely passed on the higher cost of labor to consumers in an economy in which most industries are protected from outside competition. It is not unusual for large corporate enterprises to return rates of profit varying between 7 and 12 percent as proportion of sales. For big enterprises turning over between $50 to 200 million in sales per annum in a small economy with less than 450,000 wage workers, that represents a large accumulation of profits. In 1983, for example, 20 of the larger private sector companies turned over $104 million in profits before taxes and $70 million in profits in 1982.[9] Leading 1983 profit earners in this group of 20 enterprises include Industrial Commercial Developments, Ltd. (ICD), controlled by the Matalon family, earning $19 million in profits; Desnoes and Geddes, controlled by the Desnoes and Geddes family interests, earning $7 million; Pan Jamaican Investment Trust, controlled by the Facey family interests, earning $6 million; Carreras Group, Ltd., with large shareholdings by the Hart family interests, earning $12 million; and the foreign-owned Goodyear tire company, Royal Bank, and Bank of Nova Scotia all earning, respectively, $9, $8.5, and $17 million in profits.

During the period of economic crisis in the 1970s the operating surplus or gross profits generated in the economy increased from a level of 50 percent of total wages earned in 1973 to 62 percent of total wages earned in 1980. The socialist policies of the Manley government clearly did not reduce the rate of profit accumulation in the economy as the rate of profit compared to wages increased over the 1972 to 1980 period of the Manley government. Paradoxically, in the period since 1980, after the proprivate sector government of Prime Minister Seaga came to power, the rate of profit accumulation compared to wages returned to the lower levels of the early 1970s, due mainly to the expansion of activity in areas such as construction, manufacturing, and tourism with large labor income content.

Table 6.3 gives the distribution of gross profits generated by the various sectors of the economy, as well as the respective shares of the total national wage bill broken down by sector. The comparison between 1976 and 1982 data reveals some of the differences in wage earnings and capital accumulation between the Manley period of government in the 1970s and the Seaga period in the 1980s.

Apart from the government, which contributes most to the national wage bill, manufacturing, construction, and commerce make the largest

Table 6.3 Wages and Profits by Sector

	Percent Share of Total Wages		Percent Share of Total Profits		Average Wage per Annum in $Jam.
	1976	1982	1976	1982	1982
Agriculture	6	5	16	13	2,400
Bauxite mining	3	4	17	8	19,600
Manufacturing	14	14	14	13	5,300
Construction	12	11	2	4	10,900
Commerce or distribution	12	12	23	37	3,700
Finance	8	6	4	6	n.a.
Real Estate	3	2	14	22	n.a.
Government	27	27	0	0	8,560

Note: n.a. = not available.
Source: National Income & Product, National Planning Agency, 1976-80.

contribution to total wages earned but real estate, commerce, bauxite, and agriculture turn over the largest volume of gross profits in the economy. The recession in the United States in the early 1980s and the consequent fall in demand for bauxite account for the sudden drop in bauxite profits between 1976 and 1982, but it is to be noted that trade union pressures increased the bauxite share of the national wage bill in spite of the drop in profitability. Only three sectors contribute as much or more to the national wage bill as they contribute to profits earned in the economy as a whole. These are finance where wages are very high, due to the concentration of nonmanual professional skills and construction where the strong trade union presence bids up the price of labor and manufacturing where there is also a strong trade union presence. Very large profits are earned in commerce, real estate, bauxite, and agriculture.

Except for the declining level of profits earned in bauxite, the major change between the Manley and Seaga years is the large increase in the share of profits accruing to real estate and commerce. In the case of commerce, this was due to the higher levels of consumer goods imports following the change of government which contrasted sharply with the shortages of imported consumer goods in the Manley period in the 1970s. Secondly, real estate values were repressed below replacement costs in the Manley years due to fear of communism and the feeling of insecurity surrounding ownership of property. After the proprivate sector Seaga government came to power, property values escalated massively by over 500 percent, generating bonanza profits for entrepreneurs involved in real estate. Indeed, in 1982 the least productive sectors, real estate and commerce, earned almost 60 percent of the gross profits in the economy, while in the Manley years the productive sectors earned a larger share of gross profits than they did in the 1980s. In other words, the return to economic buoyancy that accompanied the change of government from Manley to Seaga in 1980 produced a situation in which the least productive uses of capital generated bonanza gains in profits. Profits from buying and selling outpaced earnings from the more productive use of capital. In the short run, the merchants and the 'wheelers and dealers' in land came out ahead of producers and, to some extent, by hurting the profitability of farmers and manufacturers producing for the local market as real estate values increased production costs and imports displaced local production.

EMPLOYMENT

Perhaps the largest impact the accumulation of capital can make to labor is in the creation of employment in an economy persistently suffering from high levels of unemployment. This is certainly one area in which the Jamaican private sector has failed to be a catalyst for economic development. In the period since 1943, only the self-employed and the labor force employed by government have recorded large increases in the numbers of persons gainfully occupied. In the almost four decades between 1943 and 1982 the number of self-employed actually doubled and those employed by the state increased some 23 times the level of 1943. In the case of nongovernment-employed wage workers there has only been a small 18 percent increase in the numbers of persons employed over that 39-year period. The levels of employed and self-employed persons over the period are shown in Table 6.4

Indeed, after the steady increase in the number of nongovernment wage workers between 1943 and 1968, the levels fall quite precipitously in the 1970s. Such is the magnitude of the decline that by the end of the Manley years, in 1980, the number of persons employed in nongovernmental enterprises is actually less than it was in the year 1960, 20 years earlier. Had the nongovernment wage sector grown as fast as the self-employed there would be no significant open unemployment in the Jamaican economy, as a doubling of that sector would have easily absorbed the 292,000 unemployed that existed by October 1982.

Two major problems lie at the root of the difficulty. The first relates to the fact that in the development of the postwar private sector, there was significant displacement of small enterprises by larger enterprises in manufacturing and services especially. This meant that instead of adding to the employed labor force, there was considerable labor displacement. Artisan production in rural communities was particularly affected by the growth of a medium and large scale capitalist manufacturing sector that concentrated on the domestic market. Imports of cheap consumer goods also displaced large areas of artisan production. In effect, the growth of the capitalist sector was at the expense of the petty commodity producers. The result was that the net addition to the labor force was substantially reduced and the self-employed in the petty commodity sec-

Table 6.4 Increases in Labor Force

	Non-government Wage Workers	Self-employed	Government Workers
1943	285,000	156,000	4,500
1960	337,000	187,000	42,000
1968	407,000	228,000	57,000
1980	325,000	302,000	110,000
1982	338,000	314,000	104,000

Source: Census Reports, Department of Statistics, 1943 and 1960. Labor Force Survey, Department of Statistics, 1968-82.

tor were forced into buying and selling rather than productive labor as the main mode of survival outside of small scale farming.

In 1943 there were some 60,000 workers employed in manufacturing enterprises but only approximately 15,000 were located in factories. The remaining 45,000 were to be found in small artisan and petty commodity production. Exactly 40 years later, in 1983, the manufacturing sector had only grown to 90,000, at which stage the overwhelming majority were to be found in highly organized capitalist factories in enterprises of varying size. The artisan sector now represents less than 5 percent of the labor force in manufacturing, having been displaced by large, small, and medium scale capitalist enterprises.

Of course, the failure of the economic modernization effort to significantly increase the number of persons earning wages on a regular basis outside of government employment, means that the market for domestic production was even further constricted in a small economy, thereby further narrowing the prospects for production expansion and increased employment. The fact that the major manufacturing thrust was toward production for the domestic market rather than production for export aggravated this problem even further.

The second problem had to do with the ideological conflicts between the private sector and the Manley government in the 1970s that led to large scale closures of enterprises and flight of capital, resulting in a considerable net loss of nongovernmental wage workers as some 80,000 jobs were lost from the private sector.

In spite of the decline in real income in the 1970s due to the adverse terms of trade caused by the oil price increases, the fact is that opportunities for increasing production and earning profits in traditional export agriculture, nontraditional commercial farming for export, were never grasped by the Jamaican private sector, although many enterprises in services and the distributive trades recorded handsome margins of profit. The reasons had more to do with political fears and uncertainties and the absence of a climate of confidence between government and the private sector than with the objective economic realities of the period. As a result, opportunities for increasing private sector wage employment were never developed in spite of tax incentives offered by the Manley government.

There is, of course, another contributing factor that relates to the values and motivational drives of the Jamaican capitalist class and the structural blockages to entrepreneurial expansion within the owner-managing sector of middle class capitalists. A significant number of the rich families and the middle class owner managers are motivated mainly by the drive to earn enough to sustain a comfortable life-style and the acquisition of luxury goods which are the new status symbols in the society. Such expectations for high income are easily satisfied without pushing the entrepreneurs toward expansion, growth, diversification, and an urge to grasp new investment opportunities. Instead it directs some entrepreneurial efforts more toward 'get rich quick' areas of activity such as marijuana production and trade and real estate than towards manufacturing production.

The impulse to expand, diverisfy, and to build large corporate family empires is limited to a few rich families and their aggressive expansionist orientation to capitalism is resented by the complacent majority for whom consumption rather than a mastery of production is the central goal of capital accumulation. The minority within the owner managers who have genuine capitalist impulses for expansion and diversification have real difficulties getting access to long-term financing as the big capitalists tend to monopolize what long-term money is available and there are no adequate channels for raising venture capital on a scale that could fuel significant upward mobility by the more aggressive smaller capitalists into the grouping of bigger capitalists. Unfortunately so much of the real entrepreneurial dynamism in the economy is to be found among this minority of enterprising and aggressive small owner managers who cannot mobilize the financial resources to expand.

The issue is well reflected in the shoe manufacturing industry where illegal imports have wiped out many large enterprises and reduced local employment. In contrast to the general negative trend in this industry one small manufacturer, Sammy's Shoes, has been able to increase its market share and to expand output competing effectively with shoe imports while larger manufacturers were going out of business or reducing output in response to declining sales.

The dynamic small enterprise run by a father and son team has not, however, been able to secure any financing for expanding its productive capacity in spite of its healthy cash flow position. Although the enterprise has a capability to move into footwear exports, and to diversify its range of production for the domestic market, the banks have been unwilling to lend the company funds to acquire new and more modern machinery and equipment. This experience is fairly typical of problems facing small dynamic capitalist enterprises without the social contact of the big bourgeoisie. In contrast, a major bank which refused to lend money to Sammy's Shoes advanced a large unsecured $2 million loan to two members of the rich capitalist families over this same period to enable them to buy and sell a hotel for no other purpose but the realization of capital gains.

CLASS POWER

Notwithstanding all of these motivational and structural problems, Table 6.4 makes it clear that between 1960 and 1968, the period during which the proprivate sector JLP was in power (1962-72), the rate of growth of the private sector employed labor force was increasing at a rate matching that of the increase in the number of self-employed. Both subsectors grew by 21 percent over that period. Had that momentum continued in the 1970s along with the massive increase in public sector employment, the high open unemployment level in the economy would have been substantially reduced. If the private sector wage-earning group had continued expanding as fast as the self-employed between 1968 and 1982, some 220,000 additional jobs would have been created to reduce the level of the 292,000 unemployed. The policy, and ideological conflicts between Manley's PNP government and the private sector in the 1970s cost the country a considerable loss of employment generation from private sector jobs and the economy still has yet to return to the 1968 level of private sector employment.

Both labor and capital have developed in the postwar period as centers of private power of unequal magnitude. They operate as constraints on the expanding power base of the technocrats, bureaucrats, and professional politicians who have been installed in the reformed state administration as the managers of public power. Labor has developed into a relatively autonomous interest group still maintaining ties with the political parties but operating from a tradition of business unionism which de-emphasizes party politics and renders the trade union leaders accountable to the militant wage workers in both public and private sectors. Union militancy results in a heavy economic loss in terms of income, production, and wasted man hours but in the face of the depoliticization of the union movement, trade union activism and dissent provides a channel by which workers' alienation is articulated in frequent, localized apolitical strike action that might otherwise have fed into national antisystemic political protest action. The fragmentation of the union movement, while obviously a source of internal organizational weakness, restricts the political capability of labor to challenge the political directorate in the way that the labor movement spearheaded the political protests against the aristocratic colonial state in 1938.

Capitalist and owner interests are significantly more powerful than labor in the Jamaican democratic system. Both private centers of power are subject to the control and regulation of big government controlled by the technocrats and the professional politicians, who should really be seen as a new administrative class thrown up by the political changes in the postwar era. Moreso than labor, however, the owners of capital have effective means of disrupting national policy and the administrative class who control public power invariably have to seek ways and means of winning their cooperation as failure to do so runs the risk of inducing economic destabilization by capital flight as occurred in the Manley years in the 1970s.

Both labor and capital play a key role in setting limits to how far the administrative class who control big government can go in developing policies and political programs that undermine or threaten private interests in the economy without being balanced by compensatory gains or benefits. By limiting the growth of autonomy in the policy-making power domain of the public sector technocrats and politicians, these important centers of private power preserve some measure of public accountability to private interests, which is central to the achievement of the goals of democracy which seek to expand the powers of the state in ways that enhance its policy capability to benefit private interests, be they labor interests or capitalist interests.

In the power conflicts between labor and capital, capital has had to concede some of the absolute power it enjoyed under the aristocratic colonial state to labor's growing power and influence at the workplace due to the effect of the strong labor movement that developed in the postwar years. Labor's power, however, is limited to a restricted agenda of workplace areas of decision making. By having become almost completely encapsulated into collective bargaining, the labor movement has failed to develop its potential as a powerful policy lobby on national issues.

The relative power of labor and capital in Jamaican democracy has the effect, nevertheless, of setting important constraints on the power of the new class of public sector managers who have inherited a legacy of big government that sets the parameters within which labor and capital function in the economy. The articulation of power in the political system takes place mainly through tri-partite power relations between the private sector, labor, and the dominant public sector managers who have overall responsibility for leadership and management of the economy.

NOTES

1. For an insightful treatment of the early labor movement in postwar Jamaica, see George Eaton, *Alexander Bustamante and Modern Jamaica*, Kingston, Jamaica: Kingston Publishers, 1975.

2. See R.B. Davison, *Industrial Relations in Jamaica*, Kingston, Jamaica: Industrial Relations Research Association, 1973.

3. Data on workers' perceptions of trade unions are extensively discussed in Carl Stone, *Class Race and Political Behaviour in Urban Jamaica*, Kingston, Jamaica: Institute of Social and Economic Research, 1973.

4. See R.B. Davison, op. cit.

5. This research by the author is still in progress and is expected to develop as part of a detailed study of labor in Jamaica.

6. See *Report on Worker Participation*, February 1976, submitted to the Jamaican government. The author was vice-chairman of the committee which prepared this report.

7. This argument is frequently aired by the Marxist-Leninist spokesmen for the local Communist party, the WPJ.

8. In one recent case an experienced labor leader was hospitalized after a severe beating by construction workers at the cement company.

9. There are no hard data on wildcat strikes but it is estimated by Ministry of Labor officials that some 85 percent of strikes in Jamaica are wildcat strikes called by workers rather than by the trade unions. This is especially so with strikes involving the bigger unions.

7

PUBLIC OPINION AND POLITICAL AWARENESS

NATIONAL PUBLIC OPINION

An important aspect of the growth of a democracy involves the formation of an active body of national opinion among its citizenry that monitors and evaluates national political issues, public policies, and political events, both domestic and international. A number of obstacles arise in the growth of an active body of national public opinion in developing countries where parliamentary democracy has been established.

First of all, limited access to the mass media often restricts exposure to national news and coverage of events, policy issues, and public statements in the mass media. The growth of the mass media[1] is therefore a key factor facilitating the development of national public opinion. In its absence, political opinions tend to be uninformed by national events and issues and to focus instead on local community issues and personalities.

As the mass public becomes more and more aware of national political issues, political parties will respond by increasing the emphasis they place on issue debates in political campaigns, as opposed to emphases on personalities. Second, as the mass public's grasp of issues develops over time and as the media increase their focus on political coverage of policy issues in response to maturing national public opinion, issues that are salient to voters will increasingly have impact on voting patterns, in contrast to voting on the basis of party loyalties and personality appeals.

The insertion of ideological debates into the agenda of issues discussed by the political parties in a democracy has the added effect of intensifying the appeal of issues to that minority of voters[2] who become attracted to these contending party ideological doctrines. Political ideologies tend to arouse strong emotional reactions in political environments in which they are developed to speak to class, racial, or other areas of social conflict. The development of active minorities of ideologues supporting competing parties in a democracy both intensifies issue debates and enlarges the network of disseminators of political ideas.

Other obstacles toward the development of an active national public opinion in developing countries include low levels of functional literacy, isolated rural communities disconnected from each other by backward systems of transportation, and the dominance of local community identities over national identity.

In the period between the development of universal adult suffrage and political parties with mass appeal in the early 1940s and the postindependence era some important social, demographic, and political changes have facilitated the development of national public opinion in Jamaica. Not surprisingly, as national political awareness has grown, actual levels of political participation through voting have considerably increased.

In the 20-year period between between 1950 and 1970 Jamaica's urban population grew from 23 percent of the population to 36 percent. The proportion of Jamaican citizens living in areas with at least 100,000 dwellers increased from 19 percent in 1950 to 28 percent in 1970. By 1980 the interconnected growth of urban Kingston, St. Andrew, and the urban St. Catherine created a large metropolitan residential, commercial, and industrial area[3] that by 1980 included some 40 percent of the population. Another 40 percent is to be found in main road areas close to main highways and rural towns and townships. By 1980, only about 20 percent of the population lived in isolated rural communities, compared to approximately 65 perent in the 1940s. Rapid and extensive urban growth trends have facilitated the development of an active national public opinion.

Expansion in access to the electronics media has been equally impressive. In 1953 there were 27 radio receivers for every 1000 Jamaican people. By 1959 this number increased to 89 per 1000 persons. The number of radio receivers per 1000 persons climbed further to 326 by 1980. In terms of actual numbers of radio receivers, this involved an increase from 40,000 in 1953, to 150,000 in 1959 and 718,000 in 1980. By the 1970s, approximately 75 percent of the population had access to radio.

Access to television has grown rapidly in the 1970s to a level of 120,000 TV sets or 57 per 1000 persons by 1977. More recent estimates[4] suggest that some 33 percent of the Jamaican people have access to television. A major constraint in the further growth of access to television is limited access to electricity[5] in many rural areas.

Newspaper circulation doubled between the 1940s and the mid-1960s when the leading daily newspaper, the *Daily Gleaner*, had achieved a weekday circulation of 66,000, and 80,000 on weekends. Sixty-four percent of this newspaper circulation was in urban Kingston, St. Andrew, and St. Catherine. An evening tabloid[6] published by the same company had also achieved an impressive 65,000 weekday circulation.

The weekday circulation of the *Daily Gleaner* fell to 50,000 between the 1960s and the 1970s due to middle class migration and the combination of declining real incomes and escalating inflationary trends. By the early 1970s, however, survey estimates[7] indicate that at least 30 percent of the population had access to newspapers as there was extensive sharing of newspaper reading.

This expansion of access to the mass media was complemented by rapid growth of rural and urban transportation facilities. It developed around minibus services that enabled citizens to be extremely mobile and to travel frequently between areas of the country. The private motor cars increased in number from 8000 in 1938 to 100,000 by 1978, after more than doubling in the 14 years between 1964 and 1978 when the number increased from 46,000. Access to telephones increased from 16,000 in 1952 to 118,000 in 1977, also complementing the growth of mass media access and transportation facilities. The extensive growth of quick minibus travel in the areas outside of the capital city, Kingston, was especially important in eliminating the relative isolation of many rural areas.

The effects of these social infrastructural and demographic factors combined with increasing politicization of the electorate produced a significant increase in levels of voting as a percentage of the population of voting age. Between 1944 and 1962 voter turnout,[8] as a percentage of the voting age population, increased as shown in the acompanying table.

Voter Turnout as Percentage of Voting Age Population

Parliamentary Elections	Voter Turnout as Percent of Persons of Voting Age
1944	50
1949	60
1955	61
1959	62
1962	72
1967	56
1972	57
1976	72
1980	80

After a steady increase between 1944 and 1962, voter turnout fell in 1967 and 1972 because of the complicated registration system introduced to guard against fraudulent voting in a minority of urban constituencies. The abandonment of this system led to 72 percent turnout in 1976 and this increased to a very high 80 percent for the 1980 election. Paralleling the growth of media access, urbanization, and transportation facilities was a very significant growth of voter turnout from 50 percent in the early 1940s to 80 percent by 1980.

THE POLLS

The very intensive debate of both policy and ideological issues between the PNP and the JLP in the 1970s aided this process of sharpening national public opinion. This was facilitated further by the increased political content of all media organs during the period and the development of frequent quarterly public opinion polls conducted by the author for the leading newspaper the *Daily Gleaner*. These polls[9] provided feedback on public reactions to these ideological and issue debates and served to further stimulate public interest in opinion trends.

The subject matter of these polls conducted between 1976 and 1984 was distributed as follows:

Opinion Polls of the Jamaican People

Themes in Polls	Percent Share of Questions
foreign affairs	2
political leaders	5
political parties	18
policy and economic and social issues	60
citizens' mood and outlook	15

Reflecting the increasing centrality of issue debates in the country's party system as national public opinion matured in the 1970s, the polls conducted by the author concentrated heavily on measuring public opinion on issues debated in the media and by the major political parties and their spokesmen.

These polls were conducted on the basis of national samples of the Jamaican electorate varying in size mainly between 800 and 1200 voters. The sampling methodology involved the following basic steps.

1. The island's electorate is divided into approximately 1000 contiguous groupings of polling divisions with the polling divisions in each group showing a similar pattern of past voting tendencies.

2. A sample usually ranging from 40 to 90 such groupings of polling division is chosen as the basis for the voter interviews. The number of areas chosen varies according to the sample size desired. Experience establishes that a minimum of 30 such areas

widely spread geographically is necessary for accurate opinion polling. Most samples are based on 50 such areas.

3. Systematic methods of area sample selection are used to fill the quota of areas needed for the sample. Equal numbers of areas are allocated to each parish and the selection process is repeated until a sample of areas emerges that matches very closely the overall national vote in the last election.

4. The number of *voters* to be interviewed is allocated by parish according to the proportions the respective parishes represent in the national electorate.

5. An exception is made of the Metropolitan Area of Kingston in that the number of *areas* allocated is four times as many as the number of areas allocated equally to the other parishes to give more geographic representation of this more socially diverse area.

6. Interviewers are assigned to each area with overall quotas and quota controls to ensure adequate age and sex representation by area.

7. In each survey the questionnaire includes a question enquiring as to how respondents voted in the previous election. This recall vote is compared with the actual party vote in the areas to ascertain the level and direction of field errors and biases in the sample.

8. A minimum of three or four questions are used to ascertain party leanings so as to ensure validity checks on the reported responses.

All political surveys carried out by the author tend to undercount mass support for whichever party is in opposition. The size of those estimated errors can be determined by corrrecting the actual poll result with the estimated bias calculated by applying the test outlined in 7, above.

The method I developed for estimating total error was to compare the actual vote in the sample areas as a whole with how the sample of citizens said they voted in the parliamentary elections that preceded the poll. This differential allows us to compare a population statistic with a sample estimate of its dimensions. The deviation of the sample estimate from the population statistic tells us how big the total error factor is (both sampling and field errors) as the crude technique does not permit us to distinguish between the two types of error.

The method of estimating error makes two vital assumptions. First, that our respondents have truthfully recalled their past voting preference and that the electoral data on voting patterns are reliable and accurate. Areas where voting statistics are dubious due to bogus voting and fraudulent registration are therefore excluded from our area samples.

Fortunately the problem is limited to a small number of urban ghetto constituencies and accurate national samples can be drawn without including those areas. Beyond this, the error estimation method allows us the facility to exercise quality control over the field work by comparing accuracy on an area basis and by alerting us to inaccurate field work by specific interviewers or in specific areas. All of this contributes to the reduction of errors in forecasting. After each poll the error estimation allows us to calculate the size of the error factor and which party it is biased against.

With the use of this method one is able to achieve accuracy levels in election forecasting (under adverse political and field conditions) that match those of the most precise random sampling methods. In 1976 parliamentary elections our last poll corrected for a 5 percent undercounting of JLP strength to accurately predict the 57 percent PNP popular vote majority. In the three elections in which these polls were used to make predictions (1976 and 1980 parliamentary and 1981 local government) the poll forecasts corrected for this error factor produced the following levels of accuracy:

Percent difference between corrected poll forecast and actual vote

1976 parliamentary election	0
1980 parliamentary election	2
1981 local government	2
mean error	1.3

PROFILE OF CHANGES

Political development in a democracy involves more than the growth and evolution of institutions and the changes in power relationships that make the state more responsive to the needs and interests of the majority. It concerns also the formation of a body of national public opinion with enough information to make an assessment of leaders, policies, and political choices and sufficient interest in public affairs to provide a participatory and attentive audience to the main actors in the political system who manage power and compete for the opportunity to do so.

The development of national public opinion[10] has been one of the important features of the transition to democracy in Jamaica in the postwar period. It has involved some far-reaching changes in the formation and content of political opinions in the country. These changes relate to the balance of impact between national and local political issues, the salience of policy issues in political opinion formation, the increasing importance of nonpartisan opinion in election outcomes, increased levels of information and comprehension among voters, the greater salience and impact of ideological issues in political campaigns and political dis-

cussions, and a larger role for the mass media in influencing the agenda
of political debate and the information levels on politics and public affairs in the political community. Many of these changes have been influenced by the social and demographic changes that have altered the
profile of the political community. These changes in political opinion formation and the underlying social and demographic influences have had
significant effects on the pattern of voting and in the way voters perceive
political leaders, their parties, and the issues and ideological positions
they stand for. In essence, some important qualitative changes have
taken place in the Jamaican political community, especially in the postindependence period in which a maturing of the Jamaican electorate has
taken place. A large body of national survey data derived from 25 newspaper political polls and 15 other political surveys both carried out by the
author between 1971 and 1984 will be used as the source from which to
analyze some aspects of these important changes in political awareness
and public opinion trends.

In the earlier elections held under universal adult suffrage in 1944,
1949, and 1955, PNP and JLP dominance was challenged by a large number of independent candidates whose vote support was based entirely
on their personal standing within the local communities they sought to
represent. In the first such election in 1944, independent candidates and
minor political parties based on highly localized support received 35 percent of the votes and won five of the 32 parliamentary seats. In 1949 the
independents won two seats and 14 percent of the vote. In the 1955 elections, their vote share declined to 11 percent and they won no seats. In
the subsequent seven parliamentary elections (1959, 1962, 1967, 1972,
1976, 1980, and 1983) independents and localized minor parties gained
less than 1 percent of the vote and failed to win any parliamentary seats
as the two major parties succeeded in establishment of two-party dominance of the electorate.

In that earlier electoral period (between 1944 and 1955) political issues were very localized and the appeal of local candidates was as important as the standing of the national parties in influencing the mainly
rural electorate. The newspaper that had a largely middle class audience
was the main mass media organ for most of that period and the majority
of the predominantly rural political community were either uninformed
or grossly underinformed about national level events, developments, and
issues. Indeed, the open air mass meeting conducted by political parties
was the principal medium through which political information and political issues were brought to the attention of the rural communities. In
that climate local loyalties between political notables and followers, can-
didate popularity and local events and issues weighed heavily as factors
influencing voting behavior.

Even within the national parties (the PNP and the JLP) support for
those parties was heavily influenced by the personal standing of the com-

munity notables selected to represent them in parliamentary elections. Party leaders at the national level had considerable impact on local level voting behavior through the image they projected at mass meetings but many voters saw the vote as more a choice between local candidates than a choice between competing national parties. In some of the more remote rural areas the urban-based national party leaders were seen as outsiders whose credibility depended on the standing of the local political notable who represented their party.

Political campaigns in that period concentrated on personalities rather than on policy issues. Much of the political rhetoric was designed to project political opponents as dishonest, degenerate, and untrustworthy persons. The degree of personal character assassinations and personal abuse was considerable. Beyond that, the content of campaign speeches gave equal weight to local developments regarding national issues, focusing here on what benefits political parties are either failing or succeeding in delivering to voters in the local communities. To the extent that campaign rhetoric moved away from personality issues it tended to deal mainly with such 'benefit' issues as roads, water supplies, schools, health centers, community centers, relief for the poor, jobs on government projects, tickets for contract farm labor in the United States, and the provision of electricity and government housing. Candidates and parties did their best to convince voters of their superior capability to deliver these benefits to the voting communities.

To a significant degree, national political opinion did not exist in that earlier period except among the middle class and the privileged who were concerned about national issues and among sections of the working class in the capital city of Kingston where the business and administrative centers were located and an awareness of national issues was formed through intensive face-to-face political and public affairs discussions conducted in public parks, in rum shops, on street corners, and in tenement yards. This was aided by the intensive efforts at working-class politicization carrried out by the major parties in the country's capital city. It was also assisted by the impact of political trade unionism that sharpened working class political awareness in Kingston where much of the early expansion of trade union activities concentrated in the 1940s and early 1950s.

The creation of national public opinion was important in ensuring that voters took an interest in and made judgments about the management of the enormous buildup of power that was taking place in the public sector under the expanding governmental administration. As the political directorate came into a greater degree of control over the levers of domestic policy making, power, policy making, and the control over national financial and other resources became more and more centralized. For public opinion to begin to play an informed and important role in national politics, political issues and political awareness had to develop a more national focus. Citizens had to be better informed about national events. Policy issues had to become part of the diet of national public opinion and channels of communication had to develop at the national level to facilitate dialogue on issues and information flows between members of the mass public and between voters and national policy and political leaders as well as opinion leaders. As the reformed democratic state took shape, the public sector assumed a larger role in the management of economic and social affairs affecting all citizens. If the responsibilities of democratic citizenship and the right to vote for and select political representatives and leaders were to be properly exercised, a body of national opinion with some grasp, awareness, or understanding of these national policy matters had to develop.

The political parties became more national issue-oriented between the 1950s and independence in 1962 as their leaders took over responsibility for making public policy over an increasingly wider domain of policy areas. The heavy emphasis on economic policy that dominated policy formulation in the public sector in the 1960s and later decades meant that the rhetoric of the political parties increasingly shifted from localism to national policy issues in their political campaigning and political communication between the 1950s and the 1960s. As the two major parties monopolized national resources that were available to provide local level political benefits, the status and standing of political independents were completely eroded by independence. The local PNP and JLP party machine became less a domain of power controlled by a local political notable and more a branch plant of the national party in which the local political notables were as dependent on support from the political center for political survival as on support from the local community. Indeed, as resource control became more centralized by independence, the capacity to deliver local community benefits became tied to one's ability to pull the political strings at the center. This meant that local level political support that became absorbed into 'benefit politics' was now determined by how resources were managed, controlled, and allocated from the growing center of political power in the capital city. The centralization of the major political parties played a most important role in developing an awareness of national policy and political issues and in dismantling the tradition of localism that was so strong in the 1940s and the 1950s. As the major channels of political communication and information with access to some 50 percent of the electorate who represented party loyal voters, the two major political parties played a major part in shifting political awareness and political issues away from a localized focus to a more national focus between the 1950s and the mid-1960s.

The process was taken one step further, with the intense ideological debates and challenge and counter-challenge between PNP pro-socialist, pro-Third World, and radical-left party positions and policies in the 1970s and the equally intense and militant pro-Western, proprivate sector, and reformist-centrist positions of the JLP. This quite un-precedented and yet unfinished national policy and ideological debate in the 1970s was significant in three senses. First, it sought to bring the voters and citizens directly into taking positions on these sharply pola-rized ideological issues. Second, it tried to link abstract ideological de-bates to concrete issues of public policy and 'benefit politics' posing ei-ther ideological alternative as offering more benefits to the majority classes. Third, it politicized virtually every aspect of national life during this period, which forced most citizens to react to the political choices posed and to try to make some assessment of what these ideological po-sitions meant and how they translated into concrete economic and so-cial policies affecting citizens' lives. Fourth, in the effort to disseminate their respective ideologies, the parties intensely politicized their hard core followings into a sharper awareness of policy issues.

THE OPINION SUBSECTORS

Political surveys carried out by the author over the periods leading up to the 1972, 1976, and 1980 elections give a clear indication of the na-ture of the national body of public opinion that developed in Jamaica in the later postwar years. The mass public is divided into two distinct sub-groupings that share a common agenda of mainly social and economic policy issues dominating their attention. These top agenda issues relate to employment, the cost of living, the allocation of social benefits to the poorer classes, the flow of scarce benefits to hard core political supporters of the parties, and an assessment of whether life is generally getting eas-ier or more difficult for the average citizen. A secondary set of less cen-tral agenda issues relates to leadership personality and qualities, corrup-tion or mismanagement in public affairs, foreign policy, political violence, control and manipulation of the police, the style and manner in which power is being exercised by the governing party's leaders, and specific public policies that become the subject of controversy.

The first subsector of national public opinion consists of hard core activists and loyal voters supporting the two major political parties. Their opinions on national policy and political issues are determined by party loyalty to a degree that is incredible. This approximately 60 percent of the electorate look to party leaders and especially the parties' top leaders as reference point for their views on national issues. The strength of this party influence on this subsector of national public opinion can be illus-trated in a number of different political surveys.

The landing of troops by the United States, Jamaica, and certain East-ern Caribbean countries in Grenada became a very controversial issue in the late months of 1983. The PNP and its leader Michael Manley criti-cized the effort as an invasion of sovereign territory that amounted to a dangerous precedent encouraging imperialistic adventurism. The JLP government led by Prime Minister Seaga was in the vanguard of the Caribbean interests that organized the joint U.S.–Caribbean involvement in the effort, justifying it as a necessary step to containing subversive Cuban-linked Communist forces that threatened democracy and political freedoms in the Caribbean. A poll carried out by the author in December 1983 found that 86 percent of the JLP's supporters advocated the invasion and only 8 percent were against the landing of foreign troops in that country to remove the military regime which had assumed power after the assassination of Prime Minister Maurice Bishop. Among loyal PNP supporters, 60 percent were opposed to the invasion while 30 percent favored it out of hostility to the military regime which they held accountable for Bishop's death.

A major controversy developed in 1984 over the plan by the JLP government to introduce casino gambling. Both the PNP and the Jamaica Council of Chuches took the government to task on the issue. The JLP justified its proposed action in terms of likely economic gains while the church leaders and the PNP opposed casinos on moral grounds. A survey carried out by the author in May 1984 established that 81 percent of the JLP supporters favored the proposal to introduce casinos while 13 percent were opposed. Among PNP supporters 66 percent were against the introduction of casinos following the party's position, while 31 percent were for it on the grounds that the economic benefits justified it.

After the JLP government came to power in October 1980 diplomatic relations with Cuba were severed as part of the effort to remove Communist influences from Jamaica and as an expression of an assault on Caribbean Communists. The PNP, which had friendly relations with Cuba in the 1970s, insisted in certain public statements that when it was returned to power it would restore these Cuban-Jamaican diplomatic ties and resume friendly relations with Cuba. Ninety-four percent of the JLP's supporters expressed opposition to the PNP's stated intentions about restoring relations with Cuba and only 2 percent were in favor. Sixty-three percent of the PNP's supporters gave support to the party's stand on the issue, while 31 percent were opposed.

In the later months of 1983 the JLP government announced certain economic measures that the prime minister, Mr. Seaga, insisted would help to improve the chances of economic recovery. Eighty-four percent of the PNP's supporters took the view that these measures would not help the country while 11 percent expressed the opinion that they might help in some areas of the economy. Among JLP supporters 68 percent agreed that the measures would help and 22 percent were not convinced that the effects would in any way improve the economy.

The JLP party leader Prime Minister Seaga called a snap election for December 15, 1983 which the PNP leader refused to contest on the grounds that his party did not have a fair chance given the very short notice and on the basis of an objection to the decision to contest the election on the old voters' list although a new list was in the course of being prepared. The PNP leader called for fresh elections after the JLP was re-elected unopposed by the PNP in all 60 constituencies. Ninety-five percent of the PNP's supporters agreed with party leader Manley that new elections should be called once the new voters list was ready. No PNP supporters disagreed with Mr. Manley's views. Among the JLP supporters 71 percent disagreed with Mr. Manley while 25 percent supported Manley's opinion that new elections should be called. In the case of the decision to call the election on the old voters list, 99 percent of the JLP's supporters were in favor of Mr. Seaga's decision while 96 percent of the PNP's supporters opposed Mr. Seaga's actions. On the related issue of the election boycott by the PNP leaders, 98 percent of the JLP's supporters disagreed with the PNP's action while 74 percent of the PNP's supporters agreed with the boycott.

On the issue of Cuban implication or involvement in the assassination of Grenada's Prime Minister Maurice Bishop, 62 percent of the JLP's supporters agreed with the view that the Cubans were involved and 20 percent disagreed. Among PNP supporters, only 27 percent thought that the Cubans were implicated and 41 percent felt that they were not involved.

The author's July 1983 political opinion poll found that 94 percent of JLP supporters thought that Jamaica was benefiting from U.S. economic aid while a majority of 53 percent of the PNP's supporters disagreed with that view. Of the PNP supporters 44 percent agreed with the JLP view. In this as in many other opinion profiles on issues, where the nonpartisan or independent citizens show a strong majority tendency in any opinion direction, the party disagreeing with that view usually throws up between a 30 to 40 percent minority disagreeing with the majority party view. This was the case with the troop invasion of Grenada, the calling of new elections after the one-party election of December 1983, and the PNP position on restoring ties with Cuba. In each case the party view disagreeing with a strong majority position among the independent nonpartisan voters shows only small majorities disagreeing with that view and substantial minorities agreeing with positions opposed to the party. The reason, of course, is that the independents echo the opinion consensus unbiased by party loyalties and this nonpartisan consensus has a strong pull effect in influencing some partisans into deviating from their party position.

The author's November 1981 political survey found that 91 percent of the JLP's supporters agreed with the JLP government's policy of divesting government-owned enterprises while a 54 percent majority of the PNP's supporters disagreed. Independent voters (61 percent) strongly supported the JLP position and consequently 41 percent of the PNP's supporters also backed the JLP's policy position on divestment.

Worker-managed cooperatives set up by the Manley government in the 1970s in the three largest sugar estates in the country were closed down by the Seaga government in 1981 on the grounds that they were unproductive and inefficient. Sixty-six percent of the JLP's supporters agreed with the co-op closure while 22 percent disagreed. Seventy-nine percent of the PNP's supporters were opposed to the closure, while 15 percent supported it.

When the Cuban ambassador was expelled from Jamaica in 1981, the author's December 1981 political poll found that the decision was endorsed by 79 percent of the JLP's supporters and only 8 percent of the PNP's supporters. Thirteen percent of the JLP's supporters were against the expulsion while 91 percent of the PNP followers were opposed to the JLP government's action.

These many illustrations serve to emphasize the point that most issues that become position issues where the parties either take opposite sides or are perceived as having taken opposite sides will produce an opinion profile in which JLP supporters and PNP supporters disagree very sharply. This tendency towards party polarization on position issues gives the party leaders enormous influence over the captive party loyal segment of national public opinion in that party loyalty rather than personal opinions will determine where they stand on those issues. More importantly, this tendency for a large section of national public opinion to see controversial position issues in partisan terms means that it is difficult to generate public opinion debates and dialogue without the exchanges being rapidly converted into polarized JLP and PNP disagreements. The generation, therefore, of genuine national consensus on any sensitive position issue with partisan implications is rendered quite impossible because of this strong tendency for partisan feelings and emotions to cloud issues and determine where individuals stand. Public opinion exchanges on such sensitive controversial issues, therefore, get narrowed, simplified, distorted, and confused by party polarization. The major political parties contributed greatly to the creation of national public opinion but in so doing they have colonized a large section of it as a captive receptacle that merely echoes the party line on controversial political and policy issues.

FLOATING VOTERS

The independent or nonpartisan other segment of national public opinion differs from the partisan segments in several areas. They appear to be less informed than the partisan voters because they tend to show high "no opinion" categories in political surveys. When, however, we break down the category into its two groupings of swing voters who vote in elections while having no sense of party loyalties and the chronic political apathetics who refuse to vote, we find that the floating voters are less interested in politics than the partisan but are equally well informed about national events. The independent swing voters, however, are less inclined to take positions on national political issues and reflect a wide range of relatively heterogeneous political and ideological positions in contrast to the partisan groupings. They are less trusting of leaders and party politicians, and are more difficult to reach through the channels of political communication as they are less attentive in assimilating or listening to political messages through the mass media and rarely attend political mass meetings or engage in political discussions. Most importantly, their interest in politics is seasonal. It gathers strength in the intensive campaign periods leading up to elections when they will come out in favor of the more popular of the two parties. Once the party is elected, they shortly shift into neutrality and low levels of political interest, emerging from that only when the political environment warms up again with intensive party campaigning.

Surveys done in the political 'dead season' between the periods of active campaigning tend to give the mistaken impression that these voters have abandoned the two major parties. But once the campaigning intensifies, they tend to come out in favor of the more popular party faithfully reflecting the mood of the country.

Figure 7.1 illustrates the fluctuating level of political interest among the floating voters. Between 1976, when the floating voters came out in support of the PNP, and 1978, political disinterest increased the level of persons not supporting either party from 15 to 38 percent. Between 1978 and 1980, when the new campaign periods intensified, the level dropped again to 13 percent, as the floating voters shifted massively to the JLP to give that party a huge popular vote majority. Within one year of the JLP coming to power the levels rose again to 30 percent before declining once again to a 20 percent level approaching the 1983 uncontested election. Thereafter, the level of persons not supporting the JLP or the PNP increased almost predictably to 35 percent as the political temperatures cooled.

The floating voter is made up of a disproportionately large percentage of urban dwellers and younger voters. Forty percent are betweeen 18 and 25 years and 64 percent are below 30. The proportion of floating voters increases at each level of the urban rural continuum as shown in Table 7.1. The urban environment fosters less party loyalty and commitment and greater cynicism toward party politics as the urban citizens get a closer view of the enormous gap between the promises of the politicians and what they deliver and urban interests are much more dependent on party handouts and benefit politics than citizens in rural areas.

Between the earlier postindependence elections and 1980 the size of popular vote swings within the electorate as a whole has doubled from 6–7 percent to 15 percent. Indications from polls done in the 1980s sug-

Figure 7.1 End of Year Profiles of Party Support (1976–84)

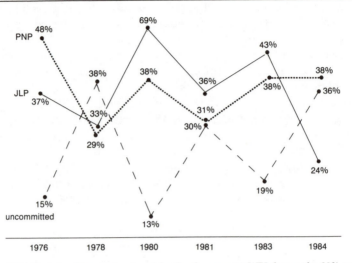

Note: In 1984 there is a 2 percent support for the Communist WPJ, hence the 98% total.
Source: From author's public opinion polls.

gest that in elections in which there is a change of government, the magnitude of popular vote swing is likely to approach a 20 percent level. Although we have no sample survey data on voters from earlier elections prior to 1972, the trend between 1972 and 1984 is one in which the percentage of floating voters clearly doubled. This sharp increase in the proportion of floating voters in the electorate compensates for the rigid party polarization characterizing the majority of the voters. These floating voters determine election outcomes by the proponderance with which they support either of the two major parties. As a result of their shifting between JLP, PNP, and uncommitted positions according to cycles of change in the two-party vote pattern, support of the two major parties usually fluctuates between 60 to 65 percent of the electorate in politically quiescent periods and increases to 80 to 85 percent levels in the heat of party campaigns. As a result, in the 1970s and 1980s the author's national survey data show PNP support shifting within a range of 28 to 47 percent and JLP support shifting within the bounds of a wider 24-to-50 percent range. These lower limits (24% for the JLP and 28% for

Table 7.1 Distribution of Floating Voters, 1984 by Percent

Deep rural areas	11
Main road areas	18
Towns	24
Urban metropolitan capital	33

Source: Author's public opinion polls.

the PNP) represent the bottom line hard core fanatically zealous support below which party strength is not likely to fall. The other half of the electorate, which includes weak party supporters and floating voters, keep the two-party system competitive by providing rapidly changing balances of support reflecting the political mood of the country.

The floating voters are mainly influenced by the top agenda issues of employment, the cost of living, the allocation of social benefits to the poor and whether life seems to be getting harder or easier for the majority. The author's earlier research[11] on voting trends, therefore, was able to establish empirical evidence correlating the level of interparty swings or fluctuations in floating voter party preference and misery index indicators such as unemployment, cost of living statistics, and changes in consumption levels. In contrast, the 1970s political survey data show that the more partisan segments of national public opinion are more influenced by the less central issues such as ideology, leadership, personality qualities and political style, mismanagement and specific policies in the foreign policy and domestic economic policy areas, all of which have high salience due to their considerable interest in politics and public affairs. These issues are deemed as less central since their impact is secondary to that of the top agenda items in shaping voting changes. These secondary issues affect how much a party is able to enthuse its hard core supporters making up 50 percent of the electorate to come out to vote. The floating voters, on the other hand, switch from party to party depending on the impact of these top agenda issues. The weak party supporters who usually bring the hard core 52 percent of the voters up to the normal 60-to-65 percent level of "dead season" support for the parties are, like the hard core voters, less likely to switch parties but will withdraw from voting if they get turned off from the party they normally support. Here the secondary or less central agenda issues, that deal more with politics than with the economic effects of policies and politics, play a key role in influencing the vote.

The issue orientation of the nonpartisan segment of national public opinion centers on a cluster of interrelated economic issues that can be seen as amounting to a dominant single issue, namely, policy results. The issue orientation of the partisan segment of national public opinion is focused on ideology, politics, and policy alternatives due to the degree to which their political awareness and impulses faithfully mirror the political cues coming from the national party leaders. Effective political communication by party leaders demands that they address both of these different political audiences to maintain maximum political support.

The increasing level of nonpartisan voters who shift support between the main parties in between "dead season" intervals of low key noncommitment comes from two sources. The lowering of the voting age in the early 1970s from 21 to 18 brought into the electorate large numbers of young voters making up about 20 to 25 percent of the electorate. These voters are at a stage in their political socialization when they have not yet developed a strong or stable commitment to any political party. Table 7.2 shows the level of uncommitted voters found in the author's December 1981 political survey broken down by age categories. It will be noted that the level of uncommitted floating voters increases significantly as one moves from older to younger age cohorts. Indeed, only 50 percent of the 17 and under teenagers approach the voting age with a clear commitment to any party. Assuming that these differences reflect life cycle rather than generational factors, it would seem to be the case that as the voter gets older the parties do quite an effective job of capturing their loyalties due to the intensity of the partisan political environment.

Beyond the impact of the youth vote in increasing the numbers of uncommitted voters since the 1970s, a significant number of weaker party loyal voters have joined the ranks of the floating voters. They tend never to return to the ranks of the party faithful once they break and join the independents.

THE MASS MEDIA IMPACT

The development of a body of national public opinion was considerably assisted by the growth and audience reach of the electronics media, in the late 1950s and the 1960s, which combined with an expanding national newspaper, created the information flow, commentary and focus on national level public affairs, policies, and political leadership necessary to sustain the diet for national public opinion. Surveys done by the author on the attentive audience for speeches by political leaders found that some 40 percent of the electorate was reached by such political messages by way of the radio media channel. Twenty-two percent assimilated such messages through the newspaper channel, and a smaller 12 percent was reached by television.

Radio, of course, has the largest audience reach given the concentration of TV and newspaper access among the upper, middle, and lower middle income strata and the more informed, literate, and higher income strata among the working class. As much as 23 percent of the political

Table 7.2 Percent Uncommitted Voters by Age (1981)

Age Groups	Percent Uncommitted Voters
Under 18	50
18–20	31
21–30	20
31–40	15
Over 40	15

Source: Author's December 1981 national survey.

community gains access to such political messages exclusively by means of radio. When one takes into account the overlap in access to media channels, some 52 percent of the political community is actually reached by some media channel transmitting political commentary and speeches by national political leaders. To be sure, the degree of attention within that media audience varies considerably. Only some 25 percent of the electorate assimilates the messages in sufficient detail as to be able to re-call what was transmitted within a period of three days afterwards. These represent a minority of highly politicized persons who maintain a close watch over political events and develop strong political opinions that tend to echo the PNP or JLP party positions quite faithfully.

But what precisely has been the qualitative impact of the mass me-dia on the country's politics and on the formation of national opinion? To begin with, both media managers and politicians accept a basic prem-ise that the mass media plays a major role in influencing public opinion. Because of this assumption, the politicians take very seriously and usually respond to how the news media project political and national events and how they develop opinion commentary on politics, politi-cians, and national affairs generally. The business elite, the national po-litical leaders, the technocrats, the managerial elite, the foreign compa-nies and the middle class generally view the news media as an institution of awesome power capable of making and breaking political leaders. Therefore, where the media tries to exert its influence, whichever in-terests feel that they are likely to be adversely affected tend to become hostile and to direct political attacks at the news media management and journalists. These attacks will vary from angry letters and telephone calls, to abuse from political platforms at mass meetings, to personal threats, and even to angry demonstrations involving militant party activists.

On the other hand, overt political biases in the news media in com-mentary and the slanting of news events presentation invariably produce skepticism and distrust and weakens the media organs' ability to in-fluence public opinion. The highly politicized partisan segments of na-tional public opinion limit very severely the exent to which political bi-ases in the media can be effectively used to influence national opinion. However, the nonpartisan floating voters are amenable to such media manipulations. The more central issue that has to be addressed is pre-cisely what is the extent of the mass media influence on the formation of national public opinion.

The mass media attempt to exert influence on public opinion in several ways. These include projecting favorable or unfavorable images about personalities, parties, and policies; influencing the agenda of na-tional political discussion by focusing on particular events and issues; promoting particular political ideas and values; and supporting political parties and leadership personalities. Perhaps the greatest area of media influence lies in the shaping of the agenda for national political discussion from the events presented in news and the commentary on political issues and personalities.

Surveys[12] carried out by the author indicate that interest in news constitutes the major reason stimulating newspaper reading and buying. Secondly, all the mass media center at least 20 percent of their local news focus on the actions, statements, and speeches of national political leaders. This heavy emphasis on public affairs statements and events is deliberate in a political culture that is highly partisan and politicized.

While the focus on these events and personalities helps to center public attention on what politicians do and say and what their policies are, the media organs are relatively less successful in influencing how people react to these phenomena. Where the media organs overtly adopt supportive or hostile coverage of policies, politicians, and political tendencies, they easily fall victim to accusations of political conspiracy and can be discredited for so doing.

In the 1970s consistent attacks on the PNP and Prime Minister Manley by the major national newspaper the *Daily Gleaner* led to aggressive counterassaults from the PNP leader and PNP activists. This political campaign against the newspaper effectively discredited it among PNP supporters and probably contributed as well to the drop in the sales of the paper during the 1970s. Sixty-two percent of the mass public expressed the view in an October 1980 poll that the *Gleaner* was then pro-JLP in its presentation of information. Only 24 percent of the electorate, who were mainly pro-JLP, thought that the *Gleaner's* news was accurate or reliable and these were mainly pro-JLP supporters and a minority of floating voters. Forty-two percent of the national sample expressed a favorable view of the *Gleaner* and supported the idea that the newspaper had served the country well. These were mainly JLP supporters and floating voters. Thirty-four percent criticized the newspaper for attacking the PNP and for publishing what were alleged to be falsehoods. The newspaper's critics were made up of a majority of pro-PNP supporters and a minority of floating voters. Political parties, therefore, have some capability to neutralize political attacks in the media. On the other hand, the most credible media organs tend to be the ones that are seen as most politically neutral, while the media organs with a strong party political image are usually discredited by persons not supportive of whichever party that media organ promotes.

Both radio stations are owned by the government but, of the two, Radio Jamaica has a nonpartisan image and is the most politically credible of the mass media institutions. The other radio station, Jamaica Broadcasting Corporation, has a long tradition of being manipulated by the two governing parties to distort news and present extremely biased political commentary. Both this radio and TV station and the second newspaper, The *Daily News* (now defunct) were extensively used to promote prosocialist PNP propaganda during the 1970s. While they both had the effect of boosting the morale of hard core PNP activists, independent voters and persons not supportive of the PNP treated most of their news coverage and commentary as party propaganda and this considerably negated any significant influence they might have had on the level of national public opinion.

A political survey in 1983 carried out by the author established that when asked about the major problems in the respective communities and local areas, there emerged a relatively common agenda of problems that focused on the following: poor roadways, unemployment, crime, growing cost of living, poor water supplies, shortage of cash, no playing fields for the youth, and police brutality. As communication and transportation contact as well as internal networks of trade and commerce brought people into a more cosmopolitan and nationally integrated political community, national awareness and national sentiments superimposed on local community attachments sharpened citizens' sense of being affected by public affairs and public policies. As the agenda of political issues became more uniform across the regions and communities that made up the political system, the basis was laid for the emergence of national public opinion.

VOTING UNIFORMITY

As a result of the development of national public opinion, the pattern of voting across the country's various regions has been altered. Strong regional differences have given way to increasing uniformity in voting and partisan support levels across these regions. The country is divided into 14 parishes that have been further subdivided into 60 parliamentary constituencies. In the earlier period there was a distinctive pattern of regional voting in which certain parishes consistently returned majorities for one of the political parties regardless of what were the overall national voting trends. Since the 1970s that tradition of distinctive regional voting patterns has been replaced by uniformity in party voting. As a result, the victorious party tends to win the overwhelming majority of parliamentary seats and the opposition parties end up being severely underrepresented as regards their share of seats compared to their share of votes. Popular vote majorities have also tended to increase as a consequence of this uniformity in voting across the parishes of the island state.

Table 7.3 shows the distribution of the parish popular vote trends for parliamentary elections held between 1959 and 1980. The data show that up to 1962 there was a minority of parishes whose popular vote deviated quite considerably from the national vote and that approximately half of the parishes up to 1967 had large deviations from the national popular vote. Between the 1972 and 1980 elections, the very large deviations from the national popular vote norm were eliminated and the overwhelming majority of the 14 parishes cluster between the small and very small deviations from the overall national popular vote distribution of partisan voting support. In effect, the country has become virtually like one single constituency, as a common agenda of national political and policy issues has replaced the strong parochial and local influences that shaped the tradition of regional party voting built up over the 1940s and 1950s. The growth of a body of national public opinion has therefore left an indelible mark of increasing uniformity on the voting patterns of the country.

Table 7.3 defines very small deviations as those falling between a 1 to 4 percent deviation from the national popular vote average for the parishes and a 5 to 9 percent deviation as a small deviation. A 9 to 12 percent deviation is classified as being large and those deviations that exceed 12 percent are considered very large. Among the 14 parishes the number of very small deviations increased from three to 11 between 1959 and 1976, while the number of very large and large deviations is reduced from five to one between 1959 and 1976. The level of uniformity in regional voting drops marginally between 1976 and 1980 but remains at a very high level. In the earlier elections held in the 1940s (as illustrated by the 1949 data) the majority of parishes fell in the large and very large deviation categories influenced both by strong regionalism in voting as well as by the impact of independent candidates. What the data show is that even after the elimination of independent candidates as an effective political force in 1959, the trend towards greater national uniformity increased considerably between the 1960s and the 1970s.

As a result of this increasing uniformity in the parish vote the concentration of parliamentary seats won by the victorious political party has increased considerably and the number of parishes in which that winning party establishes popular vote majorities has also reflected this trend toward uniformity. The trend in increasingly large popular vote majorities also follows this pattern. These trends are well illustrated in Table 7.4 which compares the seat and popular vote majorities won by the JLP in the 1962 and 1980 elections.

THE EFFECT OF IDEOLOGY

The increasing focus on political ideology in the national public opinion trends in the 1970s mirrors the increased ideological polarization between the JLP and the PNP under the leadership of Edward Seaga and Michael Manley. Precisely what the ideological labels and concepts mean to the Jamaican political community and how this insertion of ideological politics has affected political awareness within the body of national public opinion remains to be clarified.

The impact of ideology has clearly been limited to the partisan subsectors of national public opinion and to capitalist and middle class non-

Table 7.3 Parish Distribution of Popular Vote Compared to the National Vote Pattern

Parliamentary Elections	Number of Parishes Grouped by Percent Deviations from Average National JLP Share or Percent of Popular Vote for All Parishes			
	Very Small + or – 1-4 percent	Small + or – 5-9 percent	Large + or – 9-12 percent	Very Large More Than + or – 12 percent
1949 (14)	3	3	5	3
1959 (14)	3	6	2	3
1962 (14)	6	1	4	3
1967 (14)	6	3	6	0
1972 (14)	6	7	1	0
1976 (14)	11	2	1	0
1980 (14)	9	3	2	0

Source: Electoral officer's reports, (1944–1980).

Table 7.4 Comparison of Seat and Vote Majorities of the JLP
in 1962 and 1980 Elections

	1962	1980
Number of the 14 parishes in which JLP won popular vote majority	8	14
Percent national popular vote won by JLP	50	59
Percent of total parliamentary seats won by JLP	58	85

Source: Electoral officer's reports (1962, 1980).

partisan voters. The PNP's advocacy of socialism was seen by most PNP supporters within the majority classes as symbolic of the party's commitment to the uplifting of the poor in a broad populist sense. For the majority it did not imply any commitment to radical leftist policies or any programmatic approach to public policy making. The majority left it up to the party leadership to discover appropriate policies to realize that populist objective. Among a minority of approximately 20 percent of the party's hard core support, that socialist commitment had clear policy and ideological meaning in terms of a commitment to left-wing Marxist, anti-imperalist, pro-Third World, and prointernational socialist foreign policy commitments. To large sections of the capitalist class and the middle class, the PNP's seeming flirtation with Cuba and Marxism in the 1970s provided a basis on which to see the PNP as being an enemy of middle and upper income class interests.

The JLP's pro-Western, pro-United States, proprivate enterprise and anti-Marxist ideological reactions to the PNP leftward drift under Manley's leadership created two main ideological tendencies in the party's base of support. The majority saw the JLP's party philosophy as a commitment to sober, stable, efficient, pragmatic, and business-oriented public policies that would maximize the flow of long-run economic and social benefits to the poor. A minority of approximately 12 percent of that support base saw the party's ideology as implying a commitment to zealously confront and wage war against all forms of ideological radicalism of the left variety. Only the middle class and capitalist supporters of the JLP saw the party's ideology as implying a commitment to specific policies designed to promote free enterprise and the liberalizing of the constraints and controls the state had created to regulate private sector business transactions.

The impact of party ideology on most of the partisan mass public was largely limited to reinforcing and cementing party loyalties by providing some symbols that were seen as reflecting the parties' commitment to improve the lot of the majority classes. It did not have the effect of polarizing or dividing the mass public between partisans supporting divergent economic or public policy prescriptions. The typical JLP and PNP voter left it up to the party leaders to work out what policy approach was best able to achieve the party's goals of uplifting poor people and improving their life chances. Sharp polarization on ideological, foreign policy, and domestic economic and social policies emerged, however, within the political community between the party leaders, between the private sector and the middle class, on the one hand, and the PNP leaders and the minority of PNP ideological activists on the other, as these ideological positions sharpened in the 1970s. Most floating voters, however, were affected far less by ideology and much more by their perception of whether life was getting easier or more difficult, jobs were being created, purchasing power was increasing or declining, or the economy seemed to be offering hope for the future.

Where ideology had its major effects was on the management of the economy and the external supports for the political directorate. To examine these issues in detail requires an assessment of how the economy and public policy were managed by the PNP in the 1970s and what have been the new directions since the change of government to the more conservative JLP in 1980.

MEDIA OWNERSHIP AND CONTROL

Discussions of national public opinion in a democratic society invariably raise the issue of who controls or influences the main channels of communication. In Jamaica the mass media have been owned and controlled by interests that are ascendant in the domains of private and public power in the capitalist corporate economy and in the public sector. The major daily newspaper, the *Daily Gleaner* is owned and controlled by big capitalist interests (notably the Ashenheim and Clarke family interests) while the second newspaper, which went out of business after the JLP came to power, was originally owned by other big capitalist interests (the Henriques, Hendrickson, and Desnoes family interests) before it was acquired by the PNP government in the late 1970s. The major radio station was owned and controlled by foreign and local big business interests before it was also bought out by the PNP government in the 1970s. Both the television station and the radio station that operates from the same enterprise were established by government ownership and have continued under state control. Efforts by the *Daily Gleaner* newspaper to obtain a license to operate a TV station have proven fruitless as the political directorate is jealously guarding its government TV station monopoly.

Both the governing political directorate and the dominant private sector interests have direct access to the media channels and use them constantly to advocate their power and economic interests. Notwithstanding this factor, the competitiveness of the media organs and their sensitivity to meeting the information needs of the public push them often to present opinions and facts that are unfavorable to both government officials and powerful private sector interests. This element of critical journalism tends to receive considerable public encouragement through letters to newspaper editors and call-in radio programs. A small minority of independent journalists have been able to sustain this type of critical journalism in spite of the efforts by the interests who control economic and political power to control the flow of information and opinions to serve their vested interests, although some professionals within journalism have been willing to function as servants of power (both political and economic). The radio call-in programs have been especially important in providing a wide cross section of citizens (who normally would have no access to the media) an opportunity to articulate views and raise public issues. Their considerable audience provides a means by which ordinary citizens can influence public opinion.

The independent floating voters tend to be easily influenced by the news media in areas such as the promotion or discrediting of causes, policies, or politicians, particularly if the media organs are seen as credible. The Radio Jamaica radio station and the *Daily Gleaner* newspaper are the most important media resources for influencing independent voters. In the 1970s, the *Daily Gleaner* played a major role in discrediting PNP leader Manley among independent floating voters and in promoting JLP leader Eddie Seaga. Indeed, the more the PNP attacked the newspaper and discredited it among hard core PNP followers, the more independent voters and JLP supporters rallied behind the newspaper in viewing the *Gleaner* as fighting a battle for the preservation of free speech. As the only major media institution that continues to be owned by private interests, the *Gleaner* is seen by the middle class and capitalists as a major means of defending their political and economic freedoms. Radio Jamaica has a very credible and resourceful public affairs staff that is mainly pro-PNP but maintains substantial professionalism and operates with finesse that permits them to push their point of view without incurring the skepticism of most voters. Neither the PNP nor the JLP politicians have been able to manipulate the radio station's news and public affairs presentations. These two important media influences on public opinion are somewhat evenly balanced as the *Gleaner* leans towards the JLP in its political and policy thinking most of the time, while the Radio Jamaica professionals are inclined toward pro-PNP positions on national policy and public issues. The dominant media organs, therefore, mirror the country's two-party tendencies.

FACE TO FACE COMMUNICATION

The impact of the mass media, however, is severely limited in its influence on public opinion because as a small society with close face-to-face contact and interpersonal, direct communication networks, much of what messages are filtered through the media are actually reinterpreted, modified, and thereafter passed on through these informal communication channels. Secondly, most voters obtain information on public affairs, public events, and public policies from the informal communication channels rather than from the mass media.

These informal communication channels operate through street corner gatherings and groups, rum shops and marketplace areas, workplace and neighborhood friendship networks, and informal information exchanges in casual encounters such as travelling on a bus where public issues will be debated by the more politicized. A survey done by the author in December 1981 which probed information sources on the controversial issue of the so-called "Paul Burke affair"[13] found that more than 50 percent of the JLP and PNP persons who had firm views on the issue had been influenced by face-to-face communication channels. The issue involved an attempt by the JLP leader and prime minister to expose the allegedly continued PNP links with Cuba by statements claiming that a PNP activist was linked to two notorious PNP gunmen who had fled the country to seek refuge in Cuba. In contrast, only 10 percent of the less politicized independents were so influenced or informed about the issue by the informal communication channels. Clearly, the impact of these informal channels of communication is greater on partisan voters because the seasonal political interests of floating voters tend to insulate them from many of these networks. These informal political communication channels provide yet another counter to media influence on public opinion and a means by which politicians working through a national network of organized information brokers and community level grass roots opinion leaders can counter the media or bypass it with stories, rumors, claims, and accounts of events that can grip the public's imagination and seriously influence public opinion. The rumor networks are especially powerful as many citizens feel that the official media channels are carefully manipulated by the power elite and the rich and some forms of sensitive information they think can only be unearthed via such channels. Within a matter of days, stories, rumors, or accounts of important events and happenings that are channeled through the informal communication networks are able to penetrate every segment of public opinion and every area of the country provided that the content of the information is deemed important and salient enough to assimilate the messages. Where the official media organs develop deep problems of public credibility (as happened to the PNP influenced *Daily News* newspaper and the JBC radio and TV stations in the 1970s) the informal communication channels tend to thrive and become overworked with political and policy messages that often counter and neutralize what the mass media organs are trying to communicate. The clear implication here is that unlike the industrial countries where the mass media dominate communication, the extensive networks of face-to-face communication in small island states like Jamaica provide an important counterweight that limits the impact of the mass media in efforts by the political elite and the wealthy class interests to turn the communication process into a pliant servant of power. The people-to-people lines of communication inherent in these informal networks give a democratic grass-roots flavor to the communication process. These informal networks have assisted considerably in permitting opinion leaders at the various community levels to play a key role in political communication alongside the middle class professionals in the government-owned and private sector-controlled media houses.

Because national public opinion has emerged, these informal networks integrate local community communication channels into the national level of information exchanges and dialogue on issues, politics, and policies.

COMPREHENSION LEVELS

While information levels within the political community have been raised as the factors facilitating national public opinion have extended their impact on the country's politics, achieving adequate levels of information and understanding of public affairs is not easily attained. This is especially so in a society still plagued with low levels of functional literacy among the literate, appreciable levels of illiteracy among adults, and huge gaps in understanding between the majority classes, on the one hand, and the capitalists, the technocrats, and the middle class on the other. This problem of adequate information has become critical in recent years as public policy and politics have been involved more and more deeply in complex economic policy, foreign policy, and economic and social management issues. As the state's task of public management has got more and more complex and involved in economic decision making, the ability of the average citizen with a few years primary school education to grasp and comprehend these policy issues has rapidly diminished.

A survey carried out by the author in December 1981 found that 53 percent of JLP supporters, 56 percent of PNP supporters, and 54 percent of the independents admitted that they were not adequately informed about national affairs. When asked to identify the major areas of information gaps, the principal subjects mentioned were the economy, public affairs generally, government policies, and international affairs. Clearly the mass media is not doing enough to fill these information gaps but part of the problem lies in the low educational and comprehension level of large sections of the population. This partly accounts for the tendency of the mass public to concentrate entirely on policy results and their concrete manifestations rather than on discussions of or interest in analysis of policy means and policy alternatives.

More importantly, the primitive information sets and low comprehension levels within the majority of the electorate mean much of what is said about public policy is either not understood or misunderstood. Second, citizens rely on numerous opinion leaders in face to face networks to interpret and explain issues or policy matters that they cannot comprehend. Third, much of what appear on the surface as ideological politics and political education are little more than catch phrases, slogans, and superficial repetition of political rhetoric that is not understood and reflects no real level of political awareness or comprehension of what these things really mean.

Having now developed a national public opinion, the political system is faced with the more difficult task of deepening and enlarging the level of political comprehension and understanding of complex policy issues that is so important if democratic political choices are to be rationally exercised or if the average citizen is to develop the capability to distinguish sense from nonsense in the content of the channels and networks of political communication.

NOTES

1. See Daniel Lerner, *The Passing of Traditional Society; Modernizing the Middle East*, Free Press, Glencoe, Ill.: 1963.

2. Clearly, only a minority of voters are likely to be sufficiently interested in politics to pay keen attention to ideological appeals of parties. How far this minority is genuinely ideological in developing basic ideological orientations that predict their political opinions is quite another matter.

3. Although these areas are not integrated administratively, it is obvious that they constitute a single contiguous urban zone.

4. This estimate is based on the author's survey work.

5. Electricity access now exists for some 42 percent of the population.

6. The *Star* unlike the morning paper, the *Daily Gleaner*, has a majority of working class readership.

7. Based on political surveys of the author.

8. These data are taken from Carl Stone, *Jamaica at the Polls: The 1980 Parliamentary Election*, forthcoming from American Enterprise Institute in Washington.

9. For complete poll publications between 1976 and 1981, see Carl Stone, *The Political Opinions of the Jamaican People*, Kingston, Jamaica: Blacket Publishers, 1982.

10. For a full discussion of these election issues, see Carl Stone, *Jamaica at the Polls*, op. cit.

11. Ibid.

12. These surveys were done for the *Daily Gleaner* management on newspaper readership interests.

13. The JLP allegation was that Burke, the leader of the PNP's youth group, was involved in making contacts with two notorious criminals who the JLP claim are PNP gunmen who have been moving back and forth from Jamacia to Cuba.

8

FROM SOCIALIST TO CAPITALIST MANAGEMENT

Where the major political parties in a democracy appear to be sharply divided on major issues of domestic and foreign policies as well as on broad ideological directions that influence public policy, this inevitably generates some measure of stress and tension in a political system that could develop into political crisis. In liberal democracies such as Chile such ideological divisions between partisan groupings and class interests have set the stage for the collapse of democracy.

In the Jamaican case this stress area of ideological polarization is added to a second stress area that relates to the drastic decline in living standards over the 1973 to 1984 period of continuing economic crisis that has affected all classes, but especially the wage workers within the working class, the lower middle class salary earners, and the mainstream middle class. As real income levels have fallen, poverty has increased, economic and social frustration has multiplied, income sources have dried up or declined, and a climate of hopelessness akin to the 1930s has descended on the political community producing gloomy forecasts of political upheaval and disorder. Yet, in spite of these two major areas of stress, political stability has been maintained in Jamaica, indicating a capacity for crisis management. To comprehend how the democratic process has adjusted to these unfolding stresses and potential political crises we must focus in detail on the pattern of public and political management carried out by Manley's PNP in the 1970s and Seaga's JLP in the early 1980s. Jamaica, moreover, presents a case study of the role of ideology in policy formulation in a developing country, in both the domestic and foreign policy spheres. Like some other Third World states that made the transition from liberal-reformist orientations to a more leftist and radical perspective, a dominant left-leaning ideological tendency was inserted into Jamaican politics in the 1970s against the background of a severe crisis in the economy and as part of a search for an alternative development path beyond traditional neocolonial policies. The sharpening of internal ideological divisions in the country (following this development) increased the level of external intervention in the domestic political sphere as the rival cold war hemispheric interests (Cuba and the United States) consolidated ties with local allies and made Jamaican politics into an open thoroughfare for regional ideological rivalries.

The two party leaders (Manley and Seaga) see themselves as advocates of mutually antagonistic ideologies and tend to relate policy choices to their respective ideological positions with great evangelical fervor. Manley denounces neocolonialism and capitalism with great passion and projects himself as an apostle of Third World socialism and the liberation struggle against imperialism and international capitalism. Seaga, on the other hand, articulates a strong commitment to the free enterprise system of economic management and a deep faith in its appropriateness as a model for Third World development.

Both the earlier PNP party government (1972–1980) and the present JLP government have projected their respective party ideologies (PNP "socialism" and JLP "free enterprise") as policy frameworks out of which solutions to the basic economic and social problems of Jamaica can be found. Both party governments have experienced problems and gaps between the assumptions behind their policy and ideological prescriptions and the reality of political and economic structures of the Jamaican political economy and political community. More importantly, one needs to assess objectively how far the policy prescriptions put forward by the two major parties in Jamaica are likely to provide real solutions for the economic and social problems of this small, open economy. In this regard the central problems of indebtedness, balance of payments problems, shortage of investment capital, unemployment, economic dualism, and stagnation in agricultural production, as well as inflation, budget deficits, and weak public sector management all make Jamaica a fairly typical model of those problems that face most developing countries that are not blessed with oil. Comparatively, Jamaica in the 1970s had greater difficulty coping with these problems than similar Caribbean and other Third World countries. Precisely why this was so needs to be explored fully.

THE NEW PNP

Prior to 1972 when the PNP came to power, that party was a typical social democratic party that had made its peace with capitalism and private ownership but sought to achieve various programs of social reform. The latter included land reform, the broadening of educational opportunity, cooperative ownership within the petty commodity sector, progressive taxation of the affluent property-owning class and addressing the needs of the majority classes of workers and peasants by expanding government services.

The JLP represented the typical Caribbean trade union party that avoided ideology and embraced pragmatic reforms that responded to the specific social needs of the unionized workers and small peasants. Unlike the PNP, which justified the need for active involvement of the state in economic management, the JLP placed its faith in the more orthodox capitalist system of a dominant private sector.

Both parties sought support from all classes,[1] shared a common view of foreign policy as involving close links with U.S. and Western European global interests, and accepted a reformist approach to public policy that supported private business while supporting government spending to meet the social needs of the majority classes. Political liberalism and social reforms in domestic politics and policies and a unified perception of world politics provided an anchor of consensus that stabilized Jamaican party politics. The strong continuity in policy priorities between successive JLP and PNP governments meant that both parties became (over the 1944 to 1972 period) center parties with no sharp or fundamental policy differences between them. Ideological differences such as existed were mainly on the symbolic level as ideological issues were treated as debating points used to promote party images in elections and had no real implications or consequences for policy priorities. Even these symbolic ideological debates receded from the electoral arena between the early 1950s and 1972 as the parties differentiated themselves more and more in terms of competence, policy acheivements, and leadership qualities.

The only real difference in the policy area that emerged between the parties was the tendency of the PNP to increase both public spending and taxation at a faster rate than the JLP and consequently to promote a rate of increase in public employment that was higher than that achieved by the JLP.[2] On the other hand, detailed analysis[3] has shown that most social and economic policies remained intact after changes in party government.

Some fundamental changes in ideological orientation took place within the governing PNP after that party came to power in 1972. Those changes not only transformed the character of the party system but redefined the relationships between technocrats in the civil service, the private sector interest groups, and corporate interests, on the one hand, and the political directorate, on the other.

The new PNP leader Michael Manley proceeded to take the PNP beyond the bounds of the inherited social democratic tradition. His main impulse and inspiration were to try to dismantle neocolonialism and economic dependency in Jamaica. His new policy and ideological thrust were inspired both by a strong sense of economic nationalism, which saw Jamaica and Jamaicans as having to assume greater control and ownership over the local economy, and a feeling of commitment to Third World socialist trends.

Manley's thrust toward close relations with leftist Third World states (Cuba, Tanzania, Mozambique, and others) and his initiative in personally undertaking an activist stance in international affairs in relation to North-South issues represented a dramatic break from the traditional low profile foreign policy and the pro-Western foreign policy alignment[4] of the previous JLP government (1962–72). Evidence of this realignment is reflected in Jamaica's voting in the U.N. on controversial ideological issues that divided the Western capitalist countries and the United States, on the one hand, and the Communist countries and the radical Third World countries, on the other. Detailed analysis[5] of that vote pattern revealed that whereas under the JLP betwen 1960 and 1972 the Jamaican government tended to vote with the United States and with the Western bloc, under Manley's PNP party government Jamaica tended to vote with Cuba and the radical leftist Third World countries on such issues.

This radical new direction in foreign policy was followed by the cementing of close party-to-party ties with the Communist Party in Cuba and the gradual takeover of the party machinery by a new generation of younger leaders who, with the full backing of party leader, Michael Manley, injected Marxist terminology into the party's rhetoric and set itself the task of moving towards a noncapitalist path of development.

The idea of the noncapitalist path[6] to development as articulated by Soviet theoreticians and some Third World leftists does not involve a break with capitalism but envisages a set of political strategies that are designed to prepare the way toward a full break with capitalism. It involves the elimination of the monopoly of political power by the bourgeoisie (local or foreign), increasing the power of the working people in political affairs, agrarian reform, cooperative development, the creation of a strong state sector in the economy to hold in check capitalist tendencies, militant criticism of imperialism, attempts at promoting social justice and eliminating class exploitation, and the promotion of class consciousness through the dissemination of Marxist-Leninist ideas.

There was a massive swing of voters toward the PNP in the 1976 parliamentary elections within the poorer working class communities as its populist promises of social justice generated strong chords of vocal mass support. The PNP made some initiatives toward the transition stage of a noncapitalist path to development after its decisive victory at the polls in 1976. As the economy deteriorated and as the PNP government was shackled by aid dependence on the fiscally conservative International

Monetary Fund, the noncapitalist path had to be abandoned and policy directions moved back to the center while the rhetoric of the noncapitalist path continued.

Before the IMF influence became decisive, the PNP took some crucial steps both to increase the role of the state in economic management and to reduce the political influence of the bourgeoisie and the conservative petty-bourgeois technocrats in the civil service. Many bourgeois persons were removed from statutory boards and key advisory roles as a small number of the radical-left intelligentsia were recruited into the government as technocrats and advisors. Conservative civil service economists were pressured out of key positions and leftist economists were recruited to fill these positions. As the economic crisis deepened, the state took over a number of private companies to preserve jobs and the economy was brought under a regime of tight regulation and control of foreign exchange, imports, prices, and foreign currency.

Although some business interests remained on close terms with the PNP and the prime minister, the majority of the merchants, manufacturers, and big farmers, as well as professional class reacted in panic to these policy initiatives. Some migrated to Miami, while others exported foreign currency and closed or scaled down their business enterprises, or withheld tax payments.

The actual structural changes carried out by the PNP were not very far reaching although the Marxist rhetoric from the party's top leadership and leftist factions gave quite the opposite impression. Land reform plans foundered against the harsh reality of a legal system that protected property rights and made land acquisition expensive. Radical proposals to change the constitution to widen the state's powers so as to acquire land cheaply (among other things) were abandoned after the post-1976 decline in the economy weakened support for socialism and after a national poll on the subject (carried out by the author on behalf of the PNP) showed that the majority of the electorate neither had any interest in the constitutional change nor supported it.

PNP attitudes to the local private sector were quite ambivalent, vacillating, and contradictory. Patriotic appeals were made to the private sector to cooperate in the handling of the economic crisis and actual incentives were offered to stimulate exports and employment while the party leaders and leftists singled out the local bourgeoisie for ideological attacks that often trumpeted ultra-leftist declarations calling for an end to capitalism in Jamaica. The inconsistency of these overtures did nothing but accelerate the panic and flight within the bourgeoisie.

The PNP was, on the one hand, espousing the objective of creating a mixed economy in which a reduced private sector would have a place side by side with the state that was to control the commanding heights of the economy. On the other hand, party spokesmen were abusing the private sector by talking in terms of aspirations for an accelerated transition toward the noncapitalist path and thereafter to full socialism. Close party-to-party ties with Cuba encouraged the development of radical leftist rhetoric that bore no real relationship to the actual structural changes carried out by the PNP. The cosmetic of Marxist terminology served to intimidate the capitalists while pushing the government on a collision course with international capitalist agencies, although no real structural changes in the political economy were achieved beyond a reduction in capitalist political influence and an expanded role for the state in the management of the economy.

The land reform programs left most large private land holdings intact except for a modest number of property acquisitions. Most of the land obtained for redistribution were marginal lands made available on a leasehold basis and the total impact of the land reform was politically and economically negligible, especially as many projects failed miserably from a production or financial standpoint. Neither equity in land allocation nor efficiency in production were attained in the PNP's land reform initiatives.

Co-ops established in the sugar industry ran into financial and management problems, while weak trade union support for worker participation, worker apathy, and hostility by employers weakened the PNP's interest in promoting greater working class power at the workplace. In any event, the main objective sought from worker participation was the pacification of labor militancy and industrial peace rather than the promotion of worker power which would have quite the opposite effect of increasing tensions and class antagonisms in an already conflict-prone labor relations situation.

In effect, the PNP seemed not to have the political will to go through with the difficult task of pulling this conservative and highly pragmatic political culture into the stormy class conflicts that would have inevitably attended more systematic efforts at establishing an opening toward a noncapitalist path to development in Jamaica. Dependence on the IMF for balance of payments support and the tight conditions attached to IMF loans forced the PNP to scale down its designs to expand state control of the economy and to use the public sector as a means of redistributing income and social benefits to the poorer classes. The IMF conservative influence was, however, only one of several other converging forces. As the state's role in economic management increased through the larger regulatory role and the increased management burden for running public enterprises and parastatal corporations, the PNP discovered that its public sector management capability to undertake these tasks was embarrassingly limited. Capital and investment funding was simply not available to finance the state embarking on new productive enterprises, as against bailing out bankrupt businesses or keeping open (for employment purposes) companies whose owners and managers joined the exodus of people and capital out of Jamaica. Large scale migration at a rate of some 25,000 per year in a small population of 2 million left the public as well as the private sectors short of both managerial, technocratic and production skills.

The greatest strides toward the noncapitalist path were achieved in relation to political objectives. The PNP nationalized two of the three main privately owned mass media. These included a daily newspaper (The *Daily News*) and a radio station (Radio Jamaica). These were added to the government-owned radio and television station (Jamaica Broadcasting Corporation). These government-owned mass media were extensively used to propagate the PNP's ideology and to disseminate the ideas associated with the new socialist thrust, and the aspirations towards the noncapitalist path. A high level of mass mobilization was achieved within the PNP party organization and enthusiastic party activists were politicized to articulate the new ideological currents within the party. In the area of foreign policy, the Manley government closely identified with Cuba and the Third World, became one of the principal advocates of the New International Economic Order, and the radical wing in the Nonaligned Movement, and mounted verbal attacks on world imperialism and international capitalism in international forums.

THE JLP REACTION

The JLP reaction to these developments was to mount an intense campaign of attacks on socialism and Communism and to associate leftist policies with the decline in the economy. Beyond that, the JLP projected itself as a party committed to free enterprise forms of economic management. The bourgeoisie, the JLP argues, should be permitted to resume full control of the economy and the expanded role given the state by the PNP in economic management was seen by the JLP as an undesirable contributor to the economic failures of the 1970s. State regulation of the economy was portrayed as dysfunctional to economic progress and the JLP suggested that the forces of the free market must be restored to provide a more rational mechanism of resource allocation and price determination.

The JLP anchored its political position on the principle of private ownership of the means of production and the need for private investment and entrepreneurial initiative to be given the necessary incentives to move the economy forward. Private ownership, the JLP insisted, was more efficient than public ownership.

In the political sphere, the JLP reaffirmed its strong pro-Western and pro-U.S. international alignment and denounced the PNP link with Cuba as being part of a grand Communist conspiracy to overturn liberal democracy in Jamaica. Attempts by the PNP to politicize the society were derided as paving the way toward a Communist one-party state where freedom of speech and civil liberties would be destroyed as they were in Cuba. The JLP, therefore, asserted itself as the champion of the traditional liberal values that run deep in the Jamaican political culture.

The JLP, therefore, assumed the role of the defender of political liberalism and orthodox capitalist methods of economic management while the PNP moved from a center-left social democratic position towards a more leftist posture that aspired toward creating a noncapitalist path to development in Jamaica. In terms of ideological symbolism and party image, the PNP was projecting itself as the party defending the cause of the poor and the oppressed while the JLP assumed the posture of the party that stood for respected traditions, stability, gradualism, technocratic efficiency and responsible financial management. The JLP came out strongly in defense of the bourgeoisie (foreign and local) as the vital source of restimulating the economy toward a path of recovery, while the PNP placed its emphasis elsewhere on the objective of social justice for the poor.

As this pattern of two-party ideological polarization rapidly replaced the two-party consensus of the earlier period, certain tendencies emerged dominant in either party. The JLP was traditionally a party based on an alliance between pragmatic trade union leaders and business interests hostile to the PNP's advocacy of socialism. As these ideological divisions between the PNP and the JLP sharpened the business orientation within the JLP assumed dominance over the trade union segment of the party's two main tendencies. Under Edward Seaga's leadership, the ideology and dominant thinking inside the JLP moved more and more away from the JLP's traditional labor populism and more toward a business ideology and technocratic conception of managing public affairs.

In the PNP, by contrast, the traditional social democratic tendencies declined in importance as the anti-imperialist and Third World socialist perspectives swept through the corridors of thought and action inside the party. The party moderates who opposed these trends found that under Michael Manley's leadership their influence inside the party rapidly diminished in the 1970s.

PNP ECONOMIC POLICIES

These ideological differences between the JLP and the PNP formed the basis for some sharp divergencies in the public policies the two parties have brought to bear on problem solving. A focus on these concrete areas of policy difference is a crucial first step toward appraising the changes and new directions introduced by the JLP government that came to power in October 1980.

Faced with the economic crises of the 1970s, under the banner of advancing socialism, the PNP implemented a mix of economic and social policies. Some of these policies reflected the party's new ideological thrust while others mirrored conventional Western economic prescriptions derived from Keynesian theories.

As private investment declined in the early 1970s the PNP took steps to increase overseas borrowing by the government from private banks to finance capital needs. This trend is shown in Table 8.1 which outlines the dramatic fall in private foreign investment that coincided with the takeover of the government by the socialist PNP and the simultaneous and equally dramatic rise of overseas borrowing.

Immediately following the PNP's reaffirmation of socialism in 1974 and over the subsequent period (1975–80) in which radical socialist currents began to emerge in the party, foreign investment dried up completely. Only after the 1976 parliamentary elections, however, did the more militant minority of leftists in the party's leadership join the PNP cabinet. Prior to that election, the ideological moderates in the cabinet enjoyed strong influence over policy making while the party machine was effectively in the hands of the leftists. It was therefore possible to negotiate large loans from private overseas banks up to that period. These loans financed public sector economic activity. Given the balance of payments problems and the acute shortage of foreign exchange, the impact of the loans was to concentrate most of the capital formation in the public sector.

Added to this pattern of large increases in foreign borrowing was the adoption of Keynesian strategies of demand management through deficit budgeting. The object was to prime consumer spending and to keep a minimal momentum of economic activity in motion, given the fact that world inflation and the large increases in import costs had severely reduced the capacity to import. This import decline had a negative effect on the momentum of activity in the economy due to the high import dependence in both production and consumption patterns in the economy.

As can be seen from Table 8.2 the size of the budget deficit more than doubled after the PNP came to power in 1972. The impact of this budget deficit added to the large inflows of overseas loans was to increase significantly the aggregate level of government spending over GDP. Table 8.2 indicates also that the level of public spending doubled as a proportion of GDP under the expansionist budgets of the PNP in the 1970s.

The PNP also sought to develop what it defined as policies of economic self-reliance. These policies were designed to stimulate domestic

Table 8.1 Trends in Foreign Investment and Government Private Foreign Borrowing

Private foreign investment ($J million)	1970	1971	1972	1973	1974	1975	1976	1977	1978
	134	147	21	20	21	0	0	0	0

Loans from foreign commercial banks ($U.S. million)	1972	1973	1974	1975	1976	1977	1978	1979
	14	80	136	119	44	-15	15	-11

Source: Bank of Jamaica

Table 8.2 Budget Deficit and Expenditure

Budget deficit as percent of expenditure	1972	1974	1976	1978	1980
	18	25	44	40	43
Government expenditure as percent of GDP	1972	1978			
	22	41			

Source: Economic and Social Surveys (1972–1980), National Planning Agency

production as substitutes for imports that could no longer be afforded due to the balance of payments problems and the reduced capacity to import. Reduced levels of imports over the period generated shortages of many consumer goods that were normally imported or produced locally before the shortages in foreign exchange caused by oil price increases. This had two important effects. A large number of petty traders created an extensive import-export trade that brought into the island large quantities of consumer goods, some of which were banned from importation and some of which were brought in without paying the requisite import duty. Second, small peasant and middle peasant farmers increased domestic food crop production as consumers had to substitute local food items for items normally imported. In effect, one consequence of the foreign exchange crisis was an expansion of the petty commodity sector.

Out of the economic crisis, therefore, significant increases in wealth and income flows accrued to the petty commodity sector. In the commercial centers and especially in the island's capital city, Kingston, higglers made significant inroads into the market share of the middle class merchants. In some cases merchants retailed goods imported by higglers. Between 1976 and 1980 food imports (in real terms) fell from $90 million to $30 million (1972 dollars) while domestic food production grew by 26 percent from $68 million to $86 million (in 1969 dollars). Over that period also the farm gate price for domestic food crops was increasing faster than the overall price index for the economy as a whole, indicating clearly a net transfer of income to the petty commodity sector.

The expansion in income accruing to the petty commodity sector and the parallel decline in the income flows and market shares controlled by the middle class merchants were only part of the picture. The promotion of self-reliance strategies left huge gaps in the supply of consumer goods and considerable consumer alienation towards the PNP government developed on this issue over the period. Together with unemployment, the cost of living and the overall depressed state of the economy, shortages of consumer goods was one of the four major economic factors identified by voters as being among the most important election issues.

The PNP attempted to mobilize the labor force through rhetoric and emotive ideological appeals to patriotism. The effort was based on the premise that one could not rely entirely on market forces and material incentives to stimulate economic activity and that political mobilization could assist in energizing the people to scaling great heights or ambitious production targets. This policy proved to be both romantic and futile. Whereas the small peasants and middle peasants responded to market forces by increasing domestic food production, government-financed farm projects which were promoted as self-reliance strategies (but provided inadequate income and material returns to participants) resulted in underutilized land, huge expenditure over revenue deficits and poor performance in production, notwithstanding various efforts at political mobilization.

A program of industrial democracy was attempted by promoting worker participation and cooperatives. Trade union disinterest and management opposition combined with worker apathy paralyzed the worker participation initiative. The cooperative movement established in the sugar industry was a political success with respect to the establishment of worker control on the island's three largest sugar estates. But the experiment in worker controlled production was a financial failure that generated worker dissatisfaction with the meager financial rewards.

Faced with the economic crises of the period, the PNP government established government ownership and control over key areas of the economy that were vital either for overall economic management or important to the pursuit of the goal of social justice for the poor. A major foreign bank (Barclays) was nationalized. Hotels were taken over on a scale that eventually gave the government a majority ownership of the hotel rooms in the industry. The cement company was nationalized. A small number of food processing enterprises were established under government ownership. A State Trading Corporation was established with the long-term objective of permitting state control of most areas of importation. The Corporation in its initial stages monopolized the importation of basic foods, drugs, and lumber, attempting through bulk buying to pass on cheaper prices to the consumer. Rigid price and rent controls were established to control the cost of living. A wage-price policy established controls over wages as a balance to price controls.

The shortage of foreign exchange made import controls necessary as well as controls over foreign currency. Importation of goods was brought under a tight system of licensing and foreign exchange was rationed through the national bank, the Bank of Jamaica. Joint ownership was established between the government and the transnational bauxite companies and the PNP government reestablished ownership over the mined-out bauxite lands. As a response to the acute shortage of foreign exchange, the PNP government imposed a 7 percent production levy on the bauxite multinationals which generated substantial additional revenue and foreign exchange in the region of $160 to $180 million. The major urban bus company, the J.O.S., was nationalized.

The Jamaican political economy had changed in important features in the decade of the 1970s due to the cumulative impact of these PNP policies. Changing from a political economy in which the bourgeoisie was overwhelmingly dominant politically and its class interests were treated as almost synonymous with the interests of the nation, the cumulative impact of PNP policies significantly altered the balance of class power in the society. The state now assumed a dominant role in economic management both in the areas of economic regulation of business transactions and activity and in respect of the state's control over a large proportion of the flow of income in the society. Further, the state increased, quite importantly, the range and number of public enterprises that were producing goods and services in the economy, especially in crucial areas such as agriculture, trade, utilities and services, banking, bauxite, construction, tourism, and mass communication.

Table 8.3 classifies independent Caribbean English-speaking states according to the levels of state economic intervention and general ideological tendencies under various governments. Jamaica is classified as one of the political systems in which both ideological tendency and level of state economic intervention changed in the 1970s. That change was due primarily to the new currents of socialist ideology that emerged in the PNP under the leadership of Michael Manley.

Table 8.3 Commonwealth Caribbean States by Ideology and State Economic Intervention (1970s)

| Ideology | State Economic Intervention | | |
	Low	Medium	High
Liberal–pragmatic	Barbados Bahamas Grenada (under Gairy) Jamaica (under JLP) Antigua St. Lucia Dominica	St. Kitts	
Nationalist		Trinidad and Tobago	
Socialist		Jamaica (under PNP) Grenada (under Bishop)	Guyana

Source: Taken from Carl Stone, *Understanding Third World Politics and Economics,* Kingston: Earle Publishers, 1980, p. 42

Under the Manley government Jamaica moved from low levels of state economic intervention to medium levels of state economic intervention. In contrast to Guyana where the development of a Third World socialist ideological framework led to 80 percent state ownership and high levels of state intervention in the economy in all important areas, in Jamaica, considerable private sector economic power and ownership remained intact in spite of this socialist trend. Indeed, the residue of private sector economic power (based on the strength of the bourgeoisie in Jamaica) slowed down the process of socialism and promoted resistance to socialist advances. The intense conflicts between the PNP leftist intelligentsia leadership (mainly black, colored, and university educated) and the white and light-skinned bourgeoisie (mainly high school educated) generated a climate in which capital flights, tax evasions, the decapitalization of enterprises, and disinterest in investments added to the economic problems of the period. Some strong racial undertones colored these tensions as deep antagonisms developed between these elite groups.

PNP overseas borrowing shifted from private commercial banks to the IMF between the middle and the late 1970s. Indeed, it is paradoxical that after the PNP shifted somewhat to the left after the massive 1976 election victory over the JLP, the PNP got tied into extensive borrowing and consequent dependence on the conservative International Monetary Fund which was hostile to most of its policies. Further confusion and ideological antagonism was added to the political situation as policy conflicts between the IMF and the PNP leftists (who increasingly controlled PNP policy making after 1976) made it difficult to develop coherent, consistent, and predictable economic policies over the 1977 to 1980 period.

No clear winner emerged from the IMF-PNP policy and ideological conflicts. The PNP feared the impact of the stabilization policies associated with the IMF, which included currency devaluation, free trade, elimination of budget deficits, reducing inflation at the price of increasing unemployment, removal of subsidies, removal of price controls, and the scaling down of state economic intervention. But the PNP had no alternative source of foreign exchange support so the PNP had to compromise on some issues while fighting the IMF on others. The IMF, in turn was extra sensitive to its growing anti-Third World image and tried in the Jamaican case to compromise itself (in the usual hard line policies) to find a way toward working with a small influential Third World country. The real problem was that no socialist source of international financing existed to aid the PNP.

The PNP was able to maintain high budget deficits during the period of IMF borrowing. Price controls remained intact, although the list of controlled items was eventually reduced. The ceiling for wage controls was increased by the IMF after political and union pressure from a 7 percent to a 15 percent official limit. Some subsidies were cut while others remained. The PNP refused to fire or lay off public sector workers to reduce the budget deficit and broke with the IMF over that issue at a strategically designed five months before the 1980 election and proceeded to blame the IMF for its economic and political problems.

The big question that needs to be addressed was how far the PNP's policies were able to achieve the objectives and targets set. In balance, the failures were more pronounced than the successes. Between 1974, when the PNP was in power, and 1980, the last year of the PNP government led by Michael Manley, real per capita disposable income fell 30 percent, from $1,019 to $717. Over the same period per capita consumption expenditure in real terms fell 25 percent, from $737 to $557. Per capita wages in real terms also fell 25 percent, from $588 to $440.

In spite of the big increase in persons employed in the public sector due to the expansionist public spending policies of the government, the shrinkage of private sector employment and the overall decline in the economy increased unemployment from 23 percent in 1972 to 28 percent in 1980.

The self-reliance policies geared to reduce import dependence achieved modest successes between 1975 and 1977 but these gains were erased beteen 1978 and 1980 as domestic production declined dramatically. In 1974 imports represented 46 percent of GDP and this was reduced to 33 percent by 1977 due to tight import restrictions. However, by 1980 imports climbed back up to 53 percent of GDP although the value of imports in real terms dropped by over 40 percent between 1975 and 1980.

Gross capital formation fell from 35 percent of GDP (when the JLP was in power), to 26 percent in 1975 (under the PNP), and to 16 percent in 1980, thus indicating the dramatic fall in investment activities. Dependence on foreign borrowing to finance savings inceased from 30 percent when the JLP was in power in 1969, to 63 percent under the PNP in 1976, and 68 percent in 1980. In real terms domestic savings fell by approximately 35 percent between 1969 and 1980.

As can be seen from Table 8.4 the PNP's effort at price controls brought the inflation level down after the impact of the oil price increase had created double digit inflation. But the impact was short-lived as huge budget deficits, shortages, black marketeering and excessively high prices in the informal higgler controlled markets, devaluation, private sector profiteering, and imported inflation pushed domestic price increases back up to high levels. The figures show that Jamaica fared much worse than other trade dependent economies in the region in the effort to control inflation over the period. Countries with tighter controls over budget deficits (Bahamas, Barbados, and the Dominican Republic) did much better at controlling the local impact of international inflation pressures than Jamaica in these small open economic systems in the Caribbean.

Table 8.4 Comparative Inflation Levels for Jamaica and Similar Countries

Annual Percent Change in Prices 1971–1980

	1970	1971	1972	1973	1974	1975	1976	1977	1978	1979	1980
Bahamas	6	5	7	5	13	10	4	3	6	9	12
Barbados	8	12	7	17	39	20	5	8	9	13	18
Dominican Republic	4	4	8	15	13	14	8	13	3	9	17
Costa Rica	5	3	5	15	30	17	3	4	6	9	18
Jamaica	10	5	5	20	24	17	10	11	35	29	27

Source: IMF International Financial Statistics, Yearbook, 1981.

More importantly, the PNP attempt at demand Keynesian management failed to stimulate production. Due to the absence of foreign exchange which enters significantly as a prerequisite for increased output for most areas of local production, excess consumer demand induced by public spending led to increased inflation rather than increased output due to the production bottlenecks reflected most acutely in the shortage of raw materials, machinery, equipment, transportation, tools, spares, and containers. For the Keynesian multiplier to have been induced, adequate supplies of foreign exchange had to be in place.

As the debt burden mounted, more and more of the foreign borrowing and the foreign exchange earnings had to be used to pay for accumulated private and public foreign debts. Public debts were paid but large private trading debts went unpaid and creditors removed the facility of trade credit from their transactions with Jamaican companies. This factor added further to the overall decline of the economy.

Subsidies paid out by the government increased from $13 million in 1972 to $200 million in 1978. These subsidies represented the cost of financing unprofitable public enterprises and price subsidies passed on to the consumers to ease the pressures of declining real income and high inflation. The subsidy-tax burden, however, proved to be much too large for an economy in which budget deficits were climbing, real incomes falling, and tax revenue declining in real terms.

Real gains were achieved in the subsidies passed on to the consumers on basic imported food items and in the control of rental through rent control boards. A variety of areas of social legislation added to the introduction of a national minimum wage and the distribution of approximately 180,000 acres of farmland to some 46,000 farmers, and agricultural workers assisted the entire process of social survival, although the production results were not spectacular.

The State Trading Corporation functioned as an efficient bulk purchaser of imports that managed to save foreign exchange by replacing the haphazard private importing by merchants, in spite of a corruption scandal which affected its credibility.

Although the PNP's socialist economic initiatives did not produce any spectacular results, and failed to arrest the decline of the economy, it could well be that with a more activist role by the state in the economy, the economic and social pressures on the majority classes were reduced somewhat (in the short run at least) as a result of food subsidies, employment creation in special employment works, and money circulation through government social projects.

While appreciating the efforts of the PNP government to improve the lot of the urban and rural poor through socialist policies, the Jamaican electorate lost confidence in the PNP's ability to manage the economy. As a consequence, the PNP was voted out of office in the October 1980 election.

Table 8.5 gives the details of the balance of class support which voted the JLP into power. Apart from the skilled workers who gave the ideologically conservative JLP only a small majority, the JLP earned large majorities over the PNP within all the other classes and socioeconomic groupings, especially among the small farmers and the business and managerial interests.

JLP ECONOMIC POLICIES

The JLP reaction to the PNP's economic policies was to devise an alternate package of policies designed to move the economy away from socialist tendencies and structures and back to a more private sector-controlled market economy with low levels of state economic intervention.

The JLP perspective on the economy accepted entirely the need for stabilization policies and the need to remove the barriers of protection so as to create a competitive market economy, freed of government controls, and maximizing the profit incentives for local foreign capital.

The JLP took the view that budget deficits were an obstacle to proper economic management and had to be reduced. The regulatory machinery established by the PNP was seen as stifling bourgeois dynamism and initiative. The trend towards state ownership was also attacked and the JLP committed itself to divesting these enterprises. Public enterprises that had become recipients of subsidies because of inability to break even or show profits would have to be studied to either improve efficiency levels or to sell them to private interests.

The JLP came out with a strong attack on the State Trading Corporation and criticized the PNP for setting up social projects that wasted public funds.

The self-reliance concept was by implication rejected by the JLP in favor of an open economy strategy. The promotion of local ownership was replaced with an emphasis on foreign and joint local-foreign ownership. Foreign investment was seen by the JLP as a necessary prerequisite for economic recovery. Anti-imperialism and a strong Third World

Table 8.5 Percent Vote for JLP in 1980 Elections by Class and Socioeconomic Groups

Urban unemployed	60
Skilled workers	52
White collar workers	63
Business and management class	86
Farm labor	58
Small peasants	65

Source: Author's opinion poll, October 1980. Sample size = 944 voters.

political identity was to be replaced by a strong U.S. foreign policy connection as the means to motivating U.S. foreign investment and aid. Foreign policy was to be moved away from radical leftist ideological postures and toward a more pragmatic path that sought concrete economic gains.

Export emphases geared to selling products to the large U.S. market were to be the main economic strategy and this was to be carefully planned in collaboration with the U.S. government, the local bourgeois interests and U.S. corporations.

Where the PNP emphasized political and ideological mobilization, the JLP argued that what was needed was market and material incentives and greater freedom of choice by consumers, investors, and labor. A more competitive market was seen as an ideal substitute for government controls to allocate resources and determine price levels. The JLP was emphatic in pointing out how much shortages and black markets exploited the consumer and argued vehemently for supply increases to induce prices to find lower levels.

Wage controls were criticized as disturbing free labor bargaining which was projected as preferable to state regulation of labor bargaining. The JLP promised a regime of economic freedoms for all classes in which freer choice through supply/demand adjustments would improve the life chances of all individuals. Stricter financial management by the government, a climate of confidence between the government and private interests, and prospects for replacing successive years of negative growth and reduced consumption levels by a new spurt of investment activity, economic growth, employment creation, and more adequate consumer supplies would all reinforce each other and stimulate more positive orientations to production by workers, managers, owners, and investors.

The JLP, in effect, agreed entirely with both the prevailing IMF and World Bank views on what sort of economic strategies are likely to show results in Third World economies that face the problems that have been endemic in Jamaica and other Caribbean territories in the 1970s. The key to the JLP approach that parallels and agrees with the export-oriented stabilization policies of several South American economies, is the ideal of Jamaica earning its way out of the crisis by a combination of foreign investment and a reallocation of resources from import-substitution to exports.

The first task was to obtain balance of payments support through negotiating loan funding, given the fact that the earlier PNP government had broken off relations with the IMF in May of 1980 and had been unable to secure adequate loans from other sources in spite of extensive efforts by the PNP in seeking loans from private foreign banks and socialist and Third World countries. Without such loan funding the manufacturing sector, which employs 80,000 workers, would have to be shut down for factors relating to raw material shortages. Basic goods imports such as drugs, flour, cornmeal, and building materials could also not be imported. The foreign exchange shortage was rendered even more acute because as the shortage increased, the PNP government had secured advanced payments of the levy from the bauxite multinationals which left a serious cash flow problem in foreign exchange budget for the new government. The pileup of unpaid debts created by the absence of foreign exchange also meant that if loan funding could not have been secured, Jamaica's financial standing would have deteriorated due to its failure to pay debts incurred by the earlier government from the IMF, private overseas banks, and other such sources.

The JLP had in fact anticipated an election victory. Public opinion polls conducted by the author and published quarterly by the local newspaper, the *Daily Gleaner*, had consistently indicated that the JLP was likely to win the election by a wide margin. Even before the change of government and while it was still the official opposition party, the JLP leader, Seaga entered into discussions with both IMF and U.S. government officials with a view to shortening the waiting period for loans once the election was held and the party elected to office.

A new IMF loan of U.S. $625 million was secured over a three-year period in addition to a U.S. $350 million loan from the consortium of Western country interests, the Caribbean Group for Co-operation in Economic Development, chaired by the World Bank. Close ties established with the new U.S. Republican presidency and JLP support for the overall regional foreign policy designs of the Reagan administration secured an increase of U.S. economic aid from U.S. $23 million in 1980 to U.S. $93 million in 1981. The Caribbean Basin initiative of the Reagan government added another $50 million in 1982 and a total of $150 million in aid was projected for 1983.

The large increases in non-IMF loans meant that the JLP had secured enough financing to avoid having to face the problem of laying off public sector workers to reduce the budget deficit which was the center of the IMF-PNP controversy in 1980. The new IMF agreement did not relax the usual terms and conditionalities. What was different was the fact that the new administration shared the fiscal and economic policy thinking of the IMF technocrats and a harmonious relationship replaced the antagonisms of the PNP period. This new relationship increased the credibility and creditworthiness of the new government in the eyes of overseas investors, bankers, and creditors. U.S. backing was critical in significantly increasing the flow of aid to Jamaica.

Like the PNP, however, the JLP government took the view that continued large scale overseas borrowing was a necessary feature of any effort at achieving economic recovery. The active support for the new JLP government by the Reagan administration and the capitalist and "free-enterprise" ideology of the Seaga-led JLP government increased its ability to borrow from capitalist sources over and above the level of access to loan funding available to the socialist PNP government.

The change of government raised the confidence of the Jamaican bourgeoisie who now felt that a climate of confidence had been restored between the public and private sectors with the defeat of socialism in the elections and the takeover of the government by Prime Minister Seaga who both endorsed a capitalist ideology without apology but also treated the task of public management as if it were a business venture in which profitability, sound fiscal management, and efficiency were major goals in public sector activities. A survey carried out by the author among business executives in 252 companies between August and September 1981 confirmed the optimism with which the private sector interests responded to the change of government. Sixty-seven percent of the executives interviewed expressed intentions to expand their business activities subject, of course, to the availability of foreign exchange. Ninety percent expressed overall support for the policy directions being pursued by the new JLP government. Foreign exchange availability was seen as the major problem. Although much more was now available compared to 1980, the changed business climate and the start-up of new areas of economic activity increased the demand for foreign exchange over and above the increased supply. Of these executives in private sector firms 74 percent, therefore, complained about the inadequacy of foreign exchange as being the major obstacle to business expansion and the plans they had for increased output and employment.

With increased overseas borrowing and especially increased loans from the United States, the Seaga government quickly secured large increases in imported food and basic consumer items so as to remove the persistent problem of shortages faced by consumers in the earlier period. PL480 U.S. food aid, for example, doubled between 1980 and 1982. Empty shelves in rural shops and supermarkets were now filled. The estimated 50 percent of rural retail and wholesale shops that closed due to shortages during the PNP years were now reopened as supplies of consumer goods virtually doubled in volume and variety between 1980 and 1981.

These increased consumer goods supplies had two quite divergent effects on the economy. First of all, there was a dramatic fall in food prices as imported food items competed with locally produced food and bid down the price of the latter below the overall inflation level, in contrast to the PNP years when local food prices increased at a faster rate than the overall price index. High priced black markets were wiped out. The balancing of supply with demand by this import policy enabled the JLP government to bring down inflation from 27 to 5 percent, thereby achieving a most remarkable stabilizing of prices in the economy and the lowest level of inflation achieved in Jamaica since 1973.

The other effect was that the income flow to domestic food producers declined as they had to cut prices, as sales declined, and as they had to face competition from food imports. Urban consumers clearly benefited at the expense of rural small farmers and the long- or medium-term effect might be a negative and undesirable decline in local food production by small farmers who might not be able to shift output to overseas markets. In the short run these rural petty commodity producers have been rendered worse off by these JLP policies. Means, therefore, have to be found to expand domestic consumer buying to increase the demand for local food production.

On the other hand, the JLP had been able to stabilize basic goods prices in urban areas, thereby pacifying the militancy of unionized workers whose strike levels doubled during the Manley years. With a lower level of inflation the new JLP government was able to abandon the wage guidelines and to induce public sector workers to accept modest pay increases (15%) after they waited several years for an increase and as a trade-off for no lay-offs in the public sector. With a few exceptions wage settlements in the private sector were mainly within a 20% to 30% range although there are no wage guidelines and although workers have experienced a huge 30% decline in real purchasing power in the earlier period of the 1970s.

Pressure for importation of both consumer and producers' goods served to aggravate the balance of payments problem in the short run due to the time required to put in place an increased capacity to export. Export earnings have not improved. With export agriculture in decline, the balance of payments will remain a big problem until new industries and areas of production are opened up and other existing dollar earners are expanded to increase the revenue side of the foreign exchange budget. Large inflows of private foreign investment are going to be necessary to facilitate any such development and there is a great deal of uncertainty surrounding how much long-term capital inflows will be attracted to the JLP's initiative to induce private foreign investment, due to high interest rates in the United States.

Trading on the favorable North America image projected by his government's close relationship to the Reagan presidency and its enthusiastic support by the Reagan administration, Seaga set up a joint U.S.–Jamaica promotional committee to attract foreign investment. The Committee is chaired jointly by U.S. businessman David Rockefeller of Chase Manhattan Bank and Jamaican businessman Carlton Alexander, one of the more important of the leaders of the Jamaican business community. Between January and June 1981, 217 foreign investment projects and 135 local projects were submitted for processing, feasibility study, and assessment of viability. Up to March 1982 the list of (foreign) prospective investment projects had grown to 300 with a total potential capital inflow of U.S. $600 million. At least a third of these projects are planned for implementation during 1982. If most of these projects come to fruition, there should be some increase in job creation in the economy mainly in the areas of manufacturing, construction, and agriculture. To date unemployment remains as high as it was in the final years of the Manley government in the 1970s and any major initiative to reduce it will have to wait for a much larger scale of investment activity than has been occurring.

The JLP government has not been able to dismantle the infrastructure of state regulation of the economy. The continued shortage of foreign exchange makes continued licensing of imports necessary to ration what is available to priority areas. After the large increase in consumer goods experienced in the upturn of import levels in 1981, a decision has been taken to limit further increases in consumer goods imports and to allocate most of the additional foreign exchange inflows entirely to capital goods and raw materials. The JLP has, however, begun the process of scaling down government controls of imports by reducing the number of imports requiring import license. The policy is to have a phased reduction of the list of items requiring import licenses until, foreign exchange permiting, the list is entirely eliminated.

The JLP relaxed the regime of controls over rents with the result that middle and lower middle income housing prices and rents (repressed during the PNP period) escalated between a range of 50 to 200 percent increases. As a result the JLP took the decision to roll back rentals to the pre-election levels in order to control the impact on the cost of living.

In spite of the pre-election attacks on the State Trading Corporation by the JLP, the Corporation continues to function as the JLP leadership came to recognize its important role: as an efficient bulk buyer of basic food items that is able to pass on lower prices to the Jamaican consumer. Pragmatism prevailed over ideology, thereby indicating the degree of policy flexibility that remains regardless of the ideological polarization between the two political parties.

Divestment of government-owned enterprises was set in motion by the JLP government but in most cases leasehold rather than outright sale is being used as the basis for passing these enterprises from government to private management. The process of divestment is not as rapid as was anticipated, as with the exception of the hotels and a few other such commercially viable enterprises, some of the public enterprises that the government wishes to pass over to private management are not likely to be viable in terms of profitability.

The heavily indebted sugar co-ops were dismantled by the JLP but they were passed over to state management by the government-owned National Sugar Company. A decision was taken to dismantle the bankrupt state-owned urban bus company, the Jamaica Omnibus Services, and to enable private sector enterprises (mainly petty capitalist minibus operators) to fully take over transportation services in the capital city.

The JLP's economic policies center around an attempt to shift the economy from import-substitution towards a restructuring in the direction of an export orientation combined with an openly competitive flow of import trade. Local entrepreneurs accustomed to operating within protected markets are reluctant to support the policy but have no choice as without an increase in export capability the economy will have no prospect of economic recovery. The opening up of the free trade access to the U.S. market facilitated by the Reagan Basin Plan Initiative and the prospects of significant inflows of foreign investment provide an optimal context for this difficult restructuring to be attempted.

Such a restructuring is, however, a long-term strategy and requires careful planning, close public sector and private sector collaboration, and adequate financing of the structural adjustments.

Important political changes followed from the change of government. The JLP broke diplomatic ties with Cuba as the cold war hostilities in the region intensified both in the Caribbean and in Central America. Jamaica has moved full circle from being a Cuban ally under Manley to being a militant and activist ally in the U.S. regional anti-Communist crusade.

The political style has also changed. An emphasis on populism and political mobilization has given way to an emphasis on technocratic efficiency. The pursuit of long-run economic goals that can enhance economic recovery has been substituted for populist ideological posturing that seeks to maximize short-run political popularity, often at the expense of rational economic policies.

The JLP has set its sights on trying to remove the socialist strategies and infrastructure of state economic management, which are legacies of the Manley years. Given the long-term nature of the structural economic changes being attempted and the clear need for the state to engineer and guide the process of change, it seems to me that what the JLP is likely to leave behind after it loses power sometime in the future is not a full return to a low level of state economic intervention but continued medium levels of state economic intervention combined with a state capitalist system where the state uses its economic power to aid capital.

JLP POLICY PROBLEMS

Between the guarded optimism of the first two years of the JLP regime, in which an increased momentum of economic activity was established, and 1984 some major policy problems emerged that neutralized the government's economic initiatives, restored the climate of gloom and despair of the 1970s, and severely weakened the political credibility of the Seaga government. Additionally, a major political crisis developed in 1983 which has left the political system in a state of uncertainty.

A sharp decline in bauxite earnings between 1981 and 1983 combined with large increases in imports triggered a major balance-of-payments crisis. The government was forced to carry through a massive devaluation of the Jamaican dollar and to abandon the parallel market currency arrangements. The first six months of 1984 generated a 20 percent increase in the cost of living that brought the economy virtually to a standstill. As costs escalated and purchasing power dwindled consumer demand fell rapidly for all consumer goods.

The downturn in bauxite earnings also triggered a crisis in the public sector in that the gap between revenue and expenditure widened and the IMF pressured the government into agreeing to lay off over 6000 government workers and to cut back critical social and public services, such as health, education, low income housing, and all areas of local government activities relating to roads, water supply, and other such basic services. As services deteriorated and layoffs were added to an already large body of unemployed, the public's confidence in the government declined to unprecedented low levels and pessimism replaced the cautious hopes citizens had of an economic recovery.

As the foreign exchange crisis deepened, private sector interests tried to export large quantities of foreign currency thereby aggravating an already bad situation. The government reacted by imprisoning one businessman and his wife for exporting currency in transactions that involved many large corporate enterprises. Discovery of extensive currency racketeering in the private sector led to proposals to tighten up on the laws governing foreign currency and this created considerable tensions between the government and the private sector.

In order to reduce the demand for imported goods and stabilize the currency, the Seaga government imposed tight monetary policies that hiked interest rates and drastically reduced bank credit. This had the effect of bringing the momentum of private sector economic activity to a crawl and wiped out the demand for housing while imposing great hardships on all smaller business enterprises and severe cash flow problems throughout the economy. The priority that was being given to economic stabilization overturned the expectations and policies for growth and this had the effect of demoralizing the private sector as their sales and profits declined rapidly.

Big increases in taxes in the 1984–85 fiscal year designed to collect over $100 million in new taxation added further to the pressures on consumers and on the business community. Subsidies on basic food items had to be removed and in many areas government departments and enterprises could not purchase equipment and supplies, pay bills and cover essential expenses as the revenue and earnings crisis escalated in the public sector.

Continued high interest rates in the United States reduced the expected inflow of foreign exchange in the form of hard currency investments. Additionally, serious protectionist policies developed in the lucrative Trinidadian market for the local manufacturing sector and the U.S. market (opened by the C.B.I. policies) in the area of garment exports and food-processing commodities. Export earnings from traditional agriculture declined even further and although exports of fresh fruits and vegetables to the United States increased appreciably the impact was negated by the overall decline in hard currency earnings in most areas of the economy.

As the price of locally produced goods escalated in response to the devaluation and the massive markups, the demand for imports continued to rise leading to large scale illegal imports that further weakened the domestic market for locally produced goods. Excessive imports between 1981 and 1983 encouraged by the government's open economy policy and policies of liberalizing imports in response to World Bank and IMF structural adjustment prescriptions posed real problems for local manufacturers and small farmers. In 1982 domestic agriculture declined in output by some 20 percent and the sales of local manufactured items dropped by levels varying from 20 to 30 percent.

The unpredictability surrounding currency values following the policy of allowing the Jamaican dollar to float according to supply and demand for U.S. dollars led to increased currency speculation and uncertainty in business transactions which had a negative effect on investment. As the pressures built up on the local private sector this created a crisis of confidence for the government as the credibility of Seaga's economic policies declined and open resentment against the policy goals of the government replaced the spirit of cooperation that emerged in public and private sector dealings in 1981. Constant changes in monetary, fiscal, and trade policies caused by the continuing crisis led many private sector persons to lose confidence in the government and to conclude that the prime minister was both confused and incompetent at managing the nation's affairs. Seaga's image of being a financial wizard evaporated and the rumor channels of informal communication networks disseminated belittling stories about his failures to cope with the country's financial difficulties.

By the middle of 1984 a deep gloom about the prospects for economic recovery had become the dominant mood throughout the economy. The working class and the consumers who were buffeted by massive price increases began openly to express the view that life was now much harsher for them than under the Manley regime. The high profile entry of foreign experts at salaries that were between 10 to 20 times larger than what was earned by professionals in most public enterprises and government departments caused deep resentment among local professionals and public servants and led to accusations that the Seaga government

was catering only to foreigners. The unfortunate timing of these technical assistance arrangements financed largely by World Bank loans that
coincided with massive layoffs in the public sector excited great local
resentment.

A political survey carried out by the author in December 1983 found
that only 31 percent of the electorate continued to have any confidence
in the JLP government's economic policies, while 53 percent were convinced that these policies had either failed or were not likely to produce
any positive results. Another survey done in October 1983 established
that as much as 52 percent of the electorate had lost hope that life in
Jamaica would get any better over the next five to ten years, while a
much smaller 39 percent entertained cautious hopes that things might
improve. This latter political survey also found that 46 percent of the public rated the JLP government's policy performance as poor or very poor.
Thirty-seven percent thought that the performance was not bad and indicated a mixture of successes and failures, while only 17 percent thought
that the policy performance was good. When asked about whether the
JLP government was doing better or worse than the previous Manley
government in the 1970s, 40 percent expressed the view that Seaga's
government was doing worse, 23 percent thought that the performances
were similar or about the same, and 37 percent took the view that
Seaga's government was doing better.

As a result of this decline in the level of confidence in the policies
of the JLP government, political support for it fell considerably behind
the high 1980–81 levels of popularity and the opposition PNP moved
ahead of the governing JLP in popularity and voter support. The crisis
in Grenada had the effect of raising fears that if the PNP were re-elected,
similar leftist disorder might develop in Jamaica and the political community rallied behind Seaga's militant proinvasion foreign policy as fears
of Cuba and Communism were rekindled. This temporary boost in JLP
popular support toward the end of 1983 induced the JLP to call a snap
election and to hold the election on the old voters list. The PNP's refusal
to contest the election resulted in a one party parliament in which JLP
representatives won all the parliamentary seats.

Fears about large scale political violence by PNP supporters or the
challenging of the legitimacy of the JLP government have not material-
ized. In spite of the great economic hardships being experienced by the
rural and urban poor, there has been no social unrest or political turmoil
such as has developed in Chile, Brazil, Argentina, Peru, and a long list
of other Third World states experiencing severe economic problems.

Since losing the 1980 elections the PNP has moved ideologically back
to the center as the party moderates have displaced most of the leftists
and Manley himself has moderated and restrained his rhetoric and leftist political leanings. While he continues to denounce U.S. President Rea-

gan, support the Nicaraguan revolution, and extol the virtues of friendship with Cuba, both his party and himself have toned down their anti-imperialism and anti-U.S. posturing and have been actively seeking a re-embrace of U.S. liberal democrats to leave the door open for an accommodation with the United States if and when they are re-elected.

Politically, the PNP has tried to restrain and contain pressures for open confrontation with the government and to avoid militant protest action over unpopular government measures such as price increases. The rationale seems to be that any political disorder could get completely out of control and give the government and its conservative international support an excuse to suspend constitutional rights and to justify harsh military measures that could reduce the chances of free elections in the near future. This trend was broken in January 1985 when the PNP organized roadblocks to protest an increase in petroleum prices.

The absence of overt expressions of political protest and social unrest between 1980 and 1984 also reflects the mood of cynicism, hopelessness, and lack of faith in politicians, causes, and leaders that has become the basis of a rapid disinterest in politics throughout the country. Individual survival concerns have induced a significant development of political apathy and withdrawal which, added to the recency of memories about the policy failures of the Manley years, generate a feeling of deep resignation among the alienated, the disillusioned, and the disaffected. Although the PNP is ahead of the JLP in the polls, support for the PNP is lukewarm rather than intense, as the PNP up to the middle months of 1984 had yet to reactivate enthusiastic mass support in spite of its majority position and likely victory in any forthcoming parliamentary or local government elections.

To a remarkable degree the polarization between the two parties has been reduced. The PNP in opposition has acknowledged many of its political errors and Manley has been making overtures towards private sector interests to re-establish a climate of mutual trust between that section of the elite and the PNP. The PNP criticisms of JLP policy failures have de-emphasized ideological attacks and have concentrated on highlighting policy errors and their economic and social consequences. Indeed, the main thrust of the criticism has centered on challenging the JLP image as a party with managerial and financial competence rather than on the conservative orientation of the JLP leadership. Of course, both the mass public and the PNP leadership and activists have attacked the JLP leaders for not being sufficiently concerned with the suffering of the poor, while the PNP is constantly projected as the party most interested in the welfare of the masses.

The electorate has increasingly scaled down their expectations for dramatic policy changes and improvements in their quality of life after the painful period of a decade of adjustments and disillusionment with broken political promises from both parties. Moreso than any other political system in the region, the Jamaican political community has suffered severe economic and social hardships without any political upheavals. This has been aided by the degree to which both sets of party leaders have been gradually admitting that the country's problems are not likely to be solved by any simple political solutions or ideological formulas.

Of course, other factors have contributed to the political calm in Jamaica which has deviated from most of the gloomy forecasts for political and social turmoil. The governing JLP party has intimidated groups with an interest in protest action with a strong presence of heavily armed political mercenaries who killed several ghetto youth in one JLP community where plans were being put together for mounting a protest march on the country's parliament to dramatize complaints about joblessness and bias in the allocation of construction work on a major public sector building project.

The militant anti-Communist position of Prime Minister Seaga and his known strong support from U.S. President Reagan have triggered fears within the leftist minority groups in the society that any overt political turmoil mobilized by them could give the JLP an excuse for political repression against the left with full U.S. backing. After the liquidation of the remains of the Grenada revolution following the assassination of Prime Minister Bishop, the left in Jamaica and the Caribbean generally was thrown on the defensive. The failure of Cuba to either stand up to the United States or to risk an open confrontation with Reagan by coming to the defense of the Grenadian revolution has left deep anxieties among leftists in the region who feel exposed to U.S. and Reagan designs for anti-Communist offensives in the Caribbean. Additionally, Seaga has been a tough, forthright, strong and confident leader of government business who has not been afraid to make unpopular decisions and has shown no tendency to yield to opposition pressures. The left opposition within the PNP and among small fringe groups like the fledgling Communist Workers Party of Jamaica see Seaga as a ruthless leader who enjoys Washington's support and should not be provoked into taking measures to decimate the already weak support for leftist politics in the country.

The failure of the Grenadian revolution and the evident economic and social problems in Cuba arising from the massive migration from that country to Florida have destroyed the credibility of the leftist message that there exists a promising hopeful and better alternative to the existing capitalist political economies in the region. Instead of economic and social hardships creating a revival of leftist political trends, the main reactions have been increasing violent crimes against property and persons and a groundswell of support for religion and an increasing church membership as citizens lose faith in secular political and economic deliverance from their problems. The Communist WPJ, for example, has been unable to increase its popular vote strength beyond 2 percent in spite of tremendous islandwide organizational activity and the severity of the economic hardships facing the people.

Contrary to conventional theories about social deprivation leading to political unrest, in the Jamaican case the penetration of the poor communities by the main political parties and the system of dependence on political patronage increase the ties of dependency between the very poor and the party political machines during periods of economic hardship as that provides the only channel of access to benefits and social and economic opportunities for the very poor. Even when parties are in opposition and have no patronage to distribute, poor communities look to them for future patronage benefits and invest tremendous loyalty in those political machines out of a hope and expectation of realizing concrete benefits in the future. Poverty and increasing immiserization, therefore, increases the capacity of the middle class-controlled party machines to control the poor. The critical mass of heavily armed ghetto youth who become mercenaries working for both dominant political parties serve as a major deterrant or demobilization force that cools any enthusiasm by potential militant activists (unconnected to either the PNP or the JLP) who might wish to organize protest action.

All of these factors, added to the narrowing of differences between the main party leaders on ideology and policy, have sustained political stability in a period when unrest and turmoil could easily have been the reaction to the political displacement of the PNP from the parliament and the severe economic hardships that the majority have had to cope with since the late 1970s.

As the economic crisis has deepened, dependence on foreign economic and political aid has increased. The reality that aid inflows, access to markets, technological and capital transfers, and technical and financial support from international institutions and friendly governments have become necessities until the economy becomes more self-sustaining has forced both PNP and JLP leaders to seek out external allies and sources of assistance. The massively growing national debt and the vicious circle of dependence on debt financing have demoralized and weakened national confidence and have opened the door for foreign influences to exercise decisive influence over economic and social policies. In a real sense, the World Bank, the IMF, and Washington have been more important in shaping the direction of economic and social policies in the country since 1980 than any domestic interest, pressure group, or source of policy influence. While a re-elected PNP government under Manley is unlikely to so easily fit into a silent surrender of sovereignty, economic realities and deepening financial dependence in the face of a weakening capacity to earn foreign exchange will ensure continuing foreign influences over economic and social policies regardless of which party governs.

The real underlying factor behind the continuing economic crisis in the Jamaican economy and the related manifestations of political stress and polarization is the failure to expand and retain hard currency earnings. Both the PNP and the JLP have come to accept the necessity for a major economic policy emphasis on exports, although the parties are likely to pursue that goal with different policy means. The task of restructuring the economy to make it more export-oriented is a long-term one and is not amenable either to short-term solutions or simple ideological formulas. The political traditions of the country have been based on populism, which implies political solutions to economic and social problems. Manley tried with a socialist formula and failed to expand the export earnings sector which is the major determinant of economic activity in any small open economy. Seaga has similarly failed, although his export-oriented policies have been more carefully thought out and are likely to show long-run, impressive gains in the future. The central problem is that the private sector is weak, the state sector is corrupt and inefficient, and the petty commodity sectors lack mastery of modern technology. The political and economic timetables have been in fundamental conflict. The political leaders have promised short-run results in keeping with the short-run electoral political cycle. The economic problem demands a long-run solution.

The low level of understanding of the structural bases of the economic problems means that the political directorate runs into a credibility problem as it attracts blame and criticism because the people see no short-term positive gains in economic policy results and most citizens either blindly follow the party leaders' policy prescriptions or are confused regarding whether the policy means being adopted will have the desired long-run flow of positive changes and benefits. The scaling down of expectations and adjustments to the fact that the problems are chronic and deep-seated and not amenable to simple solutions has reduced the contradiction between the short-term political timetable and the longer-term timetable for economic recovery. Sustaining political order and stability under these conditions of stress will demand a more enlightened and informed electorate that is more able to understand the links between economic and social policies and economic trends in the environment. For the moment, it is the support for the major political parties and their leaders that avoids the turmoil and instability that plagued so many other countries in the region experiencing severe economic and social hardships.

THE CBI

The U.S.-Caribbean Basin Initiative which has opened up for Jamaica and the English-speaking Caribbean (and most of Central America) duty-free access to the U.S. market for a wide range of exports provides a strong incentive for shifting economic policy management in Jamaica more toward export-led growth. Indeed, this has been the single most important factor influencing the new economic policy directions of the Seaga regime. After one full year of this enlarged opportunity for exports to the United States, it is evident that the C.B.I. is not likely to have a major impact on the Jamaican economy.

The major area of increased exports to the United States are garments and winter vegetables. Expanded garment exports have been built around the 807 program based on utilizing cheap labor to assemble garments on contract to U.S. firms. By early 1985, some 7000 jobs were created in approximately 40 such enterprises. There has been a rapid growth of winter vegetable production that is projected to become a major source of foreign exchange earnings in the 1980s. Both of these opportunities for exports existed prior to the CBI.

The areas of local manufacturing production that could provide the basis for large exports into the U.S. market (shoes, leather goods, footwear, locally produced clothing) have all been excluded from duty-free CBI provisions in order to protect jobs in the United States. In addition, most other areas of Jamaican manufacturing production are not likely to be able to compete against Far East and Mexican or Brazilian exports into the U.S. market.

For the 12-month period ending December 1984, nonoil imports to the United States from CBI beneficiary countries in the region increased by 19 percent which was a mere 2 percent above the overall increase in U.S. exports for the region as a whole and including the many Latin American countries in the Southern Cone which are not CBI beneficiaries. Clearly, the increase in exports to the United States reflects the strong U.S. dollar and the trend toward increasing U.S. import dependence. Indeed, the level of Caribbean increased sales to the United States is relatively modest compared to increased U.S. exports from the Far East. While it may be premature to judge the likely long-run impact of the CBI trade provisions on the Jamaican economy, there is no evidence indicating that its impact is likely to be a significant beneficiary one. The main reason is that even with these expanded opportunities for export the Jamaican economy remains highly uncompetitive in terms of the quality of its products outside of the areas of traditional agricultural commodities such as coffee and rum and nontraditional agricultural exports such as winter vegetables.

THE BAUXITE CRISIS

A new crisis emerged in the Jamaican economy with the decline of the country's main source of foreign exchange earnings, the bauxite industry. This decline began in 1983 and accelerated in 1984 with the closure of two major bauxite companies (Reynolds and Alcoa) and is threatened even further with a likely closure of another company (Alpart). By the end of 1985, bauxite and alumina production is likely to be reduced to less than 50 percent of what it was in the 1970s. The impact is likely to aggravate the country's revenue and foreign exchange problems and render even more precarious the cautious hopes policy makers were projecting for an economic recovery in the 1980s.

This new development in bauxite reflects chronic oversupply on the world market, the increasing uncompetitiveness of U.S.-based aluminum production, the high cost of Jamaican bauxite due to the bauxite levy imposed by the Manley government in 1974, and increasing competition from other bauxite exporters, such as Guineau, Australia, and Brazil.

The consequent rapid fall in foreign exchange earnings is not likely to be offset by any gains in increased tourism and export earnings, given the economy's traditional 70 percent dependence on bauxite for foreign exchange earnings. The relatively slow rate of diversification of export earnings and the modest results from the Seaga government's efforts to attract foreign capital in export-oriented sectors of the economy all mean that the country's living standards are likely to fall very rapidly over the next few years and the problems of economic management are going to become even more crisis prone than they have been in the 1970s and early 1980s.

All of this means that the Jamaican political system faces an even greater challenge over the immediate future to maintain stability and to direct the rebuilding of this aging economy. Given the weak local private sector, the adverse world economic climate, the country's massive debt burden, the limited gains likely to come from CBI and limited interest of foreign investors in Jamaica, that challenge is an awesome one that will demand high levels of political maturity, and strong leadership, and political institutions to avert instability.

NOTES

1. The idea that the parties represented a deliberate and self-conscious multiclass coalition was first developed in Carl Stone, *Class Race and Political Behaviour in Urban Jamaica*, Kingston, Jamaica: Institute of Social and Economic Research, 1973.

2. See Carl Stone, *Democracy and Clientelism in Jamaica*, New Brunswick, N.J.: Transaction Books, 1980.

3. See Carl Stone, *Democracy and Clientelism*, op. cit.

4. Although the JLP was a member of the nonaligned movement, its position was mainly pro-Western and pro-United States on global issues, while adopting Third World positions on South Africa.

5. This U.N. vote was analyzed in detail in Carl Stone, *Profiles of Power in the Caribbean*, Philadelphia: ISHI, forthcoming.

6. See R. Ulyanovsky, *Socialism and the Newly Independent Nations*, Moscow: Progress Publishers, 1974, for a discussion of this concept.

9

CONCLUSION

The growing body of political analysis in Jamaica has produced two sharply polarized pictures of Jamaican democracy. One view[1] sees the country as having developed political stability, strong institutions, and responsive leaders who both enjoy strong mass support and have been genuinely trying to use public policy to uplift and develop the country. The second[2] view portrays Jamaica as a highly unstable and explosive society in which democracy has been used and manipulated by middle class leaders to perpetuate the power and privileges of the rich while exploiting the poor and failing to address the agenda of radical policy changes necessary to develop the country in the interests of the majority classes.

These points of view use quite different criteria to judge the success or failure of Jamaican democracy. Those who subscribe to the positive view emphasize the progress the country has made since the early plantation and colonial periods and examine the agenda of social, economic, and political gains that have accompanied the transition from a planter-dominated political system to a parliamentary democracy. The analysts who have formulated the more negative view have tended to de-emphasize these changes and to portray the political system as serving to perpetuate an evil capitalist system, class and racial exploitation, domination by foreign capital, and economic backwardness. All of these evils can only be eliminated by the development of Marxist-Leninist or non-capitalist paths towards development. Such a path, it is often suggested, will only materialize after the exploited masses take hold of their destinies by overthrowing bourgeois democracy. Such writers, therefore, insist that Jamaican democracy is fragile and unstable in that once the masses begin to see through the extent of their exploitation and begin to unite as a single coherent social class, Jamaican democracy will collapse under the weight of revolutionary pressures. In the meantime and until the revolution arrives, all attempts at policy reforms, social change, and economic development are seen as doomed to the failure of merely perpetuating capitalism which lies at the root of the country's under-development and the exploitation of its people. The political parties and their leaders are portrayed as being stooges of U.S. imperialism and the local capitalists and as being incapable of providing the type of leader-ship necessary to promote national development. Where a Marxist ideo-logical frame of reference is not the basis for analysis, the tendency is to view the society as being pathological[3] in its perpetuation of extreme inequalities and in its infection with social maladies that can be traced back to the early slave plantation period. Such inherent social weak-nesses can only be cleansed when the masses seize power from the mid-dle class and the privileged.

Any attempt to assess carefully the process of institution building, the policy reforms and changes, the evolution of the political power structure, and the development of democratic institutions cannot but ar-rive at conclusions that challenge the distorted view of the country's po-litical and social systems as not having changed fundamentally in the period since the 1930s.

A rigid caste-like social structure supported by a planter-dominated aristocratic state, racism, and a master-servant ideology that denies the inherent worth and capacity for growth and development among the black majority have been challenged by forces of political and social change. Expansion and diversification of the country's economy in the postwar period have provided opportunities for upward social mobility for blacks into the expanding middle class by way of the professions and the civil service and more recently through the opening up of opportu-nities in managerial and technical positions in the private sector. As the economy has grown, the demand for skilled jobs has created a stratum of better off wage workers whose living standards have improved con-siderably in the postwar period. Higglers, farmers, and small business-men have aggressively carved out small areas of prosperous self-employment which have enlarged the number of middle income earners.

As the upper reaches of the professions have become accessible to blacks with high education and the middle class has come to consist mainly of blacks, the earlier trends of an obsession with race have dis-appeared. The militant Rastafarian movement has now been absorbed into the mainstream of Jamaican society. The country's cultural and ar-tistic expressions have come more and more to reflect the African, black, folk, and lower class social experience, especially in music and dance, and to de-emphasize European influences. The grass roots culture has been fully articulated by the heavily Rastafarian-influenced reggae mu-sic symbolized by the creative musical genius of the late reggae star Bob

Marley, who rose from the urban ghetto of Trench Town to become an internationally recognized pop-star. Social relations are now more free and egalitarian across the social class boundaries as the lower classes have aggressively asserted their self-worth in the society. The secret ballot has given some real power to the people to choose political leaders and they have used that power to elect leaders likely to promote economic and social policies that bring benefits.

Social democratic tendencies have inspired a major growth of social policies in the postwar period that have raised the quality of life of the majority classes in the areas of health and education. The role of government in the economy has enlarged considerably over that period to protect the national interest, to monitor and regulate the economic market, to assist weak areas of the economy with economic services (small farmers, craft producers), and to develop infrastructure and services needed to expand the economy.

The early postwar period witnessed major progress in the economic, political, and social spheres up to independence. Since then, some major problem areas have emerged to slow down the path of progress. What began as a dynamic capitalist class that seemed to be moving the economy into a path towards modernization has revealed basic weaknesses in its willingness to risk capital, to innovate, and to restructure an economy. This economy was built in a period of cheap energy and low import prices and has not been able either to increase its export earnings to keep pace with import needs or to innovate and expand domestic production or reduce the dependence on imports. As a result, open unemployment has grown to massive levels of 28 percent of the labor force and crime and social violence have increased proportionately.

An escalation of political violence threatens stability as armies of unemployed youth turn to crime, have access to guns through the U.S.—Jamaica drug trade or through political parties, and have developed a lifestyle built around street gangs, guns, drugs, and violence. As a result, the conduct of elections has produced widespread killings and destruction of property, especially in urban areas in the Kingston and lower St. Andrew areas where militant PNP-supporting and JLP-supporting poor communities confront each other.

As the economy has faltered and the income base has shrunk alongside the capacity to pay for imported goods and services, the country has borrowed massively from international banks and multilateral financial institutions (IMF, World Bank, and others) while living standards have fallen since the 1970s. As a result, major new directions have occurred in the area of public policy. Successive PNP and JLP governments have had to accept rigidly conservative fiscal and monetary policies as a condition for external borrowing as well as pressures for scaling down big government and reducing the active and interventionist role of the state in the economy.

These external pressures have begun to undermine the social democratic tradition of state economic intervention, large subsidies, and other income transfers benefiting the poorer classes, the high commitment to expanding and improving social services, and the rapid growth of the public sector. Under the banner of deregulation, the Seaga regime that came to power in 1980, introduced a process of divesting state enterprises, cutting back social services, reducing public sector employment, and substituting free market or laissez-faire-type economic management for state regulation and the opening up of the economy through import liberalization in place of tight import controls. On the other hand, massive increases in U.S. aid dependence to finance capital development needs in the public sector and a new food aid welfare program have given Washington a major means of controlling the overall direction of economic and social policy. These policy changes are, however, likely to merely scale down and reduce the role of government in the economy to a level that is within the means of the economy's resources and within the capability of the public sector to manage. The balance of political and social forces supporting big government and an active role for the state in the economy will limit how far these changes can go.

Throughout the 1970s and the early 1980s the political system coped with the pressures of high unemployment, shortages of consumer goods, electoral violence, and economic stagnation. Stability was maintained and the democratic process, while under threat from violence and unregulated PNP and JLP confrontations, functioned well by permitting elections to take place that changed unpopular governments.

In spite of considerable hardships and social pressures, there have been only minor eruptions of social disorder and no major political turmoil apart from election violence and crime. Support for the party system remains strong although more voters are making choices based on issues rather than by blind party loyalties.

The majority of the Jamaican people have come to value the democratic system of mananging power and it is therefore most unlikely that these political insititutions will collapse or crumble due to diminishing mass support or revolutionary pressures from angry poor people who, some predict, will lose faith in the leaders and seek violently to take hold of power. The party systems have become institutionalized in the society and the roots of support for the leaders and the parties go very deep, especially in the poorest communities. It is indeed among the middle class, from which the radical intelligentsia springs, that there is indeed a great deal of cynicism and distrust toward the political leaders and party machines and low levels of commitment to the political institutions. Moreover, the middle class is being distanced from party politics through fear of political violence. As James Mau[4] has noted in his book on Jamaica, the myth of the threatening masses is an artifact of the anxieties and insecurities of the middle class and the privileged who mis-understand and are intimidated by the aggressive social behavior of the lower classes. The removal of the old patterns of class deference and fear of the rich and the highly educated by the lower social classes and the more assertive and confident manner of the poorer classes have been misrepresented to mean a threat to the political and social order. The writings of the intelligentsia who confidently predict the breakup of the present political social order due to expected violence from the poor are merely echoing an ideologically radical version of the anxieties and fears of lower class violence that have dominated the thoughts of the middle class and the privileged since slavery.

The negative view of Jamaican democracy distorts reality in order to delegitimize the existing political system and to create an adversary ideo-logical climate conducive to the emergence of new political leadership from the ranks of the radical intelligentsia. These self-serving polemical analyses are intended to project Marxist intellectuals as the only hope for real positive change in favor of the majority classes in a society in which Marxism is seen as repudiating values that are central to the life-style and aspirations of the poor.

On the other hand, the positive picture of Jamaican democracy fails to deal adequately with the stresses and internal contradictions in the po-litical system. Jamaican democracy was established in a period of eco-nomic buoyancy and in a climate of optimism for economic and social changes. The stagnation of the economy since the early 1970s has se-verely challenged the credibility of the country's party leaders as they have not been able to either show a track record of good economic management or to deliver the accustomed flow of benefits to their sup-porters as the economic and income base of the society has declined.

But as the official economy has declined, a large informal economy has been emerging in the hands of growing numbers of self-employed hustlers who often operate beyond the reach of either government regu-lation or taxes. Neither state-managed socialism from above, as envi-sioned by the PNP of the 1970s, nor dynamic free enterprise capitalism as envisioned by JLP's Seaga has worked in Jamaica. Instead, the drug trade, higgling, illicit imports, and hustling activities of all sorts have emerged as the sources of new wealth and income in the country. But these developments neither provide wage employment on a significant scale and new inflows of taxes nor government revenue and hard cur-rency earnings that are passed into the government's Central Bank. The assumed capacity of government to regulate economic activities and to garner a proportion of income earned to finance public sector activity has been jeopardized and questioned by these developments.

The Jamaican democratic traditions are in fact coping with severe pressures (both internal and external). Fortunately the political system has the asset of flexible leaders able to adjust to changing and variable circumstances. The notion that this political system is due for imminent collapse has been articulated by University of the West Indies social scientists for the past two decades at least. Yet the absence of any evidence that such prospects are likely to materialize has no impact on the certainty with which every new spate of Marxist writings predict the doom and collapse of the political system.

The polarized ideological positions that emerged in the 1970s have been replaced by a closer distance between the two main parties (the PNP and the JLP), converging at the political center in the 1980s. This will give the Communist left in the WPJ a full opportunity to test how far it can generate mass support operating from a far left position and competing with two center parties, with one (the PNP) being slightly left of center and the other (the JLP) slightly right of center. Predictably, even the Communist WPJ sensing the unpopularity of far left positions has begun to tone down its hard line Marxist position in seeking to prepare for its first plunge into a parliamentary election due to be held in 1988.

Contrary to expectations and predictions, the PNP between 1980 and 1984 has behaved like a loyal and exemplary opposition giving the JLP free room in which to pursue its policies. To be sure, if the Seaga government lasts until 1988, the political cycle is likely to return to militant demands for social justice which are going to be angrily returned to the agenda of policy issues and political debate by the severe austerity measures and hurried efforts at installing conservative economic policy management under the tutelage of U.S. aid, the World Bank, and the IMF.

Predictably, this period of political quiescence will be replaced by a return to political activism in the late 1980s but by then the PNP will have recovered from its present period of leadership and ideological paralysis to assume national political leadership and direction once more. The real strength of the Jamaican parliamentary system is clearly to be found in the resourcefulness of the party leadership that have shown over the years a remarkable capacity for adapting to the changing moods and trends of the political community. As long as they continue to demonstrate the leadership strength of the level displayed by past and current party leaders, democracy will continue to grow in strength in spite of foreboding Marxist predictions about political collapse.

The political parties' task of public management will be made considerably easier if and when the local bourgeoisie rediscovers the entrepreneurial dynamism that inspired its expansion and growth in the early postwar years.

Some major weaknesses, however, exist in the country's democratic system and must be addressed in the future to improve the island's capability for managing power. The first relates to the subject of leadership.

The political parties are dominated by whoever happens to be the party leader to a degree that gives those leaders an excess of personal power for which they are accountable to no organ, body, or group within their respective parties. Internal party democracy exists in theory only as this pattern of personalized one man domination of party leadership stifles the emergence of responsible collective leadership. This failure to establish a pattern in which party power is shared by the principal leaders in a party acts as a disincentive for entry into political life because power is highly concentrated in the hands of individuals who retain that dominance for long periods of time. The high incidence of political violence acts as a further disincentive for entry into party politics on the part of middle class professionals. Paradoxically, therefore, at a time when the society is producing a wide diversity of professionally trained men and women who could enrich the quality of political party leadership, the political parties are failing to attract the brightest and most creative among the trained professionals in a context in which increasingly political management of the economy has placed an enormous responsibility on the shoulders of those who govern.

The uniformity of political and voting trends across the regions and parishes of the country has meant domination of the country's parliament by whichever party wins an election because of the huge imbalance between seats and votes favoring the majority party. This means that serious thought needs to be given to introducing some element of proportional representation so as to ensure more equitable seat representation by opposition parties. This could be combined with efforts to improve the quality of constituency representation by establishing greater separation of powers between the executive and the legislature. Elected members of the legislature should perhaps specialize in representing constituent interests and the executive should be formed on the basis of a presidential system, leaving the elected chief executive free to select any outstanding citizens to serve in his or her cabinet. Such a separation of executive from legislature might revive the vigor of parliamentary life that existed in the colonial period.

The system of clientelism in which governing parties control all the spoils of office (jobs, contracts, favors, and so on) while ruthlessly victimizing persons connected to opposition parties undermines the spirit of tolerance, consensus, and respect for rights that are central to the strengthening of a democratic system. More importantly, the abuse of party patronage allocations and the punishing of political enemies create a climate in which power is used to serve short-run partisan political interests while trampling on the rights of citizens and intimidating those who maintain independent political positions. When this is added to the close connection between political gangs with guns and the political party machines, the long-run impact is to endanger democratic freedoms, and to jeopardize the right to dissent and the assurance that citizens have the right to disagree with those who govern.

Perhaps the most dangerous tendency in the country's democratic tradition is for the political community to sharply polarize between the JLP and PNP postions on all issues that are politically sensitive. The implication is that leaders elected to govern cannot rely on solid national support on any issue that the opposition parties consider politically salient and therefore requiring a ritual disagreement with the party in power. This combination of bipolarization of the political community and irresponsible opposition disagreements with anything said or done by the governing party has rendered quite precarious the capacity of the country to manage its affairs in prolonged periods of crisis. This syndrome of excessively divisive opposition tendencies severely limits the areas of public policy on which bipartisan unity can prevail and provide the broadly based national support needed to tackle many underlying social and economic problems. It inhibits the growth toward a necessary and vital agenda of consensus issues where the party leaders all agree not to disagree in the national interest so as to maximize the country's capacity for crisis management. Such policy issues as crime and violence, long-term economic goals, foreign policy, control of drugs and the illegal drug trade, minimal targets for social services (education, health, and so one), and the preservation of civil and political rights in an environment of a strong and dominant state are all matters that require such a national agenda of consensus between the parties that compete for power.

Nothwithstanding these evident weaknesses, Jamaica's democratic system has shown remarkable capacity for survival and adaptation to change over the four decades of electoral politics between 1944 and 1984. The flexibility and adaptability that have evolved over that period of consolidating democratic practices and institutions in this country suggest that the democratic trends are likely to grow rather than diminish in Jamaica in the future.

The political parties have deep roots in most social classes. The political leadership has been of outstanding quality varying from the charismatic evangelism of a Michael Manley to the managerialist and technocratic effectiveness of Eddie Seaga. The leaders have generated intense and loyal support among the poorest classes and they have in turn refashioned the organs of the state to serve majority interests. Most importantly, four decades of political change have witnessed a fundamental transformation of racist caste-like plantation social order into a highly competitive social system in which money and education rather than color and family background have become the prime currencies of influence and power.

Democracy has survived in Jamaica under Third World conditions of relatively low income and widespread poverty. Indeed, the political party machines have been adapted to the needs of a society made up of a majority of poor citizens. Contrary to what is often suggested in writings that associate democratic collapse with poverty and democratic stability with middle class affluence, the Jamaica case illustrates the adaptability of parliamentary democracy to function in a nonindustrialized environment and to develop a high level of capacity for public management (in spite of evident areas of weakness) in the face of severe and prolonged economic crises and social hardships. In light of this case study there is need to re-examine the theoretical underpinnings that seek to link democratic government exclusively with advanced industrial political cultures and to assume that democracy is endangered[5] once poverty levels increase and unemployment rates rise.

The real test of the stability and strength of a political system is not to be found in the absence of conflicts and tensions but in the political system's capacity to handle them. The combination of strong populism, clientelistic dependence on party patronage, and a high propensity toward political violence lends a certain element of turbulence to Jamaican democracy. Citizens have a paternalist view of government and entertain great expectations about government protecting and taking care of their interests. Given the limited resources available to the state to cater to rapidly growing citizens' needs and wants, significant gaps usually emerge between such expectations and the ability of any elected governments to deliver benefits. Symbolic assurances and charismatic leadership as well as ideology are often used to disguise the magnitude of the gap. In critical periods when mass discontent against unpopular governments peaks it is often articulated through controlled protest action. Such protest action or limited demonstrative violence is usually triggered by an unpopular decision that activates collective protest action by organized opposition groups and interests. Where the cause is popular, it will generate widespread public support and give the opposition party or organizations supporting it an issue on which to mobilize and crystalize antigovernment sentiment.

Since independence in 1962, there have been five such episodes of limited protest violence or protest action designed to dramatize some specific issue. These have included the following:

1. The anti-Chinese disturbances (1965)
2. The anti-government protests over the Dr. Rodney affair (1968)
3. The anti-government protests over attempts to remove street vendors (1971).
4. The first antigovernment protests over a price increase in gasoline (1979)

5. The second antigovernment protests over a price increase in gasoline (1985)

Except for the first antigovernment protests over the price increase in petroleum products, the JLP was in power in all these episodes of protest action. Four out of five episodes of protest took on an antigovernment character. The last two protests (1979, 1985) were highly organized efforts led by activists connected to the two major political parties while the first three protest actions (1965, 1968, 1971) were led by nonparty opposition activists.

Although there are some obvious critical differences between these disturbances and episodes of protest, they share some important features. They all share the character of demonstrative violence or protest that must be distinguished from revolutionary violence. Revolutionary violence embraces the use of force to capture state power or to immobilize the governing institutions. Demonstrative violence or protest attempts to influence those who exercise state power by disruptive but limited use of coercion. No direct threat is posed to those who control the state as the violence or protest action is designed to dramatize a specific issue. Because it arises out of a specific issue, the conflict it generates is usually short-lived. The disruptive action is in fact a crude political weapon to score points against a governing party or to articulate demands with a view to influencing public policy.

The 1965 disturbances began with the shooting of a black man by a Chinese grocer in a low-income area of Kingston. This was followed by three days of random looting of commercial enterprises, and physical assaults on Chinese by blacks throughout the city. The 1968 Rodney affair developed out of the deportation of the late Dr. Walter Rodney, a University of the West Indies lecturer in history who had emerged in Jamaica as the intellectual leader of a militant black power movement in the late 1960s. The protest reaction led to looting, vandalism, attacks on commercial enterprises, as well as forcible disruption of the capital city's bus service. The street vendor disturbances grew out of efforts by Kingston's mayor to remove vendors from the sidewalks. This was followed by a similar pattern of random looting, vandalism, and disruption of the bus service. In each case the targets of violence were very visible property owners whose banks, offices, shops, stores, and supermarkets symbolized the power establishment against which these urban militants were striking out to dramatize their protests. The only agents of the state who were affected were the police. Of the three, the Rodney disturbances were the most violent and disruptive, but both the Rodney episode and the protests over the street vendors would qualify as minor riots. In all three cases the turmoil dissipated in two or three days. In each case the protest action was led by militant unemployed urban youth from the capital city's ghetto areas and the actions involved were confined to the city and concentrated in the downtown commerical area.

The 1979 gas price disturbance developed a new protest methodology. It was organized by the then opposition JLP and involved the blocking of roads to paralyze all transportation and commuter traffic, and bring the economy to a standstill. It began in Kingston and spread to other rural parishes and was therefore national in scope. It had the effect of paralyzing the economy for three days before it was called off. The 1985 episode organized by the opposition PNP lasted two days and followed a similar pattern. The only difference was that the 1985 roadblocks were more violent. Seven civilians were killed compared to two in 1979. In either case party organization of protest activity attracted spontaneous support from nonpartisan citizens but the party leaders were able to call off the protests before confrontation between rival JLP and PNP activists got out of control and before demonstrators developed major confrontation with the security forces. In each case the government allowed the demonstrations without heavy security action for the first two days and thereafter heavy security action to clear the streets led to a strategic retreat by the demonstrators. In each case normalcy was restored very quickly without any major disruptive after effects. In these last two episodes of party directed protests only a minimal level of looting actually occurred, although the focus of activity was extensive throughout the capital city and the island. As in the case of the earlier disturbances, it was the urban ghetto unemployed in the capital city who provided the strike force to initiate the protest action and man the barricades in the streets.

While protest action and demonstrative violence have provided periodic channels for articulating discontent, the Jamaican political system has displayed a high capability for managing and controlling these protest episodes. Over time, the mainstream political parties have in fact co-opted and controlled the urban Lumpenproletariat forces that provide the vanguard leadership for such protest action. These disturbances, therefore, do not amount to any real threat to political stability in Jamaica and have become incorporated into the turbulent process of often violent interparty contestations for power and popular support.

In conclusion, the Jamaican experience of democratic government points to factors sustaining democratic rule that are often ignored by the political-sociological-theoretical themes that link democracy to urban, affluent, industrial societies with advanced capitalist economies. Under conditions of more poverty than affluence and a prolonged economic crisis with severe social effects, democracy has survived and thrived in Jamaica because of a number of factors often ignored in that theoretical literature. These include strong mass parties with multiple class membership and deep roots of support within the poorer classes; strong emotional ties of loyalty between activists and political leaders; unwritten rules of the political game whereby the elite and the political leadership act in support of political stability and for the preservation of democratic institutions; and a deep faith on the part of the citizens that democratic institutions operate in their interests most of the time and represent the best way of managing power.

The Jamaican experience suggests that where these factors are in place democracy will thrive under Third World conditions, even in periods of great economic crisis and social stress.

NOTES

1. This more optimistic view is well developed in Adam Kuper, *Changing Jamaica*, Kingston, Jamaica: Kingston Publishers, 1976.

2. A good example of this second view is Fitzroy Ambursley, ''Jamaica from Michael Manley to Edward Seaga,'' in F. Ambursley and R. Cohen, *Crisis in the Caribbean*, Kingston, Jamaica: Heineman, 1983; and George Beckford and Michael Witter, *Small Garden, Bitter Weed—Struggle and Change in Jamaica*, Morant Bay, Jamaica: Maroon Publishing House, 1980.

3. A good example of a non-Marxist view of the Jamaican political system that projects it as pathological is Dr. Aggrey Brown's *Color Class and Politics in Jamaica*, New Brunswick, N.J.: Transaction Books, 1979.

4. See James Mau, *Social Change and Images of the Future*, Cambridge, Mass.: Schenkman Publishing, 1968.

5. Most of the new writings on the Caribbean by North American authors make this assumption about the likely long-term decline of democracy in the region as the economies falter. See, for example, Norman Graham and Keith Edwards, *The Caribbean Basin to the Year 2000*, Boulder, Colo.: Westview Press, 1984.

INDEX

ABOUT THE AUTHOR

Carl Stone is professor of political sociology at the University of the West Indies, Kingston, Jamaica.

One of the island's leading political commentator's, Professor Stone has written extensively on economic, political, and social issues in Jamaica and the Caribbean, as well as in Latin America and the Third World.

Carl Stone holds a B.Sc. in economics from the University of the West Indies and an M.A. and Ph.D. in political science from the University of Michigan.

POLITICS IN LATIN AMERICA
A HOOVER INSTITUTION SERIES
Robert Wesson, Series Editor